The life of Horatio, Lord Nelson

The Life of Horatio, Lord Nelson

by

Robert Southey

Riverdale Books
Cumming, GA

The Life of Horatio, Lord Nelson

Riverdale Books
is an imprint of

Riverdale Electronic Books, Inc.
4420 Bonneville Drive
Cumming, GA 30041
www.riverdalebooks.com

ISBN: 978-1-932606-20-1

Published in the United States of America

Contents

Author's Dedication

To John Wilson Croker, Esq., LL.D., F.R.S., Secretary of the Admiralty; Who, by the official situation which he so ably fills is qualified to appreciate its historical accuracy; and who, as a Member of the Republic of Letters, is equally qualified to decide up its literary merits, this work is respectfully inscribed by his friend, the Author.

Introduction

Horatio Nelson (1758–1805), Vice-Admiral of the White, Viscount Nelson, Duke of Bronte, etc., remains to this day Britain's most famous naval officer.

The Royal Navy has named four ships for Nelson, starting with a 120-gun first rate built at Woolwich and launched in 1814. Converted to include steam screw propulsion in 1860, this *Nelson* would not be broken up until 1928, so that she would exist during some or all of the service of the other three. Also, like the other three, this first *Nelson* was the lead ship in a class.

The second *Nelson* was the armored cruiser of 1881. Built by John Elder & Co, at Govan, on the River Clyde in Scotland, this 7,473 ton cruiser mounted four ten-inch and eight nine-inch guns. Most of her service was spent on the Australian station.

The third ship was named *Lord Nelson*, the only one to include the title. She was the last of the Royal Navy's pre-*Dreadnought* battleships, launched in 1906, but not completed until 1908. Her main armament consisted of four twelve-inch guns with a secondary battery of ten 9.2-inch guns. *Lord Nelson* saw service in World War I, and was stricken and sold for scrapping in 1920. Ironically, she was ultimately sold to a German shipbreaker, making it entirely possible that some of her steel might have been incorporated in some of the *Kriegsmarine* ships the British would face during World War II.

The fourth *Nelson* was another battleship, launched in 1925 and commissioned in 1930. The *Nelson*s were decidedly odd looking ships, with their nine 16-inch main guns placed in three triple turrets, all mounted forward of the bridge. This was a design compromise, allowing for a smaller armor belt and reducing displacement to comply with the 1922 Washington Naval Treaty, which limited battleships to 35,000 tons. This final *Nelson* served until 1948, and was scrapped the following year.

There was also an American *Nelson*, a *Gleaves* class destroyer, but she was named for an entirely different Nelson (Rear Admiral Charles P. Nelson, USN), and is here mentioned mostly to preclude any confusion.

Another HMS *Nelson,* still extant, is not a ship but a designation given to Her Majesty's Naval Base Portsmouth, which includes Portsmouth Historic Dockyard, where Nelson's flagship at Trafalgar, HMS *Victory*, has occupied Number 2 drydock since 1922, and remains the oldest commissioned warship in the world. Presently, *Victory* serves as the flagship of the Commander-in-Chief Naval Home Command, while also being open—the wardroom, which is still used by the Navy for military purposes, being an exception—to the public as a museum.

Curiously enough, while several ships have been named for Nelson, none of the ships he commanded still exists. *Victory* was his flagship, but he did not personally command her except as one component in his fleet. While he was aboard at Trafalgar, directing the British fleet from her quarterdeck, Hardy was responsible for sailing and fighting the ship and it was his name set down on her rolls as captain.

In his own time, Nelson was wildly popular with the British public. He had the habit of winning, and, despite frequent comments in his letters suggesting he thought that his accomplishments were being ignored, this insured that he never really lacked for publicity. He was also generally popular with his contemporaries and subordinates. In the case of his fellow officers, Nelson's success in battle engendered both good will and, sometimes, envy. After reaching flag rank he was diligent in promoting subordinates following any battle, in some cases arguing in favor of officers he felt were overlooked for promotion due to technicalities.

One area where Nelson sometimes expressed a degree of dissatisfaction was in the matter of honors. At the time of his death he was Viscount and Baron Nelson, of the Nile and of Burnham Thorpe, Baron Nelson of the Nile and of Hilborough, Knight of the Most Honourable Order of the Bath, and Duke of Bronte in the Kingdom of the two Sicilies. He also held orders of chivalry from Sicily and the Ottoman Empire, was a Knight Grand Commander of the Order of St. Joachim, and in 1802 had been awarded an honorary Doctor of Civil Law degree from Oxford. Still, he had desired more, and had he lived would probably have received it.

Had Nelson survived Trafalgar, he would almost certainly have been made an Earl (the British equivalent of a Count), with a dukedom likely to follow any further major victory. It has been suggested that this slow progression through the ranks of the British peerage was the result of Nelson's consistent habit of victory. It was expected that he would accomplish much, so the rewards were handed out slowly, so as to always provide an incentive for further effort.

Additionally, Nelson was only 47 at the time of his death. In a time when flag officers frequently continued on active duty into their late sixties, it would have been considered that he might expect to serve for another decade or two, during which his continued rise in the peerage would be a matter of form, provided he kept winning battles.

Nelson's letters suggest a man with a degree of ambivalence about both titles and financial reward. He frequently suggests that he is indifferent to prize money and other financial incentives, at least for himself. But he is zealous on the subject when it comes to his subordinates. Some might, of course, suggest that this is simply a show of honorable self-deprecation, given the obvious fact that insuring his subordinates received their fair share of prize money would, in any case, also insure that the flag officer's share came to Nelson.

At the same time, he does seem to covet, and yet deride, greater honors. Perhaps this is simply the result of growing up as the son of a clergyman, and the usual Christian ambivalence about money and fame. Jesus, after all, taught that neither money nor secular honors and rewards would avail a man when seeking entrance into the next world, and might even make the application more difficult. Nelson would certainly have heard this sort of thing from his father, and he does give the appearance of having been at least somewhat religious, even if apparently willing to ignore the commandment forbidding adultery.

His quest for higher rank in the nobility may, however, be tied less to vanity and self-importance (though he seems to have possessed an adequate supply of both), than to the need to provide for his families. At that time, elevation to the peerage brought with it an annual income, and the higher the rank the greater this would be. Even more so, high rank also brought landed estates, which meant a continuing source of income from both agricultural output and rents. So being a duke would mean a fatter purse than being a mere baron or viscount.

The pensions generally lasted only for the lifetime of the first person to bear the title, or sometimes might continue for an additional one or two generations, but the title to the landed estates was normally entailed, so that it would remain in the family forever (entailed property may not be sold, and passes only through inheritance, reverting to the Crown should the family become extinct). Thus, possession of such an estate insured both a home and income for subsequent generations, or, at least, it did until the imposition of death duties (inheritance taxes) in the United Kingdom, after which these large estates often became serious liabilities to the heirs.

Nelson wasn't poor, by any means, but the need to support his estranged wife, as well as the second household he maintained with Emma Hamilton and their daughter, the additional support he provided for his brother's widow, and servicing his debts, left him with precious little extra. More income would always be useful.

This seems a good point at which to mention Emma Hamilton, particularly since Southey tends to spend no more time than necessary on anything relating to her. To his credit, he does mention her strengths, which were considerable, but says almost nothing about her background. No doubt she appreciated this.

Born Amy Lyons in Neston, Cheshire, in 1765 (possibly 1761) she was the daughter of a blacksmith. Her father died while she was still an infant. Little is known of her childhood, though at some point she changed her name to Emma Hart. While still in her teens she was a popular artists' model and, if the Romney portraits, painted a few years later, are at all accurate, a remarkably beautiful young woman. During this same period she is believed to have worked as a prostitute, and is known to have been employed as what would now be considered an exotic dancer.

She would eventually become the mistress of Charles Greville, the second son of the first Earl of Warwick. This relationship continued until Greville decided he needed to marry, at which point having a mistress would clearly present a problem. He solved this by shipping her off to his uncle, Sir William Hamilton, who had been British Envoy in Naples since 1764. Sir William would get an attractive mistress out of the deal, and his nephew's marriage to an heiress would relieve Sir William of the need to help him financially.

Rather to everyone's surprise, Sir William married Emma in 1791. Many have questioned whether he was ignorant of her past, or if he simply didn't care. His tolerance, if not encouragement, of her later affair with Nelson, carried on under his own roof, suggests the latter. It *is* known that he enjoyed showing off his young wife as she performed her "attitudes" for his guests. These might best be thought of as living approximations of classical characters, with appropriate costuming. No longer exactly a stripper, but probably showing a bit more flesh than would have been thought appropriate a few years later.

Curiously, by the time the affair with Nelson began, Emma was no longer the slender, demure looking maiden of the Romney portraits. She had put on weight, but apparently was still alluring enough for Nelson, who essentially abandoned his wife in her favor. Some have suggested that Nelson's ideal would have been to have both, but that his wife had no intention of going along with *that* idea.

After Nelson's death, the British government ignored his requests that Emma be given a pension, so she was left with the house at Merton and a small annuity from Nelson. While this might have been sufficient for some, Emma had grander ideas and would ultimately find herself in a debtors' prison. She later moved to France, dying in Calais in 1813. Horatia, Nelson's daughter with her, was taken in by his family, eventually married a clergyman, and became the mother of ten children.

The life and character of Nelson have provided both direct and indirect inspiration in the realm of popular culture. Literature and film both contain a fair number of naval officers named Nelson or Horatio, or whose fictional exploits bear a strong resemblance to Nelson's actual deeds.

In this area, C.S. Forester's Horatio Hornblower comes immediately to mind. His given name provides an obvious connection, and, like Nelson, Hornblower continually suffered from a tendency to be seasick at the beginning of a voyage. Hornblower's exploits, though, seem inspired more by those of Lord Cochrane than by Nelson.

Alexander Kent's (pen name of British author Douglas Reeman) Richard Bolitho shows more obvious parallels. To begin with, he is much more Nelson's contemporary, and even participates in some of the same battles, though usually on the periphery. Bolitho is present at the Nile and Copenhagen, and while missing Trafalgar, in his fictional saga plays an important role in events leading up to it. Also, like Nelson, Bolitho suffers from recurring bouts of fever (probably malaria), champions the rights of the common sailor, is wildly popular with both his men and the general public, and carries on a notorious relationship with a mistress. He also, again like Nelson, dies during a sea battle, the victim of a sharpshooter's bullet. The most obvious differences are that Bolitho is knighted, but never made a peer, and is buried at sea rather than being carried home to a state funeral.

Nelson has been portrayed in a number of films, perhaps most famously by Laurence, Lord Olivier, in Alexander Korda's *That Hamilton Woman* (called *Lady Hamilton* in the UK), with his then wife Vivien Leigh. Southey's biography of Nelson was directly adapted for the screen in the 1926 British production of *Nelson*, starring Sir Cedric Hardwicke as Nelson and Gertrude McCoy as Lady Hamilton. This was a remake of a 1918 film of the same title, starring Donald Calthrop and Malvina Longfellow in the same roles.

He has also appeared in other films and on television, ranging from straightforward drama, such as the 1911 *The Battle of Trafalgar*, where he was played by Sydney Booth, to comedy, such as *Blackadder's Christmas Carol*, played by Philip Pope, and the animated *Ghosts of Albion*, where he was voiced by *Star Wars*' Anthony Daniels.

A number of entirely fictional Admiral Nelsons have also turned up on film and television, not all of them really naval officers (a few have worked in outer space). The best known is probably Admiral Harriman Nelson, in Irwin Allen's *Voyage to the Bottom of the Sea*, portrayed by Walter Pidgeon in the original 1961 movie, and by Richard Basehart in the 1964 television series. This Admiral Nelson, not uncommonly among fictional incarnations, outranked the original, who died as a vice admiral.

Robert Southey (1774–1843) published his biography of Nelson in 1813, only seven years after Trafalgar, and before the final defeat of Napoleon. In the same year, Southey became Poet Laureate of England, a position he would hold until his death.

Southey's literary style was quite the norm for his period, though today it may strike the modern reader as distinctly odd. This is not so much a matter of his turn of phrase—though at times that could also apply—as in the way he constructs his sentences and, frequently, seems to entirely dispense with paragraphing. While the latter is, perhaps, not so extreme as in ancient Greek, where it was common to dispense not only with paragraphs, but also with the spaces between words, it does somewhat impede the flow of the narrative.

Early 19th Century Britons didn't always feel the need to see a new line begin with each change of speaker in dialogue, or with each new thought. Modern readers do.

Likewise, Southey's sentences often seem to run on interminably, with a plethora of colons, semi-colons, and dashes to break them up, and what seems, to the modern reader, distinctly odd punctuation between these breaks.

As an editor, I find myself somewhat torn between a desire to leave an historic document in its original form and the need to present it in a form accessible to modern readers. In that regard, I have compromised. Modern paragraphing has been introduced, which seems to enhance the flow of the narrative on the page. On the other hand, I have left the punctuation as is.

I have added fairly extensive notes throughout, covering everything from unfamiliar uses of familiar words—Southey's use of "cowboy" for a dairy worker vice the more familiar American use of the term for a ranch hand being an example—to notes on individuals, ships, and nautical terminology. Here and there Southey also gave dates without including the year, probably presuming his readers would be sufficiently familiar with these events to know when they happened. With these events now a couple of centuries in the past, the missing years have been added to the dates inside square bracket, as [1795]. Unbracketed years were, of course, included in the original text.

In addition, a translation has been provided for Southey's Greek epigram at the end of the book. With Greek and Latin at the core of British education in his time, Southey no doubt felt that his readers would be able to translate it for themselves. No such presumption prevails today and so the deficiency is supplied.

J.T. McDaniel,
Cumming, Georgia
7 November 2008

Original Introduction

Many Lives of Nelson have been written; one is yet wanting, clear and concise enough to become a manual for the young sailor, which he may carry about with him till he has treasured it up for example in his memory and in his heart. In attempting such a work I shall write the eulogy of our great national hero, for the best eulogy of Nelson is the faithful history of his actions, and the best history must be that which shall relate them most perspicuously.

Chapter 1
1758 – 1783

Nelson's Birth and Boyhood—He is entered on Board the *Raisonable*—Goes to the West Indies in a Merchant-ship; then serves in the *Triumph*—He sails in Captain Phipps' Voyage of Discovery—Goes to the East Indies in the *Seahorse*, and returns in ill Health—Serves as acting Lieutenant in the *Worcester*, and is made Lieutenant into the *Lowestoffe*, Commander into the *Badger* Brig, and Post into the *Hinchinbroke*—Expedition against the Spanish Main—Sent to the North Seas in the *Albemarle*—Services during the American War.

Horatio, son of Edmund and Catherine Nelson, was born September 29, 1758, in the parsonage-house of Burnham Thorpe, a village in the county of Norfolk, of which his father was rector. His mother was a daughter of Dr. Suckling, prebendary[1] of Westminster, whose grandmother was sister of Sir Robert Walpole, and this child was named after his godfather, the first Lord Walpole. Mrs. Nelson died in 1767, leaving eight out of eleven children.

Her brother, Captain Maurice Suckling[2], of the navy, visited the widower upon this event, and promised to take care of one of the boys. Three years afterwards, when Horatio was only twelve years of age, being

1 A cathedral canon, having an administrative role. Following the Protestant Reformation in England, this became a semi-honorary title conferred on a senior parish priest, though still retaining an administrative function in the cathedral.

2 Captain Maurice Suckling (1726–1788), was born in Barsham, Surrey. Suckling was the son of Reverend Maurice Suckling and Mary Anne Turner. His elder sister, Catherine, was Nelson's mother. In his final position as Comptroller of the Navy he was given credit for exerting significant influence in his nephew's favor, though Southey notes that at Nelson's examination for lieutenant his uncle, while present, did not identify Nelson as his nephew until *after* he had passed the examination.

at home during the Christmas holidays, he read in the county newspaper that his uncle was appointed to the *Raisonnable*[3], of sixty-four guns.

"Do, William," said he to a brother who was a year and a half older than himself, "write to my father, and tell him that I should like to go to sea with uncle Maurice."

Mr. Nelson was then at Bath, whither he had gone for the recovery of his health: his circumstances were straitened, and he had no prospect of ever seeing them bettered: he knew that it was the wish of providing for himself by which Horatio was chiefly actuated, and did not oppose his resolution; he understood also the boy's character, and had always said, that in whatever station he might be placed, he would climb if possible to the very top of the tree. Captain Suckling was written to.

"What," said he in his answer, "has poor Horatio done, who is so weak, that he, above all the rest, should be sent to rough it out at sea?—But let him come; and the first time we go into action, a cannon-ball may knock off his head, and provide for him at once."

It is manifest from these words that Horatio was not the boy whom his uncle would have chosen to bring up in his own profession. He was never of a strong body, and the ague[4], which at that time was one of the most common diseases in England, had greatly reduced his strength. Yet he had already given proofs of that resolute heart and nobleness of mind which, during his whole career of labour and of glory, so eminently distinguished him.

When a mere child, he strayed a-birds'-nesting from his grandmother's house in company with a cowboy[5]. The dinner-hour elapsed, he was absent, and could not be found, and the alarm of the family became very great, for they apprehended that he might have been carried off by gipsies.

At length, after search had been made for him in various direc-

3 This 64-gun ship-of-the-line was built at Chatham Dockyard, launched 10 December 1768. She was placed in commission on 17 November 1770, under the command of Captain Maurice Suckling. Under subsequent captains, Raisonnable saw service ont he American station during the American Revolution, as well as against the French during both the Revolution and the Napoleonic wars. In 1810 she was converted to a receiving ship, being finally broken up in 1815.

4 A general term for a fever, in Nelson's period primarily referring to malaria, which at that time was endemic in many areas where it is virtually unknown today.

5 In this context, a lad employed to look after domestic dairy cattle, and not to be confused with an American cowboy, who primarily herded beef cattle on the open range.

tions, he was discovered alone, sitting composedly by the side of a brook which he could not get over.

"I wonder, child," said the old lady when she saw him, "that hunger and fear did not drive you home."

"Fear! grandmama," replied the future hero, "I never saw fear—what is it?"

Once, after the winter holidays, when he and his brother William had set off on horseback to return to school, they came back, because there had been a fall of snow; and William, who did not much like the journey, said it was too deep for them to venture on. "If that be the case," said the father, "you certainly shall not go; but make another attempt, and I will leave it to your honour. If the road is dangerous you may return: but remember, boys, I leave it to your honour!"

The snow was deep enough to have afforded them a reasonable excuse; but Horatio was not to be prevailed upon to turn back. "We must go on," said he: "remember, brother, it was left to our honour!"

There were some fine pears growing in the schoolmaster's garden, which the boys regarded as lawful booty, and in the highest degree tempting; but the boldest among them were afraid to venture for the prize. Horatio volunteered upon this service: he was lowered down at night from the bedroom window by some sheets, plundered the tree, was drawn up with the pears, and then distributed them among his schoolfellows without reserving any for himself. "He only took them," he said, "because every other boy was afraid."

Early on a cold and dark spring morning Mr. Nelson's servant arrived at this school, at North Walsham, with the expected summons for Horatio to join his ship. The parting from his brother William, who had been for so many years his playmate and bed-fellow, was a painful effort, and was the beginning of those privations which are the sailor's lot through life.

He accompanied his father to London. The *Raisonnable* was lying in the Medway. He was put into the Chatham stage, and on its arrival was set down with the rest of the passengers, and left to find his way on board as he could. After wandering about in the cold, without being able to reach the ship, an officer observed the forlorn appearance of the boy, questioned him; and happening to be acquainted with his uncle, took him home and gave him some refreshments.

When he got on board, Captain Suckling was not in the ship, nor had any person been apprised of the boy's coming. He paced the deck the whole remainder of the day without being noticed by any one; and it was not till the second day that somebody, as he expressed it, "took compassion on him." The pain which is felt when we are first transplanted from our native soil—when the living branch is cut from the parent tree is one of the most poignant which we have to endure through life. There are after-griefs which wound more deeply, which leave behind them scars never to be effaced, which bruise the spirit, and sometimes break the heart; but never do we feel so keenly the want of love, the necessity of being loved, and the sense of utter desertion, as when we first leave the haven of home, and are, as it were, pushed off upon the stream of life.

Added to these feelings, the sea-boy has to endure physical hardships, and the privation of every comfort, even of sleep. Nelson had a feeble body and an affectionate heart, and he remembered through life his first days of wretchedness in the service.

The *Raissonable* having been commissioned on account of the dispute respecting the Falkland Islands, was paid off as soon as the difference with the court of Spain was accommodated, and Captain Suckling was removed to the *Triumph*, seventy-four, then stationed as a guard-ship in the Thames. This was considered as too inactive a life for a boy, and Nelson was therefore sent a voyage to the West Indies in a merchant-ship, commanded by Mr. John Rathbone, an excellent seaman, who had served as master's mate under Captain Suckling in the *Dreadnought*.

He returned a practical seaman, but with a hatred of the king's service, and a saying then common among the sailors, "Aft the most honour; forward the better man." Rathbone had probably been disappointed and disgusted in the navy; and, with no unfriendly intentions, warned Nelson against a profession which he himself had found hopeless.

His uncle received him on board the *Triumph* on his return, and discovering his dislike to the navy, took the best means of reconciling him to it. He held it out as a reward that, if he attended well to his navigation, he should go in the cutter and decked long-boat, which was attached to the commanding-officer's ship at Chatham. Thus he became a good pilot for vessels of that description from Chatham to the Tower, and down the Swin Channel to the North Foreland, and acquired a confidence among rocks and sands of which he often felt the value.

Nelson had not been many months on board the *Triumph*, when his love of enterprise was excited by hearing that two ships were fitting out for a voyage of discovery towards the North Pole. In consequence of the difficulties which were expected on such a service, these vessels were to take out effective men instead of the usual number of boys. This, however, did not deter him from soliciting to be received, and, by his uncle's interest, he was admitted as coxswain under Captain Lutwidge, second in command.

The voyage was undertaken in compliance with an application from the Royal Society. The Hon. Captain Constantine John Phipps, eldest son of Lord Mulgrave, volunteered his services. The *Racehorse* and *Carcass* bombs[6] were selected as the strongest ships, and, therefore, best adapted for such a voyage; and they were taken into dock and strengthened, to render them as secure as possible against the ice. Two masters of Greenlandmen were employed as pilots for each ship.

No expedition was ever more carefully fitted out; and the First Lord of the Admiralty, Lord Sandwich[7], with a laudable solicitude, went on board himself, before their departure, to see that everything had been completed to the wish of the officers. The ships were provided with a simple and excellent apparatus for distilling fresh from salt water, the invention of Dr. Irving, who accompanied the expedition. It consisted merely in fitting a tube to the ship's kettle, and applying a wet mop to the surface as the vapour was passing. By these means, from thirty-four to forty gallons were produced every day.

They sailed from the Nore on the 4th of June [1773]. On the 6th of July they were in latitude 79° 56" 39'; longitude 9° 43" 30' E. The next day, about the place where most of the old discoverers had been stopped, the *Racehorse* was beset with ice, but they hove her through with ice-anchors.

Captain Phipps continued ranging along the ice, northward and

---

6 A type of small warship mounting a heavy mortar and intended mostly for shore bombardment. The weight of the mortar and the heavy downward recoil required that these vessels be very heavily constructed, a distinct advantage in an arctic expedition, where ice could be expected. Early bombs were most often ketch rigged, but *Racehorse* and *Carcass*, in common with most later British bombs, were ship rigged. *Racehorse* was originally an eight-gun French privateer, captured in 1757. *Carcass* was an *Infernal* class bomb vessel, originally commissioned in 1759. Both vessels were additionally reinforced prior to this expedition.

7 John Montague, 4th Earl of Sandwich (1718–1792), was First Lord of the Admiralty from 1748 until 1751, and again from 1771 until 1782. The Phipps expedition took place during his second term. Sandwich is particularly noted at the patron of Captain James Cook, the Sandwich Islands (Hawaii) being named in his honor, and for his probably mythical invention of the sandwich.

westward, till the 24th; he then tried to the eastward. On the 30th he was in latitude 80° 13" longitude 18° 48" E. among the islands and in the ice, with no appearance of an opening for the ships.

The weather was exceedingly fine, mild, and unusually clear. Here they were becalmed in a large bay, with three apparent openings between the islands which formed it, but everywhere, as far as they could see, surrounded with ice. There was not a breath of air, the water was perfectly smooth, the ice covered with snow, low and even, except a few broken pieces near the edge; and the pools of water in the middle of the ice-fields just crusted over with young ice.

On the next day the ice closed upon them, and no opening was to be seen anywhere, except a hole, or lake as it might be called, of about a mile and a half in circumference, where the ships lay fast to the ice with their ice-anchors. From these ice-fields they filled their casks with water, which was very pure and soft. The men were playing on the ice all day; but the Greenland pilots, who were further than they had ever been before, and considered that the season was far advancing, were alarmed at being thus beset.

The next day there was not the smallest opening; the ships were within less than two lengths of each other, separated by ice, and neither having room to turn. The ice, which the day before had been flat and almost level with the water's edge, was now in many places forced higher than the mainyard by the pieces squeezing together.

A day of thick fog followed. It was succeeded by clear weather, but the passage by which the ships had entered from the westward was closed, and no open water was in sight, either in that or any other quarter. By the pilots' advice the men were set to cut a passage, and warp[8] through the small openings to the westward. They sawed through pieces of ice twelve feet thick, and this labour continued the whole day, during which their utmost efforts did not move the ships above three hundred yards, while they were driven, together with the ice, far to the N.E. and E. by the current. Sometimes a field of several acres square would be lifted up between two larger islands, and incorporated with them; and thus these larger pieces continued to grow by aggregation.

8 Warp: Moving the ship by towing it with a cable, often using oared ship's boats to tow, though in this instance more likely by the crew climbing down onto the ice, tailing onto the lines, and manually hauling away. Ships could also be warped into dock or against a pier using capstans or winches.

Another day passed, and there seemed no probability of getting the ships out without a strong E. or N.E. wind. The season was far advanced, and every hour lessened the chance of extricating themselves.

Young as he was, Nelson was appointed to command one of the boats which were sent out to explore a passage into the open water. It was the means of saving a boat belonging to the *Racehorse* from a singular but imminent danger. Some of the officers had fired at and wounded a walrus. As no other animal has so human-like an expression in its countenance, so also is there none that seems to possess more of the passions of humanity.

The wounded animal dived immediately, and brought up a number of its companions; and they all joined in an attack upon the boat. They wrested an oar from one of the men; and it was with the utmost difficulty that the crew could prevent them from staving or upsetting her, till the *Carcass*'s boat came up; and the walruses, finding their enemies thus reinforced, dispersed.

Young Nelson exposed himself in a more daring manner. One night, during the mid-watch, he stole from the ship with one of his comrades, taking advantage of a rising fog, and set off over the ice in pursuit of a bear. It was not long before they were missed. The fog thickened, and Captain Lutwidge and his officers became exceedingly alarmed for their safety.

Between three and four in the morning the weather cleared, and the two adventurers were seen, at a considerable distance from the ship, attacking a huge bear. The signal for them to return was immediately made.

Nelson's comrade called upon him to obey it, but in vain. His musket had flashed in the pan[9], their ammunition was expended, and a chasm in the ice, which divided him from the bear, probably preserved his life.

"Never mind," he cried; "do but let me get a blow at this devil with the butt-end of my musket, and we shall have him."

Captain Lutwidge, however, seeing his danger, fired a gun, which had the desired effect of frightening the beast, and the boy then returned, somewhat afraid of the consequences of his trespass. The captain repri-

9 That is, the spark from the flintlock ignited the priming powder, but failed to set off the powder charge in the chamber. The priming makes an obvious flash, but the bullet remains unfired.

manded him sternly for conduct so unworthy of the office which he filled, and desired to know what motive he could have for hunting a bear.

"Sir," said he, pouting his lip, as he was wont to do when agitated, "I wished to kill the bear, that I might carry the skin to my father."

A party were now sent to an island, about twelve miles off (named Walden's Island in the charts, from the midshipman who was intrusted with this service), to see where the open water lay. They came back with information that the ice, though close all about them, was open to the westward, round the point by which they came in. They said also, that upon the island they had had a fresh east wind.

This intelligence considerably abated the hopes of the crew; for where they lay it had been almost calm, and their main dependence had been upon the effect of an easterly wind in clearing the bay. There was but one alternative: either to wait the event of the weather upon the ships, or to betake themselves to the boats. The likelihood that it might be necessary to sacrifice the ships had been foreseen. The boats accordingly were adapted, both in number and size, to transport, in case of emergency, the whole crew; and there were Dutch whalers upon the coast, in which they could all be conveyed to Europe.

As for wintering where they were, that dreadful experiment had been already tried too often. No time was to be lost; the ships had driven into shoal water, having but fourteen fathoms. Should they, or the ice to which they were fast, take the ground, they must inevitably be lost; and at this time they were driving fast toward some rocks on the N.E.

Captain Phipps sent for the officers of both ships, and told them his intention of preparing the boats for going away. They were immediately hoisted out, and the fitting begun. Canvas bread-bags were made, in case it should be necessary suddenly to desert the vessels; and men were sent with the lead and line to N. and E., to sound wherever they found cracks in the ice, that they might have notice before the ice took the ground; for in that case the ships must instantly have been crushed or overset.

On the 7th of August they began to haul the boats over the ice, Nelson having command of a four-oared cutter. The men behaved excellently well, like true British seamen: they seemed reconciled to the thought of leaving the ships, and had full confidence in their officers.

About noon, the ice appeared rather more open near the vessels; and as the wind was easterly, though there was but little of it, the sails were set, and they got about a mile to the westward. They moved very slowly, and were not now nearly so far to the westward as when they were first beset. However, all sail was kept upon them, to force them through whenever the ice slacked the least. Whatever exertions were made, it could not be possible to get the boats to the water's edge before the 14th; and if the situation of the ships should not alter by that time, it would not be justifiable to stay longer by them. The commander therefore resolved to carry on both attempts together, moving the boats constantly, and taking every opportunity of getting the ships through.

A party was sent out next day to the westward to examine the state of the ice: they returned with tidings that it was very heavy and close, consisting chiefly of large fields. The ships, however, moved something, and the ice itself was drifting westward. There was a thick fog, so that it was impossible to ascertain what advantage had been gained.

It continued on the 9th; but the ships were moved a little through some very small openings: the mist cleared off in the afternoon, and it was then perceived that they had driven much more than could have been expected to the westward, and that the ice itself had driven still further. In the course of the day they got past the boats, and took them on board again.

On the morrow the wind sprang up to the N.N.E. All sail was set, and the ships forced their way through a great deal of very heavy ice. They frequently struck, and with such force that one stroke broke the shank of the *Racehorse*'s best bower-anchor, but the vessels made way; and by noon they had cleared the ice, and were out at sea.

The next day they anchored in Smeerenberg Harbour, close to that island of which the westernmost point is called Hakluyt's Headland, in honour of the great promoter and compiler of our English voyages of discovery[10]. Here they remained a few days, that the men might rest after their fatigue.

No insect was to be seen in this dreary country, nor any species of reptile—not even the common earth-worm. Large bodies of ice, called icebergs[11], filled up the valleys between high mountains, so dark as, when

10 Richard Hakluyt (c.1552–1616), author of *The Principle Navigations, Voiages, Traffiques and Discoueries of the English Nation* (1589), and *Divers Voyages Touching the Discoverie of America* (1582). He was a principle promoter of the colonization of Virginia, though he did not himself visit these shores.

11 From the description, not an iceberg, but a glacier, which is essentially a frozen river slowly flowing to the sea. It is only when a large portion of a glacier breaks off into the sea that it becomes an iceberg.

contrasted with the snow, to appear black. The colour of the ice was a lively light green. Opposite to the place where they fixed their observatory was one of these icebergs, above three hundred feet high; its side toward the sea was nearly perpendicular, and a stream of water issued from it. Large pieces frequently broke off and rolled down into the sea.

There was no thunder nor lightning during the whole time they were in these latitudes. The sky was generally loaded with hard white clouds, from which it was never entirely free even in the clearest weather. They always knew when they were approaching the ice long before they saw it, by a bright appearance near the horizon, which the Greenlandmen called the blink of the ice. The season was now so far advanced that nothing more could have been attempted, if indeed anything had been left untried; but the summer had been unusually favourable, and they had carefully surveyed the wall of ice, extending for more than twenty degrees between the latitudes of 80° and 81", without the smallest appearance of any opening.

The ships were paid off shortly after their return to England; and Nelson was then placed by his uncle with Captain Farmer, in the *Seahorse*, of twenty guns[12], then going out to the East Indies in the squadron under Sir Edward Hughes. He was stationed in the foretop at watch and watch. His good conduct attracted the attention of the master (afterwards Captain Surridge), in whose watch he was; and upon his recommendation the captain rated him as midshipman.

At this time his countenance was florid, and his appearance rather stout and athletic; but when he had been about eighteen months in India, he felt the effects of that climate, so perilous to European constitutions. The disease baffled all power of medicine; he was reduced almost to a skeleton; the use of his limbs was for some time entirely lost; and the only hope that remained was from a voyage home.

Accordingly he was brought home by Captain Pigot, in the *Dolphin*; and had it not been for the attentive and careful kindness of that officer on the way, Nelson would never have lived to reach his native shores. He had formed an acquaintance with Sir Charles Pole, Sir Thomas Troubridge, and other distinguished officers, then, like himself, beginning

12 Southey here appears to be confusing the earlier *Seahorse* of 1712, and stricken in 1748, with the *Seahorse* of 1748, in which Nelson served. Both sixth rates, the earlier *Seahorse* was rated at 20 guns, while Nelson's ship was rated at 24 guns, mounting 22 nine-pounders on the upper deck and a pair of three-pounders on the quarterdeck.

their career: he had left them pursuing that career in full enjoyment of health and hope, and was returning, from a country in which all things were to him new and interesting, with a body broken down by sickness, and spirits which had sunk with his strength.

Long afterwards, when the name of Nelson was known as widely as that of England itself, he spoke of the feelings which he at this time endured. "I felt impressed," said he, "with a feeling that I should never rise in my profession. My mind was staggered with a view of the difficulties I had to surmount and the little interest I possessed. I could discover no means of reaching the object of my ambition. After a long and gloomy reverie, in which I almost wished myself overboard, a sudden glow of patriotism was kindled within me, and presented my king and country as my patron. 'Well then,' I exclaimed, 'I will be a hero! and, confiding in Providence, I will brave every danger!'"

Long afterwards Nelson loved to speak of the feelings of that moment; and from that time, he often said, a radiant orb was suspended in his mind's eye, which urged him onward to renown. The state of mind in which these feelings began, is what the mystics mean by their season of darkness and desertion. If the animal spirits fail, they represent it as an actual temptation. The enthusiasm of Nelson's nature had taken a different direction, but its essence was the same. He knew to what the previous state of dejection was to be attributed; that an enfeebled body, and a mind depressed, had cast this shade over his soul; but he always seemed willing to believe that the sunshine which succeeded bore with it a prophetic glory, and that the light which led him on was "light from heaven."

His interest, however, was far better than he imagined. During his absence, Captain Suckling had been made Comptroller of the Navy, his health had materially improved upon the voyage, and as soon as the *Dolphin* was paid off, he was appointed acting lieutenant in the *Worcester*[13], sixty-four, Captain Mark Robinson, then going out with convoy to Gibraltar.

Soon after his return, on the 8th of April 1777, he passed his examination for a lieutenancy. Captain Suckling sat at the head of the board, and when the examination had ended, in a manner highly honourable to Nelson, rose from his seat, and introduced him to the examining

13 Having been launched in 1769, *Worcester* was still a relatively new ship at this time.

captains as his nephew. They expressed their wonder that he had not informed them of this relationship before.

He replied that he did not wish the younker to be favoured—he knew his nephew would pass a good examination, and he had not been deceived. The next day Nelson received his commission as second lieutenant of the *Lowestoffe* frigate[14], Captain William Locker, then fitting out for Jamaica.

American and French privateers, under American colours, were at that time harassing our trade in the West Indies. Even a frigate was not sufficiently active for Nelson, and he repeatedly got appointed to the command of one of the *Lowestoffe*'s tenders. During one of their cruises, the *Lowestoffe* captured an American letter-of-marque[15].

It was blowing a gale, and a heavy sea running. The first lieutenant, being ordered to board the prize, went below to put on his hanger. It happened to be mislaid and, while he was seeking it, Captain Locker came on deck. Perceiving the boat still alongside, and in danger every moment of being swamped, and being extremely anxious that the privateer should be instantly taken in charge, because he feared that it would otherwise founder, he exclaimed, "Have I no officer in the ship who can board the prize?"

Nelson did not offer himself immediately, waiting, with his usual sense of propriety, for the first lieutenant's return. But hearing the master volunteer, he jumped into the boat, saying, "It is my turn now, and if I come back, it is yours."

The American, who had carried a heavy press of sail in hope of escaping, was so completely water-logged that the *Lowestoffe*'s boat went in on deck and out again with the sea.

---

14 HMS *Lowestoffe*: More recent ships in this line have spelled the name "*Lowestoft*." Nelson was appointed to the fifth of nine Royal Navy ships to bear this name (only eight of which saw actual service, the sixth being canceled before completion). Nelson's *Lowestoffe* was a 32-gun frigate, mounting 12-pounders in the main battery and 6-pounders on the quarterdeck and forecastle. The Deptford built *Lowestoffe* served from 1761 until 1801. The last *Lowestoft* was a Type 12 frigate, in commission from 1961 and sunk as a torpedo test target in 1986.

15 A letter of marque is a document from a government authorizing an individual or group to outfit and operate a private man of war, primarily for the purpose of commerce raiding, the ships generally not being sufficiently armed to take on warships. Also, as the crews were normally paid in shares following the sale of the prize and its cargo, merchant vessels were not only easier targets, but paid a better return. It was common practice to refer to the privateer itself as a letter-of-marque.

About this time he lost his uncle. Captain Locker, however, who had perceived the excellent qualities of Nelson, and formed a friendship for him which continued during his life, recommended him warmly to Sir Peter Parker[16], then commander-in-chief upon that station. In consequence of this recommendation he was removed into the *Bristol*[17] flag-ship, and Lieutenant Cuthbert Collingwood[18] succeeded him in the *Lowestoffe.*

Sir Peter Parker was the friend of both, and thus it happened that whenever Nelson got a step in rank, Collingwood succeeded him. The former soon became first lieutenant and, on the 8th of December 1778, was appointed commander of the *Badger* brig[19], Collingwood taking his place in the *Bristol.*

While the *Badger* was lying in Montego Bay, Jamaica, the *Glasgow* of twenty guns came in and anchored there, and in two hours was in flames, the steward having set fire to her while stealing rum out of the after-hold. Her crew were leaping into the water, when Nelson came up in his boats, made them throw their powder overboard and point their guns upward, and by his presence of mind and personal exertions prevented the loss of life which would otherwise have ensued.

On the 11th of June 1779 he was made post into the *Hinchinbrook*[20],

---

16 Admiral Sir Peter Parker, Bart. (1721–1811), would continue to sponsor Nelson throughout his career, and served as Chief Mourner at his funeral. He became Admiral of the Fleet in 1799, succeeding Lord Howe as the most senior on the list of flag officers.

17 Entering service in 1775, the 50-gun *Bristol* was the third ship to bear that name. She became a prison ship in 1794 (some sources say a hospital ship), and was broken up in 1810.

18 Collingwood (1748–1810) was two years senior to Nelson as a lieutenant, but would not be promoted to captain until 1780, two years after Nelson. The two were good friends and served together on a number of occasions. Collingwood was Nelson's second in command at Trafalgar, flying his flag in *Royal Sovereign*. Following Nelson's death, Collingwood became Commander-in-Chief, Mediterranean. He held that post until 1810, when he was finally relieved, only to die during the voyage home. He is buried in St. Paul's Cathedral in London.

19 This brig (a vessel with two masts, carrying square sails on both), was originally the American merchantman Defence, purchased into the Royal Navy in Jamaica in 1777, and replacing a previous HMS *Badger*, which had been condemned as unfit for further service. The rather sketchy records on this vessel suggest that she mounted twelve gun. *Badger* was sold out of the service at Jamaica in 1782.

20 HMS Hinchinbroke was formerly the French Astrée, captured in 1779. Southey notes that she was "sheathed in wood," meaning that the underwater part of the hull was covered by an extra layer of planking to protect the actual hull from marine worms.

of twenty-eight guns, an enemy merchantman, sheathed with wood, which had been taken into the service. Collingwood was then made commander into the *Badger.*

A short time after he left the *Lowestoffe,* that ship, with a small squadron, stormed the fort of St. Fernando de Omoa, on the south side of the Bay of Honduras, and captured some register ships which were lying under its guns. Two hundred and fifty quintals of quicksilver[21], and three millions of piastres, were the reward of this enterprise, and it is characteristic of Nelson that the chance by which he missed a share in such a prize is never mentioned in any of his letters, nor is it likely that it ever excited even a momentary feeling of vexation.

Nelson was fortunate in possessing good interest at the time when it could be most serviceable to him. His promotion had been almost as rapid as it could be, and before he had attained the age of twenty-one he had gained that rank which brought all the honours of the service within his reach[22]. No opportunity, indeed, had yet been given him of distinguishing himself, but he was thoroughly master of his profession, and his zeal and ability were acknowledged wherever he was known.

Count d'Estaing, with a fleet of one hundred and twenty-five sail, men of war and transports, and a reputed force of five-and twenty thousand men, threatened Jamaica from St. Domingo. Nelson offered his services to the Admiral and to Governor-General Dalling, and was appointed

---

This was becoming an old-fashioned practice by this time, and most Royal Navy ships were sheathed in copper, which served the same purpose much more effectively. While Nelson was made post into her on 11 June 1779, he did not actually take up his command until 1 September, as the ship was at sea and did not return to Jamaica until that date. It was during this period that Nelson was given command of the shore batteries at Port Royal.

21 An old name for mercury, it comes from the appearance of the silvery metal, which is liquid at normal room temperatures.

22 Advancement from midshipman through captain was essentially by merit, though influence could certainly play a part. Once an officer was made a Post Captain (that is, a captain by actual rank, and not merely the courtesy title afforded an officer of lesser rank who commanded a vessel), further advancement was entirely by seniority. Thus, provided he managed to outlive everyone with a lower position on the captains list, a captain would eventually advance through all flag ranks until he became Admiral of the Fleet. The chief disadvantage of this system, which is that an outstanding captain could not be promoted until everyone above him on the list had either died or been promoted, was known even then. It was not unusual for captains or flag officers to be promoted to the next higher rank, and then not employed, in order to promote a man who was lower on the list be deemed more useful to the service.

to command the batteries of Fort Charles, at Port Royal.

Not more than seven thousand men could be mustered for the defence of the island,—a number wholly inadequate to resist the force which threatened them. Of this Nelson was so well aware, that when he wrote to his friends in England, he told them they must not be surprised to hear of his learning to speak French.

D'Estaing, however, was either not aware of his own superiority, or not equal to the command with which he was intrusted. He attempted nothing with his formidable armament, and General Dalling was thus left to execute a project which he had formed against the Spanish colonies.

This project was to take Fort San Juan on the river of that name, which flows from Lake Nicaragua into the Atlantic, make himself master of the lake itself, and of the cities of Granada and Leon, and thus cut off the communication of the Spaniards between their northern and southern possessions in America. Here it is that a canal between the two seas may most easily be formed—a work more important in its consequences than any which has ever yet been effected by human power[23].

Lord George Germaine, at that time secretary of state for the American Department, approved the plan, and as discontents at that time were known to prevail in the Nuevo Reyno, in Popayan, and in Peru, the more sanguine part of the English began to dream of acquiring an empire in one part of America, more extensive than that which they were on the point of losing in another.

General Dalling's plans were well formed, but the history and the nature of the country had not been studied as accurately as its geography. The difficulties which occurred in fitting out the expedition delayed it till the season was too far advanced, and the men were thus sent to adventure themselves, not so much against an enemy, whom they would have beaten, as against a climate which would do the enemy's work.

Early in the year 1780, five hundred men destined for this service were convoyed by Nelson from Port Royal to Cape Gracias a Dios, in Honduras. Not a native was to be seen when they landed—they had been

23 The idea of building a canal through Nicaragua was promoted for many years before a canal was finally built across the Isthmus of Panama. The idea continues to interest various parties, including the Nicaraguan government, with a Nicaraguan canal seen as a potential competitor to, or even a replacement for, the Panama Canal, which is currently undergoing an enormous expansion project, as the old locks can no longer accommodate many modern ships.

taught that the English came with no other intent than that of enslaving them, and sending them to Jamaica. After a while, however, one of them ventured down, confiding in his knowledge of one of the party, and by his means the neighbouring tribes were conciliated with presents, and brought in.

The troops were encamped on a swampy and unwholesome plain, where they were joined by a party of the 79th regiment from Black River, who were already in a deplorable state of sickness. Having remained here a month, they proceeded, anchoring frequently, along the Mosquito shore, to collect their Indian allies, who were to furnish proper boats for the river, and to accompany them.

They reached the river San Juan, March 24th and here, according to his orders, Nelson's services were to terminate. But not a man in the expedition had ever been up the river, or knew the distance of any fortification from its mouth, and he not being one who would turn back when so much was to be done, resolved to carry the soldiers up.

About two hundred, therefore, were embarked in the Mosquito shore craft and in two of the *Hinchinbrook*'s boats, and they began their voyage. It was the latter end of the dry season, the worst time for such an expedition. The river was consequently low.

Indians were sent forward through narrow channels between shoals and sandbanks, and the men were frequently obliged to quit the boats and exert their utmost strength to drag or thrust them along. This labour continued for several days.

When they came into deeper water, they had then currents and rapids to contend with, which would have been insurmountable but for the skill of the Indians in such difficulties. The brunt of the labour was borne by them and by the sailors—men never accustomed to stand aloof when any exertion of strength or hardihood is required. The soldiers, less accustomed to rely upon themselves, were of little use. But all equally endured the violent heat of the sun, rendered more intense by being reflected from the white shoals, while the high woods, on both sides of the river, were frequently so close as to prevent any refreshing circulation of air, and during the night all were equally exposed to the heavy and unwholesome dews[24].

24 At this time the causes of disease were still mostly unknown, and it was still presumed that many tropical fevers, now known to bacterial or parasitic in origin and most often carried by insects, were caused by unwholesome elements in the atmosphere.

On the 9th of April they reached an island in the river, called San Bartolomeo, which the Spaniards had fortified as an outpost, with a small semicircular battery, mounting nine or ten swivels, and manned with sixteen or eighteen men. It commanded the river in a rapid and difficult part of the navigation. Nelson, at the head of a few of his seamen, leaped upon the beach. The ground upon which he sprung was so muddy that he had some difficulty in extricating himself, and lost his shoes.

Bare-footed, however, he advanced, and, in his own phrase, *boarded the battery*. In this resolute attempt he was bravely supported by Despard, at that time a captain in the army, afterward unhappily executed for his schemes of revolutionary treason[25]. The castle of San Juan is situated about 16 miles higher up. The stores and ammunition, however, were landed a few miles below the castle, and the men had to march through woods almost impassable.

One of the men was bitten under the eye by a snake, which darted upon him from the bough of a tree. He was unable to proceed from the violence of the pain and when, after a short while, some of his comrades were sent back to assist him, he was dead, and the body already putrid.

Nelson himself narrowly escaped a similar fate. He had ordered his hammock to be slung under some trees, being excessively fatigued, and was sleeping, when a monitor lizard passed across his face. The Indians

---

"Malaria," for example, is Italian for "bad air." It was known at the time that draining swamps could reduce the incidence of many of these diseases, though it would still be some years before it was recognized that the link was in eliminating breeding areas for mosquitoes, and from eliminating supposedly unhealthy emanations from the swamp itself.

25 Colonel Edward Marcus Despard, Esq., (1751–1803), was an Irish born British officer. He served in Honduras, rising to the rank of colonel, and serving as governor before being recalled to England. In 1802, Despard was arrested on a charge of treason, stemming from a supposed plot to overthrow the British government. Though the plot, if it even existed, does not appear to have gone much beyond the stage of drunken complaining and idealistic correspondence, Despard and six others were convicted and sentenced to be hanged, drawn, and quartered, a sentence that had not been imposed in many years. Nelson, among others, petitioned the government for clemency in Despard's case. Their pleas resulted in only a minor mitigation of sentence. It was agreed that the prisoners would be hanged until they were dead, then have their heads cut off, rather than being hanged until almost dead, disemboweled, and made to watch their entrails being burned, after which they were beheaded and their bodies cut into four pieces. The sentence was carried out on 21 February 1803. In keeping with his station, Despard was buried in St. Paul's Cathedral, which provoked its own controversy at the time.

happily observed the reptile, and knowing what it indicated, awoke him. He started up, and found one of the deadliest serpents of the country coiled up at his feet.

He suffered from poison of another kind, for drinking at a spring in which some boughs of the *manchineel*[26] had been thrown, the effects were so severe as, in the opinion of some of his friends, to inflict a lasting injury upon his constitution.

The castle of San Juan is 32 miles below the point where the river issues from the Lake of Nicaragua, and 69 from its mouth. Boats reach the sea from thence in a day and a-half, but their navigation back, even when unladen, is the labour of nine days. The English appeared before it on the 11th, two days after they had taken San Bartolomeo.

Nelson's advice was that it should instantly be carried by assault, but Nelson was not the commander, and it was thought proper to observe all the formalities of a siege. Ten days were wasted before this could be commenced. It was a work more of fatigue than of danger, but fatigue was more to be dreaded than the enemy.

The rains set in, and could the garrison have held out a little longer, diseases would have rid them of their invaders. Even the Indians sunk under it, the victims of unusual exertion, and of their own excesses.

The place surrendered on the 24th. But victory procured to the conquerors none of that relief which had been expected. The castle was worse than a prison, and it contained nothing which could contribute to the recovery of the sick, or the preservation of those who were yet unaffected. The huts which served for hospitals were surrounded with filth, and with the putrefying hides of slaughtered cattle—almost sufficient of themselves to have engendered pestilence—and when at last orders were given to erect a convenient hospital, the contagion had become so general that there were none who could work at it, for besides the few who were able to perform garrison duty, there were not orderly men enough to assist the sick.

Added to these evils, there was the want of all needful remedies for, though the expedition had been amply provided with hospital stores, river craft enough had not been procured for transporting the requisite

---

26 Called in modern Spanish *manzanilla de la muerte*, or "little apple of death," the *manchineel* is a toxic tree. The liquid sap can blister skin, as can smoke from burning the tree. The sap was used as blowgun dart poison by Carib Indians, and branches from the tree were used to poison water supplies.

baggage. And when much was to be left behind, provision for sickness was that which of all things men in health would be most ready to leave. Now, when these medicines were required, the river was swollen, and so turbulent that its upward navigation was almost impracticable.

At length even the task of burying the dead was more than the living could perform, and the bodies were tossed into the stream, or left for beasts of prey, and for the *gallinazos*[27]—those dreadful carrion birds, which do not always wait for death before they begin their work.

Five months the English persisted in what may be called this war against nature. They then left a few men, who seemed proof against the climate, to retain the castle till the Spaniards should choose to retake it and make them prisoners. The rest abandoned their baleful conquest. Eighteen hundred men were sent to different posts upon this wretched expedition—not more than three hundred and eighty ever returned. The *Hinchinbrook*'s complement consisted of two hundred men. Eighty-seven took to their beds in one night, and of the whole crew not more than ten survived.

The transports' men all died, and some of the ships, having none left to take care of them, were sunk in the harbour. But transport ships were not wanted, for the troops which they had brought were no more. They had fallen, not by the hand of an enemy, but by the deadly influence of the climate.

Nelson himself was saved by a timely removal. In a few days, after the commencement of the siege, he was seized with the prevailing dysentery. Meantime Captain Glover (son of the author of *Leonidas*[28]) died, and Nelson was appointed to succeed him in the *Janus*, of forty-four guns, Collingwood being then made post into the *Hinchinbrook*.

He returned to the harbour the day before San Juan surrendered, and immediately sailed for Jamaica in the sloop which brought the news of his appointment. He was, however, so greatly reduced by the disorder that, when they reached Port Royal, he was carried ashore in his cot, and finding himself, after a partial amendment, unable to retain

27 Turkey vultures (*Cathartes Aura*), though the suggestion that the birds would begin feeding before the victim had died suggests that a different species may have been observed.

28 An epic poem, published in 1737 by Richard Glover (1712–1785), taking as its subject King Leonidas of Sparta and the defense of Thermopylae. *Leonidas* was one of Southey's favorite poems.

the command of his new ship, he was compelled to ask leave to return to England, as the only means of recovery. Captain (afterwards Admiral) Cornwallis took him home in the *Lion,* and to his care and kindness Nelson believed himself indebted for his life.

He went immediately to Bath, in a miserable state—so helpless that he was carried to and from his bed—and the act of moving him produced the most violent pain. In three months he recovered and immediately hastened to London, and applied for employment. After an interval of about four months he was appointed to the *Albemarle,* of twenty-eight guns, a French merchantman which had been purchased from the captors for the king's service.

His health was not yet thoroughly re-established; and while he was employed in getting his ship ready, he again became so ill as hardly to be able to keep out of bed. Yet in this state, still suffering from the fatal effect of a West Indian climate, as if it might almost be supposed, he said, to try his constitution, he was sent to the North Seas, and kept there the whole winter.

The asperity with which he mentioned this so many years afterwards evinces how deeply he resented a mode of conduct equally cruel to the individual and detrimental to the service. It was during the armed neutrality; and when they anchored off Elsinore, the Danish Admiral sent on board, desiring to be informed what ships had arrived, and to have their force written down.

"The *Albemarle,*" said Nelson to the messenger, "is one of his Britannic Majesty's ships: you are at liberty, sir, to count the guns as you go down the side; and you may assure the Danish Admiral that, if necessary, they shall all be well served."

During this voyage he gained a considerable knowledge of the Danish coast and its soundings, greatly to the advantage of his country in after-times. The *Albemarle* was not a good ship, and was several times nearly overset in consequence of the masts having been made much too long for her. On her return to England they were shortened, and some other improvements made at Nelson's suggestion. Still he always insisted that her first owners, the French, had taught her to run away, as she was never a good sailer except when going directly before the wind.

On their return to the Downs, while he was ashore visiting the senior officer, there came on so heavy a gale that almost all the vessels drove, and a store-ship came athwart-hawse of the *Albemarle.* Nelson feared she would drive on the Goodwin Sands; he ran to the beach; but even the Deal boatmen thought it impossible to get on board, such was the violence of the storm. At length some of the most intrepid offered to make the attempt for fifteen guineas; and to the astonishment and fear of all the beholders, he embarked during the height of the tempest. With great difficulty and imminent danger he succeeded in reaching her. She lost her bowsprit and foremast, but escaped further injury.

He was now ordered to Quebec, where his surgeon told him he would certainly be laid up by the climate. Many of his friends urged him to represent this to Admiral Keppel; but having received his orders from Lord Sandwich, there appeared to him an indelicacy in applying to his successor to have them altered. Accordingly he sailed for Canada.

During her first cruise on that station the *Albemarle* captured a fishing schooner, which contained in her cargo nearly all the property that her master possessed, and the poor fellow had a large family at home, anxiously expecting him. Nelson employed him as a pilot in Boston Bay, then restored him the schooner and cargo, and gave him a certificate to secure him against being captured by any other vessel.

The man came off afterwards to the *Albemarle*, at the hazard of his life, with a present of sheep, poultry, and fresh provisions. A most valuable supply it proved, for the scurvy was raging on board: this was in the middle of August, and the ship's company had not had a fresh meal since the beginning of April. The certificate was preserved at Boston in memory of an act of unusual generosity; and now that the fame of Nelson has given interest to everything connected with his name, it is regarded as a relic.

The *Albemarle* had a narrow escape upon this cruise. Four French sail of the line and a frigate, which had come out of Boston harbour, gave chase to her; and Nelson, perceiving that they beat him in sailing, boldly ran among the numerous shoals of St. George's Bank, confiding in his own skill in pilotage. Captain Salter, in the *Sta. Margaretta*, had escaped the French fleet by a similar manoeuvre not long before. The frigate alone continued warily to pursue him; but as soon as he perceived that this enemy was unsupported, he shortened sail and hove to; upon which the Frenchman thought it advisable to give over the pursuit, and sail in quest of his consorts.

At Quebec Nelson became acquainted with Alexander Davison,

by whose interference he was prevented from making what would have been called an imprudent marriage. The *Albemarle* was about to leave the station, her captain had taken leave of his friends, and was gone down the river to the place of anchorage; when the next morning, as Davison was walking on the beach, to his surprise he saw Nelson coming back in his boat.

Upon inquiring the cause of this reappearance, Nelson took his arm to walk towards the town, and told him that he found it utterly impossible to leave Quebec without again seeing the woman whose society had contributed so much to his happiness there, and offering her his hand.

"If you do," said his friend, "your ruin must inevitably follow."

"Then let it follow," cried Nelson, "for I am resolved to do it."

"And I," replied Davison, "am resolved you shall not."

Nelson, however, upon this occasion, was less resolute than his friend, and suffered himself to be led back to the boat.

The *Albemarle* was under orders to convoy a fleet of transports to New York. "A very pretty job," said her captain, "at this late season of the year" (October was far advanced), "for our sails are at this moment frozen to the yards."

On his arrival at Sandy Hook, he waited on the commander-in-chief, Admiral Digby, who told him he was come on a fine station for making prize money.

"Yes, sir," Nelson made answer, "but the West Indies is the station for honour."

Lord Hood, with a detachment of Rodney's victorious fleet, was at that time at Sandy Hook: he had been intimate with Captain Suckling; and Nelson, who was desirous of nothing but honour, requested him to ask for the *Albemarle*, that he might go to that station where it was most likely to be obtained.

Admiral Digby reluctantly parted with him. His professional merit was already well known; and Lord Hood, on introducing him to Prince William Henry[29], as the Duke of Clarence was then called, told the prince,

29 Prince William Henry (1765–1837) was the third son of King George III. William would be created Duke of Clarence in 1789. It being presumed that his royal duties would be rather limited, having two elder brothers, he entered the Navy as a midshipman at the age of 13, rising to captain by 1786. Seniority would then see him rise to Admiral, and finally Admiral of the Fleet, though he held no commands at sea after reaching flag rank. In 1830 he ascended the throne as King William IV, his two

if he wished to ask any questions respecting naval tactics, Captain Nelson could give him as much information as any officer in the fleet.

The Duke—who, to his own honour, became from that time the firm friend of Nelson—describes him as appearing the merest boy of a captain he had ever seen, dressed in a full laced uniform, an old-fashioned waistcoat with long flaps, and his lank unpowdered hair tied in a stiff Hessian tail of extraordinary length; making altogether so remarkable a figure, that, says the duke, "I had never seen anything like it before, nor could I imagine who he was, nor what he came about. But his address and conversation were irresistibly pleasing; and when he spoke on professional subjects, it was with an enthusiasm that showed he was no common being."

It was expected that the French would attempt some of the passages between the Bahamas; and Lord Hood, thinking of this, said to Nelson, "I suppose, sir, from the length of time you were cruising among the Bahama Keys, you must be a good pilot there."

He replied, with that constant readiness to render justice to every man which was so conspicuous in all his conduct through life, that he was well acquainted with them himself, but that in that respect his second lieutenant was far his superior.

The French got into Puerto Cabello, on the coast of Venezuela. Nelson was cruising between that port and La Guapra, under French colours, for the purpose of obtaining information; when a king's launch, belonging to the Spaniards, passed near, and being hailed in French, came alongside without suspicion, and answered all questions that were asked concerning the number and force of the enemy's ships.

The crew, however, were not a little surprised when they were taken on board and found themselves prisoners. One of the party went by the name of the Count de Deux-Ponts. He was, however, a prince of the German empire, and brother to the heir of the Electorate of Bavaria: his companions were French officers of distinction, and men of science, who

---

elder brothers, Prince Frederick and King George IV, having died without legitimate issue. He remained throughout his life a strong partisan of the Royal Navy, and the order allowing naval officers at sea to drink to loyal toast while seated is most reliably dated to his reign (though generations of novelists have suggested that it was already in effect decades earlier). William also having no surviving legitimate children or grand-children, he was succeeded on the throne by his niece, Victoria, upon his death in 1837.

had been collecting specimens in the various branches of natural history.

Nelson, having entertained them with the best his table could afford, told them they were at liberty to depart with their boat, and all that it contained: he only required them to promise that they would consider themselves as prisoners if the commander-in-chief should refuse to acquiesce in their being thus liberated: a circumstance which was not likely to happen.

Tidings soon arrived that the preliminaries of peace had been signed; and the *Albemarle* returned to England and was paid off.

Nelson's first business, after he got to London, even before he went to see his relations, was to attempt to get the wages due to his men for the various ships in which they had served during the war. "The disgust of seamen to the navy," he said, "was all owing to the infernal plan of turning them over from ship to ship; so that men could not be attached to their officers, nor the officers care the least about the men." Yet he himself was so beloved by his men that his whole ship's company offered, if he could get a ship, to enter for her immediately.

He was now, for the first time, presented at court. After going through this ceremony, he dined with his friend Davison at Lincoln's Inn. As soon as he entered the chambers, he threw off what he called his iron-bound coat; and, putting himself at ease in a dressing gown, passed the remainder of the day in talking over all that had befallen them since they parted on the shore of the River St. Lawrence.

Chapter 2
1784–1793

Nelson goes to France—Reappointed to the *Boreas* at the Leeward Islands in the *Boreas*—His firm conduct concerning the American Interlopers and the Contractors—Marries and returns to England—Is on the point of quitting the Service in Disgust—Manner of Life while unemployed—Appointed to the *Agamemnon* on the breaking out of the War of the French Revolution.

I have closed the war," said Nelson in one of his letters, "without a fortune; but there is not a speck in my character. True honour, I hope, predominates in my mind far above riches."

He did not apply for a ship, because he was not wealthy enough to live on board in the manner which was then become customary. Finding it, therefore, prudent to economise on his half-pay[30] during the peace, he went to France, in company with Captain Macnamara of the navy, and took lodgings at St. Omer's.

The death of his favourite sister, Anne, who died in consequence of going out of the ball-room at Bath when heated with dancing, affected his father so much that it had nearly occasioned him to return in a few weeks. Time, however, and reason and religion, overcame this grief in the old man; and Nelson continued at St. Omer's long enough to fall in love with the daughter of an English clergyman.

---

30 During this period, naval officers received full pay only when assigned to a ship, or to specific duties ashore. Officers who fit into neither of these categories drew half-pay, on which they were expected to maintain themselves until such time as they were able to obtain an appointment. Unless officers were wealthy, or had been fortunate in prize money, it was not unusual for them to seek other employment during these periods. The enlisted sailors, of course, were simply discharged and left to their own devices.

This second attachment appears to have been less ardent than the first, for upon weighing the evils of a straitened income to a married man, he thought it better to leave France, assigning to his friends something in his accounts as the cause. This prevented him from accepting an invitation from the Count of Deux-Ponts to visit him at Paris, couched in the handsomest terms of acknowledgment for the treatment which he had received on board the *Albemarle*.

The self-constraint which Nelson exerted in subduing this attachment made him naturally desire to be at sea; and when, upon visiting Lord Howe at the Admiralty, he was asked if he wished to be employed, he made answer that he did. Accordingly in March, he was appointed to the *Boreas*, twenty-eight guns, going to the Leeward Islands as a cruiser on the peace establishment.

Lady Hughes and her family went out with him to Admiral Sir Richard Hughes, who commanded on that station.

His ship was full of young midshipmen, of whom there were not less than thirty on board; and happy were they whose lot it was to be placed with such a captain. If he perceived that a boy was afraid at first going aloft, he would say to him in a friendly manner, "Well, sir, I am going a race to the mast-head, and beg that I may meet you there."

The poor little fellow instantly began to climb, and got up how he could,—Nelson never noticed in what manner, but when they met in the top, spoke cheerfully to him, and would say how much any person was to be pitied who fancied that getting up was either dangerous or difficult.

Every day he went into the school-room to see that they were pursuing their nautical studies; and at noon he was always the first on deck with his quadrant[31]. Whenever he paid a visit of ceremony, some of these youths accompanied him; and when he went to dine with the governor at Barbadoes, he took one of them in his hand, and presented him, saying, "Your Excellency must excuse me for bringing one of my midshipmen. I make it a rule to introduce them to all the good company I can, as they have few to look up to, besides myself, during the time they are at sea."

When Nelson arrived in the West Indies, he found himself senior

31 A navigational instrument, used to determine the elevation of celestial bodies. By this time it had generally been replaced by the more convenient and compact octant, which in turn would be replaced by the modern sextant. The names of each of these instruments derives from the length of their arc, being one quarter, one eighth, or one sixth of a circle.

captain, and consequently second in command on that station. Satisfactory as this was, it soon involved him in a dispute with the admiral, which a man less zealous for the service might have avoided.

He found the *Latona* in English Harbour, Antigua, with a broad pendant hoisted; and upon inquiring the reason, was presented with a written order from Sir R. Hughes, requiring and directing him to obey the orders of Resident Commissioner Moutray during the time he might have occasion to remain there; the said resident commissioner being in consequence, authorised to hoist a broad pendant on board any of his Majesty's ships in that port that he might think proper. Nelson was never at a loss how to act in any emergency.

"I know of no superior officers," said he, "besides the Lords Commissioners of the Admiralty, and my seniors on the post list." Concluding, therefore, that it was not consistent with the service for a resident commissioner, who held only a civil situation, to hoist a broad pendant, the moment that he had anchored he sent an order to the captain of the *Latona* to strike it, and return it to the dock-yard.

He went on shore the same day, dined with the commissioner, to show him that he was actuated by no other motive than a sense of duty, and gave him the first intelligence that his pendant had been struck. Sir Richard sent an account of this to the Admiralty; but the case could admit of no doubt, and Captain Nelson's conduct was approved.

He displayed the same promptitude on another occasion. While the *Boreas*, after the hurricane months were over, was riding at anchor in Nevis Roads, a French frigate passed to leeward, close along shore. Nelson had obtained information that this ship was sent from Martinico[32], with two general officers and some engineers on board, to make a survey of our sugar islands. This purpose he was determined to prevent them from executing, and therefore he gave orders to follow them.

The next day he came up with them at anchor in the roads of St. Eustatia, and anchored at about two cables' length on the frigate's quarter. Being afterwards invited by the Dutch governor to meet the French officers at dinner, he seized that occasion of assuring the French captain that, understanding it was his intention to honour the British possessions with a visit, he had taken the earliest opportunity in his power to accompany him, in his Majesty's ship the *Boreas*, in order that such atten-

32 Martinico is located on the island of Hispaniola, in what is today the Dominican Republic.

tion might be paid to the officers of his Most Christian Majesty as every Englishman in the islands would be proud to show.

The French, with equal courtesy, protested against giving him this trouble; especially, they said, as they intended merely to cruise round the islands without landing on any. But Nelson, with the utmost politeness, insisted upon paying them this compliment, followed them close in spite of all their attempts to elude his vigilance, and never lost sight of them; till, finding it impossible either to deceive or escape him, they gave up their treacherous purpose in despair, and beat up for Martinico.

A business of more serious import soon engaged his attention. The Americans were at this time trading with our islands, taking advantage of the register of their ships, which had been issued while they were British subjects. Nelson knew that, by the Navigation Act[33], no foreigners, directly or indirectly, are permitted to carry on any trade with these possessions. He knew, also, that the Americans had made themselves foreigners with regard to England; they had disregarded the ties of blood and language when they acquired the independence which they had been led on to claim, unhappily for themselves before they were fit for it; and he was resolved that they should derive no profit from those ties now. Foreigners they had made themselves, and as foreigners they were to be treated.

"If once," said he, "they are admitted to any kind of intercourse with our islands, the views of the loyalists, in settling at Nova Scotia, are entirely done away; and when we are again embroiled in a French war, the Americans will first become the carriers of these colonies, and then have possession of them. Here they come, sell their cargoes for ready money, go to Martinico, buy molasses, and so round and round. The loyalist cannot do this, and consequently must sell a little dearer. The residents here are Americans by connection and by interest, and are inimical to Great Britain. They are as great rebels as ever were in America, had they the power to show it."

In November, when the squadron, having arrived at Barbadoes, was to separate, with no other orders than those for examining anchor-

33 The Navigation Acts were a set of laws restricting trade with Britain or its colonies to English ships. The requirement that imports from Europe, and exports to Europe, be first landed in England for the purpose of collecting duties, significantly adding to the cost of goods to the colonies and was one of the causes of the American Revolution. The Navigation Acts remained in effect until 1849.

ages, and the usual inquiries concerning wood and water, Nelson asked his friend Collingwood, then captain of the *Mediator*, whose opinions he knew upon the subject, to accompany him to the commander-in-chief, whom he then respectfully asked, whether they were not to attend to the commerce of the country, and see that the Navigation Act was respected—that appearing to him to be the intent of keeping men-of-war upon this station in time of peace?

Sir Richard Hughes replied, he had no particular orders, neither had the Admiralty sent him any Acts of Parliament. But Nelson made answer, that the Navigation Act was included in the statutes of the Admiralty, with which every captain was furnished, and that Act was directed to admirals, captains, &c., to see it carried into execution.

Sir Richard said he had never seen the book. Upon this Nelson produced the statutes, read the words of the Act, and apparently convinced the commander-in-chief, that men-of-war, as he said, "were sent abroad for some other purpose than to be made a show of." Accordingly orders were given to enforce the Navigation Act.

Major-General Sir Thomas Shirley was at this time governor of the Leeward Islands; and when Nelson waited on him, to inform him how he intended to act, and upon what grounds, he replied, that "old generals were not in the habit of taking advice from young gentlemen."

"Sir," said the young officer, with that confidence in himself which never carried him too far, and always was equal to the occasion, "I am as old as the prime minister of England[34], and I think myself as capable of commanding one of his Majesty's ships as that minister is of governing the state."

He was resolved to do his duty, whatever might be the opinion or conduct of others; and when he arrived upon his station at St. Kitt's, he sent away all the Americans, not choosing to seize them before they had been well apprised that the Act would be carried into effect, lest it might seem as if a trap had been laid for them.

The Americans, though they prudently decamped from St. Kitt's, were emboldened by the support they met with, and resolved to resist his orders, alleging that king's ships had no legal power to seize them without having deputations from the customs. The planters were to a man against him; the governors and the presidents of the different islands, with only a

34 In fact, Nelson was some eight months older than William Pitt, the Younger (1759–1806), who had become Prime Minister in 1783.

single exception, gave him no support; and the admiral, afraid to act on either side, yet wishing to oblige the planters, sent him a note, advising him to be guided by the wishes of the president of the council.

There was no danger in disregarding this, as it came unofficially, and in the form of advice. But scarcely a month after he had shown Sir Richard Hughes the law, and, as he supposed, satisfied him concerning it, he received an order from him, stating that he had now obtained good advice upon the point, and the Americans were not to be hindered from coming, and having free egress and regress, if the governor chose to permit them. An order to the same purport had been sent round to the different governors and presidents; and General Shirley and others informed him, in an authoritative manner, that they chose to admit American ships, as the commander-in-chief had left the decision to them.

These persons, in his own words, he soon "trimmed up, and silenced;" but it was a more delicate business to deal with the admiral: "I must either," said he, "disobey my orders, or disobey Acts of Parliament. I determined upon the former, trusting to the uprightness of my intentions, and believing that my country would not let me be ruined for protecting her commerce."

With this determination he wrote to Sir Richard; appealed again to the plain, literal, unequivocal sense of the Navigation Act; and in respectful language told him, he felt it his duty to decline obeying these orders till he had an opportunity of seeing and conversing with him. Sir Richard's first feeling was that of anger, and he was about to supersede Nelson; but having mentioned the affair to his captain, that officer told him he believed all the squadron thought the orders illegal, and therefore did not know how far they were bound to obey them. It was impossible, therefore, to bring Nelson to a court-martial, composed of men who agreed with him in opinion upon the point in dispute; and luckily, though the admiral wanted vigour of mind to decide upon what was right, he was not obstinate in wrong, and had even generosity enough in his nature to thank Nelson afterwards for having shown him his error.

Collingwood in the *Mediator*, and his brother, Wilfred Collingwood, in the *Rattler*, actively co-operated with Nelson. The custom-houses were informed that after a certain day all foreign vessels found in the ports would be seized; and many were, in consequence, seized, and condemned in the Admiralty Court. When the *Boreas* arrived at Nevis, she found four American vessels deeply laden, and what are called the island colours flying—white, with a red cross. They were ordered to hoist their proper flag, and depart within 48 hours; but they refused to obey, denying that they were Americans.

Some of their crews were then examined in Nelson's cabin, where the Judge of Admiralty happened to be present. The case was plain; they confessed that they were Americans, and that the ships, hull and cargo, were wholly American property; upon which he seized them. This raised a storm: the planters, the custom-house, and the governor, were all against him. Subscriptions were opened, and presently filled, for the purpose of carrying on the cause in behalf of the American captains; and the admiral, whose flag was at that time in the roads, stood neutral.

But the Americans and their abettors were not content with defensive law. The marines, whom he had sent to secure the ships, had prevented some of the masters from going ashore; and those persons, by whose depositions it appeared that the vessels and cargoes were American property, declared that they had given their testimony under bodily fear, for that a man with a drawn sword in his hand had stood over them the whole time. A rascally lawyer, whom the party employed, suggested this story; and as the sentry at the cabin door was a man with a drawn sword, the Americans made no scruple of swearing to this ridiculous falsehood, and commencing prosecutions against him accordingly.

They laid their damages at the enormous amount of £40,000; and Nelson was obliged to keep close on board his own ship, lest he should be arrested for a sum for which it would have been impossible to find bail. The marshal frequently came on board to arrest him, but was always prevented by the address of the first lieutenant, Mr. Wallis. Had he been taken, such was the temper of the people that it was certain he would have been cast for the whole sum. One of his officers, one day, in speaking of the restraint which he was thus compelled to suffer, happened to use the word *pity*!

"Pity!" exclaimed Nelson: "Pity! did you say? I shall live, sir, to be envied! and to that point I shall always direct my course."

Eight weeks remained in this state of duresse. During that time the trial respecting the detained ships came on in the court of Admiralty. He went on shore under a protection for the day from the judge; but, notwithstanding this, the marshal was called upon to take that opportunity of arresting him, and the merchants promised to indemnify him for so doing. The judge, however, did his duty, and threatened to send the marshal to prison if he attempted to violate the protection of the court.

Mr. Herbert, the president of Nevis, behaved with singular generosity upon this occasion. Though no man was a greater sufferer by the measures which Nelson had pursued, he offered in court to become his bail for £10,000 if he chose to suffer the arrest. The lawyer whom he had chosen proved to be an able as well as an honest man; and notwithstanding the opinions and pleadings of most of the counsel of the different islands, who maintained that ships of war were not justified in seizing American vessels without a deputation from the customs, the law was so explicit, the case so clear, and Nelson pleaded his own cause so well, that the four ships were condemned.

During the progress of this business he sent a memorial home to the King, in consequence of which orders were issued that he should be defended at the expense of the crown. And upon the representation which he made at the same time to the Secretary of State, and the suggestions with which he accompanied it, the Register Act was framed. The sanction of Government, and the approbation of his conduct which it implied, were highly gratifying to him; but he was offended, and not without just cause, that the Treasury should have transmitted thanks to the commander-in-chief for his activity and zeal in protecting the commerce of Great Britain.

"Had they known all," said he, "I do not think they would have bestowed thanks in that quarter, and neglected me. I feel much hurt that, after the loss of health and risk of fortune, another should be thanked for what I did against his orders. I either deserved to be sent out of the service, or at least to have had some little notice taken of what I had done. They have thought it worthy of notice, and yet have neglected me. If this is the reward for a faithful discharge of my duty, I shall be careful, and never stand forward again. But I have done my duty, and have nothing to accuse myself of."

The anxiety which he had suffered from the harassing uncertainties of law is apparent from these expressions. He had, however, something to console him, for he was at this time wooing the niece of his friend the president, then in her eighteenth year, the widow of Dr. Nisbet, a physician. She had one child, a son, by name Josiah, who was three years old.

One day Mr. Herbert, who had hastened half-dressed to receive Nelson, exclaimed, on returning to his dressing-room, "Good God! if I did not find that great little man, of whom everybody is so afraid, playing in the next room, under the dining-table, with Mrs. Nisbet's child!"

A few days afterwards Mrs. Nisbet herself was first introduced to him, and thanked him for the partiality which he had shown to her little boy. Her manners were mild and winning; and the captain, whose heart was easily susceptible of attachment, found no such imperious necessity for subduing his inclinations as had twice before withheld him from marrying.

They were married on March 11, 1787: Prince William Henry, who had come out to the West Indies the preceding winter, being present, by his own desire, to give away the bride.

Mr. Herbert, her uncle, was at this time so much displeased with his only daughter, that he had resolved to disinherit her, and leave his whole fortune, which was very great, to his niece. But Nelson, whose nature was too noble to let him profit by an act of injustice, interfered, and succeeded in reconciling the president to his child.

"Yesterday," said one of his naval friends the day after the wedding, "the navy lost one of its greatest ornaments by Nelson's marriage. It is a national loss that such an officer should marry: had it not been for this, Nelson would have become the greatest man in the service." The man was rightly estimated; but he who delivered this opinion did not understand the effect of domestic love and duty upon a mind of the true heroic stamp.

"We are often separate," said Nelson, in a letter to Mrs. Nisbet a few months before their marriage; "but our affections are not by any means on that account diminished. Our country has the first demand for our services; and private convenience or happiness must ever give way to the public good. Duty is the great business of a sea officer: all private considerations must give way to it, however painful."

"Have you not often heard," says he in another letter, "that salt water and absence always wash away love? Now I am such a heretic as not to believe that article, for, behold, every morning I have had six pails of salt water poured upon my head, and instead of finding what seamen say to be true, it goes on so contrary to the prescription, that you may, perhaps, see me before the fixed time."

More frequently his correspondence breathed a deeper strain. "To write letters to you," says he, "is the next greatest pleasure I feel to receiving them from you. What I experience when I read such as I am sure are the pure sentiments of your heart, my poor pen cannot express; nor, indeed, would I give much for any pen or head which could express feelings of that kind. Absent from you, I feel no pleasure: it is you who are everything to me. Without you, I care not for this world; for I have found, lately, nothing in it but vexation and trouble. These are my present sentiments. God Almighty grant they may never change! Nor do I think they will. Indeed there is, as far as human knowledge can judge, a moral certainty that they cannot; for it must be real affection that brings us together, not interest or compulsion."

Such were the feelings, and such the sense of duty, with which Nelson became a husband.

During his stay upon this station he had ample opportunity of observing the scandalous practices of the contractors, prize-agents, and other persons in the West Indies connected with the naval service. When he was first left with the command, and bills were brought him to sign for money which was owing for goods purchased for the navy, he required the original voucher, that he might examine whether those goods had been really purchased at the market price; but to produce vouchers would not have been convenient, and therefore was not the custom.

Upon this Nelson wrote to Sir Charles Middleton, then Comptroller of the Navy, representing the abuses which were likely to be practised in this manner. The answer which he received seemed to imply that the old forms were thought sufficient; and thus, having no alternative, he was compelled, with his eyes open, to submit to a practice originating in fraudulent intentions.

Soon afterwards two Antigua merchants informed him that they were privy to great frauds which had been committed upon government in various departments; at Antigua, to the amount of nearly £500,000; at Lucie, £300,000; at Barbadoes, £250,000; at Jamaica, upwards of a million. The informers were both shrewd sensible men of business; they did not affect to be actuated by a sense of justice, but required a per-centage upon so much as government should actually recover through their means.

Nelson examined the books and papers which they produced, and was convinced that government had been most infamously plundered. Vouchers, he found, in that country, were no check whatever: the principle was, that "a thing was always worth what it would bring;" and the merchants were in the habit of signing vouchers for each other, without even the appearance of looking at the articles. These accounts he sent home to the different departments which had been defrauded; but the peculators were too powerful, and they succeeded not merely in impeding inquiry, but even in raising prejudices against Nelson at the Board of Admiralty, which it was many years before he could subdue.

Owing probably, to these prejudices, and the influence of the peculators, he was treated, on his return to England, in a manner which had nearly driven him from the service. During the three years that the *Boreas* had remained upon a station which is usually so fatal, not a single officer or man of her whole complement had died. This almost unexampled instance of good health, though mostly, no doubt, imputable to a healthy season, must in some measure, also, be ascribed to the wise conduct of the captain.

He never suffered the ships to remain more than three or four weeks at a time at any of the islands; and when the hurricane months confined him to English Harbour, he encouraged all kinds of useful amusements—music, dancing, and cudgelling among the men; theatricals among the officers; anything which could employ their attention, and keep their spirits cheerful.

The *Boreas* arrived in England in June. Nelson, who had many times been supposed to be consumptive when in the West Indies, and perhaps was saved from consumption by that climate, was still in a precarious state of health[35]; and the raw wet weather of one of our ungenial summers brought on cold, and sore throat, and fever; yet his vessel was kept at the Nore from the end of June till the end of November, serving as a slop and receiving ship. This unworthy treatment, which more probably proceeded from inattention than from neglect, excited in Nelson the strongest indignation.

During the whole five months he seldom or never quitted the ship, but carried on the duty with strict and sullen attention. On the morning when orders were received to prepare the *Boreas* for being paid off, he expressed his joy to the senior officer in the Medway, saying, "It will release me for ever from an ungrateful service; for it is my firm and unalterable determination never again to set my foot on board a king's ship.

35 Whatever the cause of Nelson's condition, it was probably not consumption (tuberculosis), which even today cannot be treated effectively by a change of climate, rest, or any other measures short of powerful antibiotics. Nelson recovered, which suggests some sort of tropical parasite may have been to blame.

Immediately after my arrival in town I shall wait on the First Lord of the Admiralty, and resign my commission."

The officer to whom he thus communicated his intentions behaved in the wisest and most friendly manner; for finding it in vain to dissuade him in his present state of feeling, he secretly interfered with the First Lord to save him from a step so injurious to himself, little foreseeing how deeply the welfare and honour of England were at that moment at stake. This interference produced a letter from Lord Howe the day before the ship was paid off, intimating a wish to see Captain Nelson as soon as he arrived in town; when, being pleased with his conversation, and perfectly convinced, by what was then explained to him, of the propriety of his conduct, he desired that he might present him to the king on the first levee-day; and the gracious manner in which Nelson was then received effectually removed his resentment.

Prejudices had been, in like manner, excited against his friend, Prince William Henry. "Nothing is wanting, sir," said Nelson, in one of his letters, "to make you the darling of the English nation but truth. Sorry am I to say, much to the contrary has been dispersed."

This was not flattery, for Nelson was no flatterer. The letter in which this passage occurs shows in how wise and noble a manner he dealt with the prince. One of his royal highness's officers had applied for a court-martial upon a point in which he was unquestionably wrong. His royal highness, however, while he supported his own character and authority, prevented the trial, which must have been injurious to a brave and deserving man.

"Now that you are parted," said Nelson, "pardon me, my prince, when I presume to recommend that he may stand in your royal favour as if he had never sailed with you, and that at some future day you will serve him. There only wants this to place your conduct in the highest point of view. None of us are without failings—his was being rather too hasty; but that, put in competition with his being a good officer, will not, I am bold to say, be taken in the scale against him. More able friends than myself your royal highness may easily find, and of more consequence in the state; but one more attached and affectionate is not so easily met with: Princes seldom, very seldom, find a disinterested person to communicate their thoughts to: I do not pretend to be that person; but of this be assured, by a man who, I trust, never did a dishonourable act, that I am interested only that your royal highness should be the greatest and best man this country ever produced."

Encouraged by the conduct of Lord Howe, and by his reception at court, Nelson renewed his attack upon the peculators with fresh spirit. He had interviews with Mr. Rose, Mr. Pitt, and Sir Charles Middleton, to all of whom he satisfactorily proved his charges. In consequence, it is said, these very extensive public frauds were at length put in a proper train to be provided against in future; his representations were attended to; and every step which he recommended was adopted; the investigation was put into a proper course, which ended in the detection and punishment of some of the culprits; an immense saving was made to government, and thus its attention was directed to similar peculations in other parts of the colonies.

But it is said also that no mark of commendation seems to have been bestowed upon Nelson for his exertion. It has been justly remarked that the spirit of the navy cannot be preserved so effectually by the liberal honours bestowed on officers when they are worn out in the service, as by an attention to those who, like Nelson at this part of his life, have only their integrity and zeal to bring them into notice.

A junior officer, who had been left with the command at Jamaica, received an additional allowance, for which Nelson had applied in vain. Double pay was allowed to every artificer and seaman employed in the naval yard: Nelson had superintended the whole business of that yard with the most rigid exactness, and he complained that he was neglected.

"It was most true," he said, "that the trouble which he took to detect the fraudulent practices then carried on was no more than his duty; but he little thought that the expenses attending his frequent journeys to St. John's upon that duty (a distance of twelve miles) would have fallen upon his pay as captain of the *Boreas*."

Nevertheless, the sense of what he thought unworthy usage did not diminish his zeal. "I," said he, "must buffet the waves in search of—What? Alas! that they called honour is thought of no more. My fortune, God knows, has grown worse for the service; so much for serving my country! But the devil, ever willing to tempt the virtuous, has made me offer, if any ships should be sent to destroy his Majesty of Morocco's ports, to be there; and I have some reason to think that, should any more come of it, my humble services will be accepted. I have invariably laid down, and followed close, a plan of what ought to be uppermost in the breast of an officer,—that it is much better to serve an ungrateful country than to give up his own fame. Posterity will do him justice. A uniform course of honour and integrity seldom fails of bringing a man to the goal of fame at last."

The design against the Barbary pirates, like all other designs against them, was laid aside; and Nelson took his wife to his father's parsonage, meaning only to pay him a visit before they went to France; a project which he had formed for the sake of acquiring a competent knowledge of the French language.

But his father could not bear to lose him thus unnecessarily. Mr. Nelson had long been an invalid, suffering under paralytic and asthmatic affections, which, for several hours after he rose in the morning, scarcely permitted him to speak. He had been given over by his physicians for this complaint nearly forty years before his death; and was, for many of his latter years, obliged to spend all his winters at Bath. The sight of his son, he declared, had given him new life.

"But, Horatio," said he, "it would have been better that I had not been thus cheered, if I am so soon to be bereaved of you again. Let me, my good son, see you whilst I can. My age and infirmities increase, and I shall not last long."

To such an appeal there could be no reply. Nelson took up his abode at the parsonage, and amused himself with the sports and occupations of the country. Sometimes he busied himself with farming the glebe[36]; sometimes spent the greater part of the day in the garden, where he would dig as if for the mere pleasure of wearying himself. Sometimes he went a birds'-nesting, like a boy; and in these expeditions Mrs. Nelson always, by his expressed desire, accompanied him. Coursingwas his favourite amusement[37]. Shooting, as he practised it, was far too dangerous for his companions; for he carried his gun upon the full cock, as

36 Lands belonging to the incumbent pastor's parish or parishes, but treated as if they were the personal property of the incumbent. Rents and agricultural output were used to support the pastor.

37 A form of hunting with dogs, in which the dogs chase down and kill the game. Sight hounds, such as grayhounds, are employed, rather than scent hunters such as foxhounds. Depending upon the type of dog used, game can range from small animals, such as rabbits, to very large game, including deer and wolves, hence the various breeds referred to as wolfhounds, staghounds, boarhounds, and so forth. A more modern usage refers to a form of grayhound racing, now generally outlawed, using a live rabbit instead of a mechanical lure.

if he were going to board an enemy; and the moment a bird rose, he let fly without ever putting the fowling-piece to his shoulder. It is not, therefore, extraordinary that his having once shot a partridge should be remembered by his family among the remarkable events of his life.

But his time did not pass away thus without some vexatious cares to ruffle it. The affair of the American ships was not yet over, and he was again pestered with threats of prosecution.

"I have written them word," said he, "that I will have nothing to do with them, and they must act as they think proper. Government, I suppose, will do what is right, and not leave me in the lurch. We have heard enough lately of the consequences of the Navigation Act to this country. They may take my person; but if sixpence would save me from a prosecution, I would not give it."

It was his great ambition at this time to possess a pony; and having resolved to purchase one, he went to a fair for that purpose. During his absence two men abruptly entered the parsonage and inquired for him: they then asked for Mrs. Nelson; and after they had made her repeatedly declare that she was really and truly the captain's wife, presented her with a writ, or notification, on the part of the American captains, who now laid their damages at £20,000, and they charged her to give it to her husband on his return.

Nelson, having bought his pony, came home with it in high spirits. He called out his wife to admire the purchase and listen to all its excellences: nor was it till his glee had in some measure subsided that the paper could be presented to him.

His indignation was excessive; and in the apprehension that he should be exposed to the anxieties of the suit and the ruinous consequences which might ensue, he exclaimed, "This affront I did not deserve! But I'll be trifled with no longer. I will write immediately to the Treasury, and if government will not support me, I am resolved to leave the country."

Accordingly, he informed the Treasury that, if a satisfactory answer were not sent him by return of post, he should take refuge in France. To this he expected he should be driven, and for this he arranged everything with his characteristic rapidity of decision. It was settled that he should depart immediately, and Mrs. Nelson follow, under the care of his elder brother Maurice, ten days after him. But the answer which he received from government quieted his fears: it stated that Captain Nelson was a very good officer, and needed to be under no apprehension, for he would assuredly be supported.

Here his disquietude upon this subject seems to have ended. Still he was not at ease; he wanted employment, and was mortified that his applications for it produced no effect.

"Not being a man of fortune," he said, "was a crime which he was unable to get over, and therefore none of the great cared about him."

Repeatedly he requested the Admiralty that they would not leave him to rust in indolence. During the armament which was made upon occasion of the dispute concerning Nootka Sound[38], he renewed his application; and his steady friend, Prince William, who had then been created Duke of Clarence, recommended him to Lord Chatham.

The failure of this recommendation wounded him so keenly that he again thought of retiring from the service in disgust; a resolution from which nothing but the urgent remonstrances of Lord Hood induced him to desist. Hearing that the *Raisonnable*, in which he had commenced his career, was to be commissioned, he asked for her. This also was in vain; and a coolness ensued, on his part, toward Lord Hood, because that excellent officer did not use his influence with Lord Chatham upon this occasion.

Lord Hood, however, had certainly sufficient reasons for not interfering; for he ever continued his steady friend. In the winter of 1792, when we were on the eve of the revolutionary war, Nelson once more offered his services, earnestly requested a ship, and added, that if their lordships should be pleased to appoint him to a cockle-boat he should feel satisfied.

He was answered in the usual official form: "Sir, I have received your letter of the 5th instant, expressing your readiness to serve, and have read the same to my Lords Commissioners of the Admiralty."

On the 12th of December he received this dry acknowledgment. The fresh mortification did not, however, affect him long; for, by the joint interest of the Duke and Lord Hood, he was appointed, on the 30th of January following, to the *Agamemnon*, of sixty-four guns.

38 Nootka Sound is located on the west coast of Vancouver Island, in British Colombia, Canada. In the late 1780s Spain's attempts to enforce a trade monopoly with Asia, including seizing British ships and facilities in Nootka Sound, very nearly led to war with Spain. War was averted, and a series of conventions would establish colonial rights on the Pacific coast of North America, which in turn led to establishing British colonies in what would become western Canada.

Chapter 3
1793–1795

The *Agamemnon* sent to the Mediteranean—Commencement of Nelson's Aquaintance with Sir W. Hamilton—He is sent to Corsica, to co-operate with Paoli—State of Affairs in that Island—Nelson undertakes the Siege of Bastia, and reduces it—Takes a distinguished part in the Siege of Calvi, where he loses an Eye—Admiral Hotham's Action—The *Agamemnon* ordered to Genoa, to co-operate with the Austrian and Sardinian Forces—Gross Misconduct of the Austrian General.

"There are three things, young gentleman," said Nelson to one of his midshipmen, "which you are constantly to bear in mind. First, you must always implicitly obey orders, without attempting to form any opinion of your own respecting their propriety; secondly, you must consider every man your enemy who speaks ill of your king; and, thirdly, you must hate a Frenchman as you do the devil." With these feelings he engaged in the war. Josiah, his son-in-law, went with him as a midshipman.

The *Agamemnon* was ordered to the Mediterranean under Lord Hood[39]. The fleet arrived in those seas at a time when the south of France would willingly have formed itself into a separate republic, under the protection of England.

But good principles had been at that time perilously abused by ignorant and profligate men; and, in its fear and hatred of democracy, the English Government abhorred whatever was republican. Lord Hood

39 Vice Admiral Samuel Hood, at that time Baron Hood, and to become the 1st Viscount Hood in 1796, was appointed Commander-in-Chief, Mediterranean in May 1793. Previous to this appointment he had served on the Board of Admiralty.

could not take advantage of the fair occasion which presented itself; and which, if it had been seized with vigour, might have ended in dividing France:—but he negotiated with the people of Toulon, to take possession provisionally of their port and city; which, fatally for themselves, was done.

Before the British fleet entered, Nelson was sent with despatches to Sir William Hamilton, our envoy at the Court of Naples. Sir William, after his first interview with him, told Lady Hamilton he was about to introduce a little man to her, who could not boast of being very handsome; but such a man as, he believed, would one day astonish the world.

"I have never before," he continued, "entertained an officer at my house; but I am determined to bring him here. Let him be put in the room prepared for Prince Augustus."

Thus that acquaintance began which ended in the destruction of Nelson's domestic happiness. It seemed to threaten no such consequences at its commencement. He spoke of Lady Hamilton, in a letter to his wife, as a young woman of amiable manners, who did honour to the station to which she had been raised[40]; and he remarked, that she had been exceedingly kind to Josiah.

The activity with which the envoy exerted himself in procuring troops from Naples, to assist in garrisoning Toulon, so delighted him, that he is said to have exclaimed, "Sir William, you are a man after my own heart!—you do business in my own way:" and then to have added, "I am now only a captain; but I will, if I live, be at the top of the tree."

Here, also, that acquaintance with the Neapolitan court commenced, which led to the only blot upon Nelson's public character. The king, who was sincere at that time in his enmity to the French, called the English the saviours of Italy, and of his dominions in particular. He paid the most flattering attentions to Nelson, made him dine with him, and seated him at his right hand.

Having accomplished this mission, Nelson received orders to join Commodore Linzee at Tunis. On the way, five sail of the enemy were discovered off the coast of Sardinia, and he chased them. They proved to be three forty-four gun frigates, with a corvette of twenty-four and a brig of twelve.

40 "Raised" is something of an understatement. Whether Nelson was actually familiar with Emma Hamilton's background at this time is questionable, though one might expect he would have at least heard rumors.

The *Agamemnon* had only 345 men at quarters, having landed part of her crew at Toulon, and others being absent in prizes. He came near enough one of the frigates to engage her, but at great disadvantage, the Frenchman manoeuvring well and sailing greatly better.

A running fight of three hours ensued, during which the other ships, which were at some distance, made all speed to come up. By this time the enemy was almost silenced, when a favourable change of wind enabled her to get out of reach of the *Agamemnon*'s guns; and that ship had received so much damage in the rigging that she could not follow her.

Nelson, conceiving that this was but the forerunner of a far more serious engagement, called his officers together, and asked them if the ship was fit to go into action against such a superior force without some small refit and refreshment for the men. Their answer was, that she certainly was not.

He then gave these orders,—"Veer the ship, and lay her head to the westward: let some of the best men be employed in refitting the rigging, and the carpenter in getting crows and capstan-bars to prevent our wounded spars from coming down: and get the wine up for the people, with some bread, for it may be half an hour good before we are again in action."

But when the French came up, their comrade made signals of distress, and they all hoisted out their boats to go to her assistance, leaving the *Agamemnon* unmolested.

Nelson found Commodore Linzee at Tunis, where he had been sent to expostulate with the Dey upon the impolicy of his supporting the revolutionary government of France. Nelson represented to him the atrocity of that government.
Such arguments were of little avail in Barbary; and when the Dey was told that the French had put their sovereign to death, he drily replied, that "Nothing could be more heinous; and yet, if historians told the truth, the English had once done the same[41]."

This answer had doubtless been suggested by the French about him: they had completely gained the ascendancy, and all negotiation on our part proved fruitless. Shortly afterward, Nelson was detached with a small squadron, to co-operate with General Paoli and the Anti-Gallican party in Corsica.

41 A reference to the execution of Charles I on 30 January 1649.

Some thirty years before this time the heroic patriotism of the Corsicans, and of their leader Paoli, had been the admiration of England.

The history of these brave people is but a melancholy tale. The island which they inhabit has been abundantly blessed by nature; it has many excellent harbours; and though the *malaria*, or pestilential atmosphere, which is so deadly in many parts of Italy and of the Italian islands, prevails on the eastern coast, the greater part of the country is mountainous and healthy.

It is about 150 miles long, and from 40 to 50 broad; in circumference, some 320; a country large enough, and sufficiently distant from the nearest shores, to have subsisted as an independent state, if the welfare and happiness of the human race had ever been considered as the end and aim of policy. The Moors, the Pisans, the kings of Aragon, and the Genoese, successively attempted, and each for a time effected its conquest.

The yoke of the Genoese continued longest, and was the heaviest. These petty tyrants ruled with an iron rod; and when at any time a patriot rose to resist their oppressions, if they failed to subdue him by force they resorted to assassination. At the commencement of the last century they quelled one revolt by the aid of German auxiliaries, whom the Emperor Charles VI sent against a people who had never offended him, and who were fighting for whatever is most dear to man.

In 1734 the war was renewed; and Theodore, a Westphalian baron, then appeared upon the stage.

In that age men were not accustomed to see adventurers play for kingdoms, and Theodore became the common talk of Europe. He had served in the French armies; and having afterwards been noticed both by Ripperda and Alberoni, their example, perhaps, inflamed a spirit as ambitious and as unprincipled as their own.

He employed the whole of his means in raising money and procuring arms; then wrote to the leaders of the Corsican patriots, to offer them considerable assistance, if they would erect Corsica into an independent kingdom, and elect him king. When he landed among them, they were struck with his stately person, his dignified manners, and imposing talents. They believed the magnificent promises of foreign assistance which he held out, and elected him king accordingly.

Had his means been as he represented them, they could not have acted more wisely than in thus at once fixing the government of their country, and putting an end to those rivalries among the leading families, which had so often proved pernicious to the public weal. He struck money, conferred titles, blocked up the fortified towns which were held by the Genoese, and amused the people with promises of assistance for about eight months: then, perceiving that they cooled in their affections towards him in proportion as their expectations were disappointed, he left the island, under the plea of expediting himself the succours which he had so long awaited.

Such was his address, that he prevailed upon several rich merchants in Holland, particularly the Jews, to trust him with cannon and warlike stores to a great amount. They shipped these under the charge of a supercargo[42].

Theodore returned with this supercargo to Corsica, and put him to death on his arrival, as the shortest way of settling the account. The remainder of his life was a series of deserved afflictions.

He threw in the stores which he had thus fraudulently obtained; but he did not dare to land, for Genoa had now called in the French to their assistance, and a price had been set upon his head. His dreams of royalty were now at an end; he took refuge in London, contracted debts, and was thrown into the King's Bench.

After lingering there many years, he was released under an act of insolvency, in consequence of which he made over the kingdom of Corsica for the use of his creditors, and died shortly after his deliverance.

The French, who have never acted a generous part in the history of the world, readily entered into the views of the Genoese, which accorded with their own policy: for such was their ascendancy at Genoa, that in subduing Corsica for these allies, they were in fact subduing it for themselves.

They entered into the contest, therefore, with their usual vigour, and their usual cruelty. It was in vain that the Corsicans addressed a most affecting memorial to the court of Versailles; that remorseless government persisted in its flagitious project. They poured in troops; dressed a part of them like the people of the country, by which means they deceived

42 A person carried aboard a ship, but neither a passenger nor a member of the crew, who has been placed in charge of the cargo being hauled. He is employed by the cargo's owner, and represents his interest. In this case, the supercargo represented the Dutch merchants who had financed the equipment and arms.

and destroyed many of the patriots; cut down the standing corn[43], the vines, and the olives; set fire to the villages, and hung all the most able and active men who fell into their hands.

A war of this kind may be carried on with success against a country so small and so thinly peopled as Corsica. Having reduced the island to perfect servitude, which they called peace, the French withdrew their forces.

As soon as they were gone, men, women, and boys rose at once against their oppressors. The circumstances of the times were now favourable to them; and some British ships, acting as allies of Sardinia, bombarded Bastia and San Fiorenzo, and delivered them into the hands of the patriots.

This service was long remembered with gratitude: the impression made upon our own countrymen was less favourable.

They had witnessed the heartburnings of rival chiefs, and the dissensions among the patriots; and perceiving the state of barbarism to which continual oppression, and habits of lawless turbulence, had reduced the nation, did not recollect that the vices of the people were owing to their unhappy circumstances, but that the virtues which they displayed arose from their own nature.

This feeling, perhaps, influenced the British court, when, in 1746, Corsica offered to put herself under the protection of Great Britain: an answer was returned, expressing satisfaction at such a communication, hoping that the Corsicans would preserve the same sentiments, but signifying also that the present was not the time for such a measure.

These brave islanders then formed a government for themselves, under two leaders, Gaffori and Matra, who had the title of protectors. The latter is represented as a partisan of Genoa, favouring the views of the oppressors of his country by the most treasonable means.

Gaffori was a hero worthy of old times. His eloquence was long remembered with admiration. A band of assassins was once advancing against him; he heard of their approach, went out to meet them; and, with a serene dignity which overawed them, requested them to hear him.

He then spake to them so forcibly of the distresses of their country, her intolerable wrongs, and the hopes and views of their brethren in

43 In British usage, any type of grain, including, but not limited to *maize*, which was called "Indian corn" in Britain. In the context of this incident, probably wheat.

arms, that the very men who had been hired to murder him, fell at his feet, implored his forgiveness, and joined his banner.

While he was besieging the Genoese in Corte, a part of the garrison perceiving the nurse with his eldest son, then an infant in arms, straying at a little distance from the camp, suddenly sallied out and seized them. The use they made of their persons was in conformity to their usual execrable conduct.

When Gaffori advanced to batter the walls, they held up the child directly over that part of the wall at which the guns were pointed. The Corsicans stopped: but Gaffori stood at their head, and ordered them to continue the fire. Providentially the child escaped, and lived to relate, with becoming feeling, a fact so honourable to his father.

That father conducted the affairs of the island till 1753, when he was assassinated by some wretches, set on, it is believed, by Genoa, but certainly pensioned by that abominable government after the deed. He left the country in such a state that it was enabled to continue the war two years after his death without a leader: the Corsicans then found one worthy of their cause in Pasquale de Paoli.

Paoli's father was one of the patriots who effected their escape from Corsica when the French reduced it to obedience. He retired to Naples, and brought up his youngest son in the Neapolitan service.

The Corsicans heard of young Paoli's abilities, and solicited him to come over to his native country, and take the command. He did not hesitate long: his father, who was too far advanced in years to take an active part himself, encouraged him to go; and when they separated, the old man fell on his neck, and kissed him, and gave him his blessing.

"My son," said he, "perhaps I may never see you more; but in my mind I shall ever be present with you. Your design is great and noble; and I doubt not but God will bless you in it. I shall devote to your cause the little remainder of my life in offering up my prayers for your success."

When Paoli assumed the command, he found all things in confusion: he formed a democratical government, of which he was chosen chief: restored the authority of the laws; established a university; and took such measures, both for repressing abuses and moulding the rising generation, that, if France had not interfered, upon its wicked and detestable principle of usurpation, Corsica might at this day have been as free, and flourishing and happy a commonwealth as any of the Grecian states in the days of their prosperity.

The Genoese were at this time driven out of their fortified towns, and must in a short time have been expelled. France was indebted some millions of livres to Genoa: it was not convenient to pay this money; so the French minister proposed to the Genoese, that she should discharge the debt by sending six battalions to serve in Corsica for four years.

The indignation which this conduct excited in all generous hearts was forcibly expressed by Rousseau, who, with all his errors, was seldom deficient in feeling for the wrongs of humanity.

"You Frenchmen," said he, writing to one of that people, "are a thoroughly servile nation, thoroughly sold to tyranny, thoroughly cruel and relentless in persecuting the unhappy. If you knew of a freeman at the other end of the world, I believe you would go thither for the mere pleasure of extirpating him."

The immediate object of the French happened to be purely mercenary: they wanted to clear off their debt to Genoa; and as the presence of their troops in the island effected this, they aimed at doing the people no farther mischief.

Would that the conduct of England had been at this time free from reproach! but a proclamation was issued by the English government, after the peace of Paris[44], prohibiting any intercourse with the rebels of Corsica.

Paoli said, he did not expect this from Great Britain. This great man was deservedly proud of his country. "I defy Rome, Sparta, or Thebes," he would say, "to show me thirty years of such patriotism as Corsica can boast!"

Availing himself of the respite which the inactivity of the French and the weakness of the Genoese allowed, he prosecuted his plans of civilising the people. He used to say, that though he had an unspeakable pride in the prospect of the fame to which he aspired; yet if he could but render his countrymen happy, he could be content to be forgotten. His own importance he never affected to undervalue.

"We are now to our country," said he, "like the prophet Elisha stretched over the dead child of the Shunamite,—eye to eye, nose to nose, mouth to mouth. It begins to recover warmth, and to revive: I hope

44 The 1763 Treaty of Paris ended the Seven Years War (French and Indian War). There have been several other Treaties of Paris, starting in the 13th Century and continuing through the 20th, including the 1783 Treaty of Paris that ended the American Revolution.

it will yet regain full health and vigour."

But when the four years were expired, France purchased the sovereignty of Corsica from the Genoese for forty millions of livres; as if the Genoese had been entitled to sell it; as if any bargain and sale could justify one country in taking possession of another against the will of the inhabitants, and butchering all who oppose the usurpation!

Among the enormities which France has committed, this action seems but as a speck; yet the foulest murderer that ever suffered by the hand of the executioner has infinitely less guilt upon his soul than the statesman who concluded this treaty, and the monarch who sanctioned and confirmed it.

A desperate and glorious resistance was made, but it was in vain; no power interposed in behalf of these injured islanders, and the French poured in as many troops as were required. They offered to confirm Paoli in the supreme authority, only on condition that he would hold it under their government.

His answer was, that "the rocks which surrounded him should melt away before he would betray a cause which he held in common with the poorest Corsican."

This people then set a price upon his head. During two campaigns he kept them at bay: they overpowered him at length; he was driven to the shore, and having escaped on shipboard, took refuge in England. It is said that Lord Shelburne[45] resigned his seat in the cabinet because the ministry looked on without attempting to prevent France from succeeding in this abominable and important act of aggrandizement.

In one respect, however, our country acted as became her. Paoli was welcomed with the honours which he deserved, a pension of £1,200 was immediately granted him, and provision was liberally made for his elder brother and his nephew.

About twenty years Paoli remained in England, enjoying the friendship of the wise and the admiration of the good. But when the French Revolution began, it seemed as if the restoration of Corsica was at hand.

The whole country, as if animated by one spirit, rose and demanded liberty; and the National Assembly passed a decree recognising the island as a department of France, and therefore entitled to all the privileges of

45 William Petty-FitzMaurice, 2nd Ear of Shelburne, 1st Marquess of Lansdowne (1737–1805). Shelburne was First Lord of Trade in 1763. He would later serve as Prime Minister from 1782 to 1783.

the new French constitution. This satisfied the Corsicans, which it ought not to have done; and Paoli, in whom the ardour of youth was passed, seeing that his countrymen were contented, and believing that they were about to enjoy a state of freedom, naturally wished to return to his native country.

He resigned his pension in the year 1790, and appeared at the bar of the Assembly with the Corsican deputies, when they took the oath of fidelity to France.

But the course of events in France soon dispelled those hopes of a new and better order of things, which Paoli, in common with so many of the friends of human-kind, had indulged; and perceiving, after the execution of the king, that a civil war was about to ensue, of which no man could foresee the issue, he prepared to break the connection between Corsica and the French Republic.

The convention suspecting such a design, and perhaps occasioning it by their suspicions, ordered him to their bar. That way he well knew led to the guillotine; and returning a respectful answer, he declared that he would never be found wanting in his duty, but pleaded age and infirmity as a reason for disobeying the summons.

Their second order was more summary; and the French troops, who were in Corsica, aided by those of the natives, who were either influenced by hereditary party feelings, or who were sincere in Jacobinism, took the field against him.

But the people were with him. He repaired to Corte, the capital of the island, and was again invested with the authority which he had held in the noonday of his fame. The convention upon this denounced him as a rebel, and set a price upon his head. It was not the first time that France had proscribed Paoli.

Paoli now opened a correspondence with Lord Hood, promising, if the English would make an attack upon St. Fiorenzo from the sea, he would at the same time attack it by land. This promise he was unable to perform; and Commodore Linzee, who, in reliance upon it, was sent upon this service, was repulsed with some loss.

Lord Hood, who had now been compelled to evacuate Toulon, suspected Paoli of intentionally deceiving him. This was an injurious suspicion.

Shortly afterwards he dispatched Lieutenant-Colonel (afterward Sir John) Moore and Major Koehler to confer with him upon a plan of operations. Sir Gilbert Elliot accompanied them; and it was agreed that, in consideration of the succours, both military and naval, which his Britannic Majesty should afford for the purpose of expelling the French, the island of Corsica should be delivered into the immediate possession of his Majesty, and bind itself to acquiesce in any settlement he might approve of concerning its government, and its future relation with Great Britain.

While this negotiation was going on, Nelson cruised off the island with a small squadron, to prevent the enemy from throwing in supplies.

Close to St. Fiorenzo the French had a storehouse of flour near their only mill: he watched an opportunity, and landed 120 men, who threw the flour into the sea, burnt the mill, and re-embarked before 1,000 men, who were sent against him, could occasion them the loss of a single man.

While he exerted himself thus, keeping out all supplies, intercepting despatches, attacking their outposts and forts, and cutting out vessels from the bay,—a species of warfare which depresses the spirit of an enemy even more than it injures them, because of the sense of individual superiority which it indicates in the assailants—troops were landed, and St. Fiorenzo was besieged. The French finding themselves unable to maintain their post sunk one of their frigates, burnt another, and retreated to Bastia.

Lord Hood submitted to General Dundas, who commanded the land forces, a plan for the reduction of this place: the general declined co-operating, thinking the attempt impracticable without a reinforcement of 2,000 men, which he expected from Gibraltar. Upon this Lord Hood determined to reduce it with the naval force under his command; and leaving part of his fleet off Toulon, he came with the rest to Bastia.

He showed a proper sense of respect for Nelson's services, and of confidence in his talents, by taking care not to bring with him any older captain[46].

A few days before their arrival, Nelson had had what he called a brush with the enemy. "If I had had with me 500 troops," he said, "to a certainty I should have stormed the town; and I believe it might have been carried. Armies go so slow that seamen think they never mean to

46 That is, none of the captains who accompanied Hood to Bastia were senior to Nelson, so that he remained the senior captain on that station.

get forward; but I daresay they act on a surer principle, although we seldom fail."

During this partial action our army appeared upon the heights; and having reconnoitered the place, returned to St. Fiorenzo.

"What the general could have seen to make a retreat necessary," said Nelson, "I cannot comprehend. A thousand men would certainly take Bastia: with five hundred and the *Agamemnon* I would attempt it. My seamen are now what British seamen ought to be—almost invincible. They really mind shot no more than peas."

General Dundas had not the same confidence. "After mature consideration," he said in a letter to Lord Hood, "and a personal inspection for several days of all circumstances, local as well as others, I consider the siege of Bastia, with our present means and force, to be a most visionary and rash attempt; such as no officer would be justified in undertaking."

Lord Hood replied that nothing would be more gratifying to his feelings than to have the whole responsibility upon himself; and that he was ready and willing to undertake the reduction of the place at his own risk with the force and means at present there.

General D'Aubant, who succeeded at this time to the command of the army, coincided in opinion with his predecessor, and did not think it right to furnish his lordship with a single soldier, cannon, or any stores. Lord Hood could only obtain a few artillerymen; and ordering on board that part of the troops who, having been embarked as marines, were borne on the ships' books as part of their respective complements, he began the siege with 1,183 soldiers, artillerymen, and marines, and 250 sailors.

"We are but few," said Nelson, "but of the right sort; our general at St. Fiorenzo not giving us one of the five regiments he has there lying idle."

These men were landed on the 4th of April [1794], under Lieutenant-Colonel Villettes and Nelson, who had now acquired from the army the title of brigadier. Guns were dragged by the sailors up heights where it appeared almost impossible to convey them—a work of the greatest difficulty, and which Nelson said could never, in his opinion, have been accomplished by any but British seamen.

The soldiers, though less dexterous in such service, because not accustomed, like sailors, to habitual dexterity, behaved with equal spirit.

"Their zeal," said the brigadier, "is almost unexampled. There is not a man but considers himself as personally interested in the event, and deserted by the general. It has, I am persuaded, made them equal to double their numbers."

This is one proof, of many, that for our soldiers to equal our seamen, it is only necessary for them to be equally well commanded. They have the same heart and soul, as well as the same flesh and blood. Too much may, indeed, be exacted from them in a retreat; but set their face toward a foe, and there is nothing within the reach of human achievement which they cannot perform.

The French had improved the leisure which our military commander had allowed them; and before Lord Hood commenced his operations, he had the mortification of seeing that the enemy were every day erecting new works, strengthening old ones, and rendering the attempt more difficult.

La Combe St. Michel, the commissioner from the national convention, who was in the city, replied in these terms to the summons of the British admiral—"I have hot shot for your ships, and bayonets for your troops. When two-thirds of our men are killed, I will then trust to the generosity of the English."

The siege, however, was not sustained with the firmness which such a reply seemed to augur. On the 19th of May a treaty of capitulation was begun; that same evening the troops from St. Fiorenzo made their appearance on the hills; and, on the following morning, General d'Aubant arrived with the whole army to take possession of Bastia.

The event of the siege had justified the confidence of the sailors; but they themselves excused the opinion of the generals when they saw what they had done.

"I am all astonishment," said Nelson, "when I reflect on what we have achieved; 1,000 regulars, 1,500 national guards, and a large party of Corsican troops, 4,000 in all, laying down their arms to 1,200 soldiers, marines, and seamen! I always was of opinion, have ever acted up to it, and never had any reason to repent it, that one Englishman was equal to three Frenchmen. Had this been an English town, I am sure it would not have been taken by them."

When it had been resolved to attack the place, the enemy were supposed to be far inferior in number; and it was not till the whole had been arranged, and the siege publicly undertaken, that Nelson received certain information of the great superiority of the garrison. This intelligence he kept secret, fearing lest, if so fair a pretext were afforded, the attempt would be abandoned.

"My own honour," said he to his wife, "Lord Hood's honour, and the honour of our country, must have been sacrificed had I mentioned what I knew; therefore you will believe what must have been my feelings during the whole siege, when I had often proposals made to me to write to Lord Hood to raise it."

Those very persons who thus advised him, were rewarded for their conduct at the siege of Bastia: Nelson, by whom it may truly be affirmed that Bastia was taken, received no reward. Lord Hood's thanks to him, both public and private, were, as he himself said, the handsomest which man could give; but his signal merits were not so mentioned in the despatches as to make them sufficiently known to the nation, nor to obtain for him from government those honours to which they so amply entitled him. This could only have arisen from the haste in which the despatches were written; certainly not from any deliberate purpose, for Lord Hood was uniformly his steady and sincere friend.

One of the cartel's ships, which carried the garrison of Bastia to Toulon, brought back intelligence that the French were about to sail from that port; such exertions had they made to repair the damage done at the evacuation, and to fit out a fleet. The intelligence was speedily verified.

Lord Hood sailed in quest of them toward the islands of Hieres. The *Agamemnon* was with him.

"I pray God," said Nelson, writing to his wife, "that we may meet their fleet. If any accident should happen to me, I am sure my conduct will be such as will entitle you to the royal favour; not that I have the least idea but I shall return to you, and full of honour: if not, the Lord's will be done. My name shall never be a disgrace to those who may belong to me. The little I have, I have given to you, except a small annuity—I wish it was more; but I have never got a farthing dishonestly: it descends from clean hands. Whatever fate awaits me, I pray God to bless you, and preserve you, for your son's sake."

With a mind thus prepared, and thus confident, his hopes and wishes seemed on the point of being gratified, when the enemy were discovered close under the land, near St. Tropez. The wind fell, and prevented Lord Hood from getting between them and the shore, as he designed: boats came out from Antibes and other places to their assistance, and towed them within the shoals in Gourjean Roads, where they were protected by the batteries on isles St. Honoré and St. Marguerite, and on Cape Garousse. Here the English admiral planned a new mode of attack, meaning to double on five of the nearest ships; but the wind again died away, and it was found that they had anchored in compact order, guarding the only passage for large ships. There was no way of effecting this passage, except by towing or warping the vessels; and this rendered the attempt impracticable. For this time the enemy escaped; but Nelson bore in mind the admirable plan of attack which Lord Hood had devised, and there came a day when they felt its tremendous effects.

The *Agamemnon* was now despatched to co-operate at the siege of Calvi with General Sir Charles Stuart; an officer who, unfortunately for his country, never had an adequate field allotted him for the display of those eminent talents which were, to all who knew him, so conspicuous. Nelson had less responsibility here than at Bastia; and was acting with a man after his own heart, who was never sparing of himself, and slept every night in the advanced battery.

But the service was not less hard than that of the former siege. "We will fag ourselves to death," said he to Lord Hood, "before any blame shall lie at our doors. I trust it will not be forgotten, that twenty-five pieces of heavy ordnance have been dragged to the different batteries, mounted, and, all but three, fought by seamen, except one artilleryman to point the guns."

The climate proved more destructive than the service; for this was during the lion sun, as they call our season of the dog-days. Of 2,000 men, above half were sick, and the rest like so many phantoms. Nelson described himself as the reed among the oaks, bowing before the storm when they were laid low by it.

"All the prevailing disorders have attacked me," said he, "but I have not strength enough for them to fasten on."

The loss from the enemy was not great; but Nelson received a serious injury: a shot struck the ground near him, and drove the sand and small gravel into one of his eyes. He spoke of it slightly at the time: writing the same day to Lord Hood, he only said that he had got a little hurt that morning, not much; and the next day, he said, he should be able to attend his duty in the evening. In fact, he suffered it to confine him only one day; but the sight was lost.

After the fall of Calvi, his services were, by a strange omission, altogether overlooked; and his name was not even mentioned in the list of wounded. This was no ways imputable to the admiral, for he sent home to government Nelson's journal of the siege, that they might fully understand the nature of his indefatigable and unequalled exertions. If those exertions were not rewarded in the conspicuous manner which they deserved, the fault was in the administration of the day, not in Lord Hood.

Nelson felt himself neglected. "One hundred and ten days," said he, "I have been actually engaged at sea and on shore against the enemy; three actions against ships, two against Bastia in my ship, four boat actions, and two villages taken, and twelve sail of vessels burnt. I do not know that any one has done more. I have had the comfort to be always applauded by my Commander-in-Chief, but never to be rewarded; and, what is more mortifying, for services in which I have been wounded, others have been praised, who, at the same time, were actually in bed, far from the scene of action. They have not done me justice. But never mind, I'll have a *Gazette* of my own." How amply was this second-sight of glory realised!

The health of his ship's company had now, in his own words, been miserably torn to pieces by as hard service as a ship's crew ever performed: 150 were in their beds when he left Calvi; of them he lost 54 and believed that the constitutions of the rest were entirely destroyed.

He was now sent with despatches to Mr. Drake, at Genoa, and had his first interview with the Doge. The French had, at this time, taken possession of Vado Bay, in the Genoese territory; and Nelson foresaw that, if their thoughts were bent on the invasion of Italy, they would accomplish it the ensuing spring.

"The allied powers," he said, "were jealous of each other; and none but England was hearty in the cause."

His wish was for peace on fair terms, because England he thought was draining herself to maintain allies who would not fight for themselves.

Lord Hood had now returned to England, and the command devolved on Admiral Hotham[47].

47 William Hotham, 1st Baron Hotham (1736–1813), was a vice admiral when he replaced Hood as Commander-in-Chief, Mediterranean. He was promoted to full admiral shortly thereafter, and was elevated to the Irish peerage in 1797.

The affairs of the Mediterranean wore at this time a gloomy aspect. The arts, as well as the arms of the enemy, were gaining the ascendancy there. Tuscany concluded peace relying upon the faith of France, which was, in fact, placing itself at her mercy. Corsica was in danger. We had taken that island for ourselves, annexed it formally to the crown of Great Britain, and given it a constitution as free as our own.

This was done with the consent of the majority of the inhabitants; and no transaction between two countries was ever more fairly or legitimately conducted: yet our conduct was unwise;—the island is large enough to form an independent state, and such we should have made it, under our protection, as long as protection might be needed; the Corsicans would then have felt as a nation; but when one party had given up the country to England, the natural consequence was that the other looked to France. The question proposed to the people was, to which would they belong?

Our language and our religion were against us; our unaccommodating manners, it is to be feared, still more so. The French were better politicians. In intrigue they have ever been unrivalled; and it now became apparent that, in spite of old wrongs, which ought never to have been forgotten nor forgiven, their partisans were daily acquiring strength.

It is part of the policy of France, and a wise policy it is, to impress upon other powers the opinion of its strength, by lofty language: and by threatening before it strikes; a system which, while it keeps up the spirit of its allies, and perpetually stimulates their hopes, tends also to dismay its enemies.

Corsica was now loudly threatened. "The French, who had not yet been taught to feel their own inferiority upon the seas, braved us in contempt upon that element." They had a superior fleet in the Mediterranean, and they sent it out with express orders to seek the English and engage them.

Accordingly, the Toulon fleet, consisting of seventeen ships of the line and five smaller vessels, put to sea. Admiral Hotham received this information at Leghorn, and sailed immediately in search of them. He had with him fourteen sail of the line, and one Neapolitan seventy-four; but his ships were only half-manned, containing but 7,650 men, whereas the enemy had 16,900.

He soon came in sight of them: a general action was expected; and Nelson, as was his custom on such occasions, wrote a hasty letter to his wife, as that which might possibly contain his last farewell. "The lives of all," said he, "are in the hand of Him who knows best whether to preserve mine or not; my character and good name are in my own keeping."

But however confident the French government might be of their naval superiority, the officers had no such feeling; and after manoeuvring for a day in sight of the English fleet, they suffered themselves to be chased.

One of their ships, the *Ça Ira*, of eighty-four guns, carried away her main and fore top-masts. The *Inconstant* frigate fired at the disabled ship, but received so many shot that she was obliged to leave her. Soon afterwards a French frigate took the *Ça Ira* in tow; and the *Sans-Culottes*, one hundred and twenty, and the *Jean Barras*, seventy-four, kept about gunshot distance on her weather bow.

The *Agamemnon* stood towards her, having no ship of the line to support her within several miles. As she drew near, the *Ça Ira* fired her stern guns so truly, that not a shot missed some part of the ship; and latterly, the masts were struck by every shot.

It had been Nelson's intention not to fire before he touched her stern; but seeing how impossible it was that he should be supported, and how certainly the *Agamemnon* must be severely cut up if her masts were disabled, he altered his plan according to the occasion. As soon, therefore, as he was within a hundred yards of her stern, he ordered the helm to be put a-starboard, and the driver and after-sails to be brailed up and shivered; and, as the ship fell off, gave the enemy her whole broadside.

They instantly braced up the after-yards, put the helm a-port, and stood after her again. This manoeuvre he practised for two hours and a quarter, never allowing the *Ça Ira* to get a single gun from either side to bear on him; and when the French fired their after-guns now, it was no longer with coolness and precision, for every shot went far ahead.

By this time her sails were hanging in tatters, her mizen-top-mast, mizen-top-sail, and cross-jack-yards shot away. But the frigate which had her in tow hove in stays, and got her round. Both these French ships now brought their guns to bear, and opened their fire.

The *Agamemnon* passed them within half-pistol shot; almost every shot passed over her, for the French had elevated their guns for the rigging, and for distant firing, and did not think of altering the elevation. As soon as the *Agamemnon*'s after-guns ceased to bear, she hove in stays, keeping a constant fire as she came round; and being worked, said Nelson, with as much exactness as if she had been turning into Spithead.

On getting round, he saw that the *Sans-Culottes*, which had wore, with many of the enemy's ships, was under his lee bow, and standing to leeward. The admiral, at the same time, made the signal for the van ships to join him. Upon this Nelson bore away, and prepared to set all sail; and the enemy, having saved their ship, hauled close to the wind, and opened upon him a distant and ineffectual fire.

Only seven of the *Agamemnon*'s men were hurt—a thing which Nelson himself remarked as wonderful: her sails and rigging were very much cut, and she had many shots in her hull, and some between wind and water. The *Ça Ira* lost 110 men that day, and was so cut up that she could not get a top-mast aloft during the night.

At daylight on the following morning, the English ships were taken aback with a fine breeze at N.W., while the enemy's fleet kept the southerly wind. The body of their fleet was about five miles distant; the *Ça Ira* and the *Censeur*, seventy-four, which had her in tow, about three and a half.

All sail was made to cut these ships off; and as the French attempted to save them, a partial action was brought on. The *Agamemnon* was again engaged with her yesterday's antagonist; but she had to fight on both sides the ship at the same time. The *Ça Ira* and the *Censeur* fought most gallantly: the first lost nearly 300 men, in addition to her former loss; the last, 350.

Both at length struck; and Lieutenant Andrews, of the *Agamemnon*, brother to the lady to whom Nelson had become attached in France, and, in Nelson's own words, "as gallant an officer as ever stepped a quarter-deck," hoisted English colours on board them both.

The rest of the enemy's ships behaved very ill. As soon as these vessels had struck, Nelson went to Admiral Hotham and proposed that the two prizes should be left with the *Illustrious* and *Courageux*, which had been crippled in the action, and with four frigates, and that the rest of the fleet should pursue the enemy, and follow up the advantage to the utmost. But his reply was—"We must be contented: we have done very well."

"Now," said Nelson, "had we taken ten sail, and allowed the eleventh to escape, when it had been possible to have got at her, I could never have called it well done. Goodall backed me; I got him to write to the admiral; but it would not do. We should have had such a day as, I believe, the annals of England never produced."

In this letter the character of Nelson fully manifests itself. "I wish," said he, "to be an admiral, and in the command of the English fleet: I should very soon either do much, or be ruined: my disposition cannot bear tame and slow measures. Sure I am, had I commanded on the 14th, that either the whole French fleet would have graced my triumph, or I should have been in a confounded scrape."

What the event would have been, he knew from his prophetic feelings and his own consciousness of power; and we also know it now, for Aboukir and Trafalgar have told it.

The *Ça Ira* and *Censeur* probably defended themselves with more obstinacy in this action, from a persuasion that, if they struck, no quarter would be given; because they had fired red-hot shot, and had also a preparation sent, as they said, by the convention from Paris, which seems to have been of the nature of the Greek fire; for it became liquid when it was discharged, and water would not extinguish its flames. This combustible was concealed with great care in the captured ships; like the red-hot shot, it had been found useless in battle.

Admiral Hotham's action saved Corsica for the time; but the victory had been incomplete, and the arrival at Toulon of six sail of the line, two frigates, and two cutters from Brest, gave the French a superiority which, had they known how to use it, would materially have endangered the British Mediterranean fleet. That fleet had been greatly neglected at the Admiralty during Lord Chatham's administration: and it did not, for some time, feel the beneficial effect of his removal.

Lord Hood had gone home to represent the real state of affairs, and solicit reinforcements adequate to the exigencies of the time, and the importance of the scene of action. But that fatal error of under-proportioning the force to the service; that ruinous economy, which, by sparing a little, renders all that is spent useless, infected the British councils; and Lord Hood, not being able to obtain such reinforcements as he knew were necessary, resigned the command.

"Surely," said Nelson, "the people at home have forgotten us."

Another Neapolitan seventy-four joined Admiral Hotham, and Nelson observed with sorrow that this was matter of exultation to an English fleet. When the store-ships and victuallers from Gibraltar arrived, their escape from the enemy was thought wonderful; and yet, had they not escaped, "the game," said Nelson, "was up here. At this moment our operations are at a stand for want of ships to support the Austrians in getting possession of the sea-coast of the king of Sardinia; and behold our admiral does not feel himself equal to show himself, much less to give assistance in their operations."

It was reported that the French were again out with 18 or 20 sail. The combined British and Neapolitan were but sixteen; should the enemy be only eighteen, Nelson made no doubt of a complete victory; but if they were twenty, he said, it was not to be expected; and a battle, without complete victory, would have been destruction, because another mast was not to be got on that side Gibraltar.

At length Admiral Man arrived with a squadron from England.

"What they can mean by sending him with only five sail of the line," said Nelson, "is truly astonishing; but all men are alike, and we in this country do not find any amendment or alteration from the old Board of Admiralty. They should know that half the ships in the fleet require to go to England; and that long ago they ought to have reinforced us."

About this time Nelson was made colonel of marines[48]; a mark of approbation which he had long wished for rather than expected. It came in good season, for his spirits were oppressed by the thought that his services had not been acknowledged as they deserved; and it abated the resentful feeling which would else have been excited by the answer to an application to the War-office.

During his four months' land service in Corsica, he had lost all his ship furniture, owing to the movements of a camp. Upon this he wrote to the Secretary at War, briefly stating what his services on shore had been, and saying, he trusted it was not asking an improper thing to request that the same allowance might be made to him which would be made to a land officer of his rank, which, situated as he was, would be that of a brigadier-general: if this could not be accorded, he hoped that his additional expenses would be paid him.

The answer which he received was, that "no pay had ever been issued under the direction of the War-office to officers of the navy serving with the army on shore."

He now entered upon a new line of service. The Austrian and Sardinian armies, under General de Vins, required a British squadron to

48 In the Royal Navy of this period, it was sometimes the practice to give a favored captain and appointment as colonel of Marines. The position was a sinecure, having no real duties, but providing an additional income for the officer.

co-operate with them in driving the French from the Riviera di Genoa; and as Nelson had been so much in the habit of soldiering, it was immediately fixed that the brigadier should go.

He sailed from St. Fiorenzo on this destination; but fell in, off Cape del Mele, with the enemy's fleet, who immediately gave his squadron chase. The chase lasted four-and-twenty hours; and, owing to the fickleness of the wind, the British ships were sometimes hard pressed; but the want of skill on the part of the French gave Nelson many advantages.

Nelson bent his way back to St. Fiorenzo, where the fleet, which was in the midst of watering and refitting, had, for seven hours, the mortification of seeing him almost in possession of the enemy, before the wind would allow them to put out to his assistance.

The French, however, at evening, went off, not choosing to approach nearer the shore.

During the night, Admiral Hotham, by great exertions, got under weigh; and, having sought the enemy four days, came in sight of them on the fifth.

Baffling winds and vexatious calms, so common in the Mediterranean, rendered it impossible to close with them; only a partial action could be brought on; and then the firing made a perfect calm. The French being to windward, drew inshore; and the English fleet was becalmed six or seven miles to the westward.

L'Acide, of seventy-four guns, struck; but before she could be taken possession of, a box of combustibles in her fore-top took fire, and the unhappy crew experienced how far more perilous their inventions were to themselves than to their enemies. So rapid was the conflagration, that the French in their official account say, the hull, the masts, and sails, all seemed to take fire at the same moment; and though the English boats were put out to the assistance of the poor wretches on board, not more than 200 could be saved.

The *Agamemnon*, and Captain Rowley in the *Cumberland*, were just getting into close action a second time, when the admiral called them off, the wind now blowing directly into the Gulf of Frejus, where the enemy anchored after the evening closed.

Nelson now proceeded to his station with eight sail of frigates under his command. Arriving at Genoa, he had a conference with Mr. Drake, the British envoy to that state; the result of which was, that the object of the British must be to put an entire stop to all trade between Genoa, France, and the places occupied by the French troops; for unless this trade were stopped, it would be scarcely possible for the allied armies to hold their situation, and impossible for them to make any progress in driving the enemy out of the Riviera di Genoa.

Mr. Drake was of opinion that even Nice might fall for want of supplies, if the trade with Genoa were cut off. This sort of blockade Nelson could not carry on without great risk to himself. A captain in the navy, as he represented to the envoy, is liable to prosecution for detention and damages. This danger was increased by an order which had then lately been issued; by which, when a neutral ship was detained, a complete specification of her cargo was directed to be sent to the secretary of the Admiralty, and no legal process instituted against her till the pleasure of that board should be communicated.

This was requiring an impossibility. The cargoes of ships detained upon this station, consisting chiefly of corn, would be spoiled long before the orders of the Admiralty could be known; and then, if they should happen to release the vessel, the owners would look to the captain for damages.

Even the only precaution which could be taken against this danger, involved another danger not less to be apprehended: for if the captain should direct the cargo to be taken out, the freight paid for, and the vessel released, the agent employed might prove fraudulent, and become bankrupt; and in that case the captain became responsible.

Such things had happened: Nelson therefore required, as the only means for carrying on that service, which was judged essential to the common cause, without exposing the officers to ruin, that the British envoy should appoint agents to pay the freight, release the vessels, sell the cargo, and hold the amount till process was had upon it: government thus securing its officers.

"I am acting," said Nelson, "not only without the orders of my commander-in-chief, but, in some measure, contrary to him. However, I have not only the support of his Majesty's ministers, both at Turin and Genoa, but a consciousness that I am doing what is right and proper for the service of our king and country. Political courage, in an officer abroad, is as highly necessary as military courage."

This quality, which is as much rarer than military courage as it is more valuable, and without which the soldier's bravery is often of little avail, Nelson possessed in an eminent degree. His representations were attended to as they deserved. Admiral Hotham commended him for what he had done; and the attention of government was awakened to the injury which the cause of the allies continually suffered from the frauds of neutral vessels.

"What changes in my life of activity!" said the indefatigable man. "Here I am, having commenced a co-operation with an old Austrian general, almost fancying myself charging at the head of a troop of horse! I do not write less than from ten to twenty letters every day; which, with the Austrian general and *aides-de-camp*, and my own little squadron, fully employ my time. This I like; active service or none."

It was Nelson's mind which supported his feeble body through these exertions. He was at this time almost blind, and wrote with very great pain. "Poor *Agamemnon*," he sometimes said, "was as nearly worn out as her captain; and both must soon be laid up to repair."

When Nelson first saw General de Vins, he thought him an able man, who was willing to act with vigour. The general charged his inactivity upon the Piedmontese and Neapolitans, whom, he said, nothing could induce to act; and he concerted a plan with Nelson for embarking a part of the Austrian army, and landing it in the rear of the French.

But the English commodore soon began to suspect that the Austrian general was little disposed to any active operations. In the hope of spurring him on, he wrote to him, telling him that he had surveyed the coast to the W. as far as Nice, and would undertake to embark 4,000 or 5,000 men, with their arms and a few days' provisions, on board the squadron, and land them within two miles of St. Remo, with their field-pieces.

Respecting further provisions for the Austrian army, he would provide convoys, that they should arrive in safety; and if a re-embarkation should be found necessary, he would cover it with the squadron.

The possession of St. Remo, as headquarters for magazines of every kind, would enable the Austrian general to turn his army to the eastward or westward. The enemy at Oneglia would be cut off from provisions, and men could be landed to attack that place whenever it was judged necessary.

St. Remo was the only place between Vado and Ville Franche where the squadron could lie in safety, and anchor in almost all winds. The bay was not so good as Vado for large ships; but it had a mole, which Vado had not, where all small vessels could lie, and load and unload their cargoes. This bay being in possession of the allies, Nice could be completely blockaded by sea.

General de Vins affecting, in his reply, to consider that Nelson's proposal had no other end than that of obtaining the bay of St. Remo as a station for the ships, told him, what he well knew, and had expressed before, that Vado Bay was a better anchorage; nevertheless, if *Monsieur le Commandant* Nelson was well assured that part of the fleet could winter there, there was no risk to which he would not expose himself with pleasure, for the sake of procuring a safe station for the vessels of his Britannic Majesty.

Nelson soon assured the Austrian commander that this was not the object of his memorial. He now began to suspect that both the Austrian Court and their general had other ends in view than the cause of the allies.

"This army," said he, "is slow beyond all description; and I begin to think that the Emperor is anxious to touch another £4,000,000 of English money. As for the German generals, war is their trade, and peace is ruin to them; therefore we cannot expect that they should have any wish to finish the war. The politics of courts are so mean, that private people would be ashamed to act in the same way; all is trick and finesse, to which the common cause is sacrificed. The general wants a loop-hole; it has for some time appeared to me that he means to go no further than his present position, and to lay the miscarriage of the enterprise against Nice, which has always been held out as the great object of his army, to the non-co-operation of the British fleet and of the Sardinians."

To prevent this plea, Nelson again addressed De Vins, requesting only to know the time, and the number of troops ready to embark; then he would, he said, dispatch a ship to Admiral Hotham, requesting transports, having no doubt of obtaining them, and trusting that the plan would be successful to its fullest extent.

Nelson thought at the time that, if the whole fleet were offered him for transports, he would find some other excuse; and Mr. Drake, who was now appointed to reside at the Austrian headquarters, entertained the same idea of the general's sincerity. It was not, however, put so clearly to the proof as it ought to have been.

He replied that, as soon as Nelson could declare himself ready with the vessels necessary for conveying 10,000 men, with their artillery and baggage, he would put the army in motion.

But Nelson was not enabled to do this: Admiral Hotham, who was highly meritorious in leaving such a man so much at his own discretion, pursued a cautious system, ill according with the bold and comprehensive views of Nelson, who continually regretted Lord Hood, saying that the nation had suffered much by his resignation of the Mediterranean command. The plan which had been concerted, he said, would astonish the French, and perhaps the English.

There was no unity in the views of the allied powers, no cordiality in their co-operation, no energy in their councils. The neutral powers assisted France more effectually than the allies assisted each other.

The Genoese ports were at this time filled with French privateers, which swarmed out every night, and covered the gulf; and French vessels were allowed to tow out of the port of Genoa itself, board vessels which were coming in, and then return into the mole. This was allowed without a remonstrance; while, though Nelson abstained most carefully from offering any offence to the Genoese territory or flag, complaints were so repeatedly made against his squadron, that, he says, it seemed a trial who should be tired first; they of complaining, or he of answering their complaints.

But the question of neutrality was soon at an end. An Austrian commissary was travelling from Genoa towards Vado; it was known that he was to sleep at Voltri, and that he had £10,000 with him—a booty which the French minister in that city, and the captain of a French frigate in that port, considered as far more important than the word of honour of the one, the duties of the other, and the laws of neutrality.

The boats of the frigate went out with some privateers, landed, robbed the commissary, and brought back the money to Genoa. The next day men were publicly enlisted in that city for the French army: 700 men were embarked, with 7,000 stand of arms, on board the frigates and other vessels, who were to land between Voltri and Savona. There a detachment from the French army was to join them, and the Genoese peasantry were to be invited to insurrection—a measure for which everything had been prepared.

The night of the 13th was fixed for the sailing of this expedition; the Austrians called loudly for Nelson to prevent it; and he, on the evening of the 13th, arrived at Genoa.

His presence checked the plan: the frigate, knowing her deserts, got within the merchant-ships, in the inner mole; and the Genoese government did not now even demand of Nelson respect to the neutral port, knowing that they had allowed, if not connived at, a flagrant breach of neutrality, and expecting the answer which he was prepared to return, that it was useless and impossible for him to respect it longer.

But though this movement produced the immediate effect which was designed, it led to ill consequences, which Nelson foresaw, but for want of sufficient force was unable to prevent. His squadron was too small for the service which it had to perform.

He required two seventy-fours and eight or ten frigates and sloops; but when he demanded this reinforcement, Admiral Hotham had left the command. [Vice-Admiral] Sir Hyde Parker had succeeded till the new commander should arrive; and he immediately reduced it to almost nothing, leaving him only one frigate and a brig.

This was a fatal error. While the Austrian and Sardinian troops, whether from the imbecility or the treachery of their leaders, remained inactive, the French were preparing for the invasion of Italy.

Not many days before Nelson was thus summoned to Genoa, he chased a large convoy into Alassio. Twelve vessels he had formerly destroyed in that port, though 2,000 French troops occupied the town. This former attack had made them take new measures of defence; and there were now above 100 sail of victuallers, gun-boats, and ships of war.

Nelson represented to the Admiral how important it was to destroy these vessels; and offered, with his squadron of frigates, and the *Culloden* and *Courageux*, to lead himself in the *Agamemnon*, and take or destroy the whole. The attempt was not permitted; but it was Nelson's belief that, if it had been made, it would have prevented the attack upon the Austrian army, which took place almost immediately afterwards.

General de Vins demanded satisfaction of the Genoese government for the seizure of his commissary; and then, without waiting for their reply, took possession of some empty magazines of the French, and pushed his sentinels to the very gates of Genoa. Had he done so at first, he would have found the magazines full; but, timed as the measure was, and useless as it was to the cause of the allies, it was in character with the whole of the Austrian general's conduct; and it is no small proof of the dexterity with which he served the enemy, that in such circumstances he could so act with Genoa as to contrive to put himself in the wrong.

Nelson was at this time, according to his own expression, placed in a cleft stick. Mr. Drake, the Austrian minister, and the Austrian general, all joined in requiring him not to leave Genoa; if he left that port unguarded, they said, not only the imperial troops at St. Pier d'Arena and Voltri would be lost, but the French plan for taking post between Voltri and Savona would certainly succeed; if the Austrians should be worsted in the advanced posts, the retreat of the Bocchetta would be cut off; and if this happened, the loss of the army would be imputed to him, for having left Genoa.

On the other hand, he knew that if he were not at Pietra, the enemy's gun-boats would harass the left flank of the Austrians, who, if they were defeated, as was to be expected, from the spirit of all their operations, would, very probably, lay their defeat to the want of assistance from the *Agamemnon*.

Had the force for which Nelson applied been given him, he could have attended to both objects; and had he been permitted to attack the convoy in Alassio, he would have disconcerted the plans of the French, in spite of the Austrian general.

He had foreseen the danger, and pointed out how it might be prevented; but the means of preventing it were withheld. The attack was made as he foresaw; and the gun-boats brought their fire to bear upon the Austrians.

It so happened, however, that the left flank, which was exposed to them, was the only part of the army that behaved well: this division stood its ground till the centre and the right wing fled, and then retreated in a soldierlike manner. General de Vins gave up the command in the middle of the battle, pleading ill health.

"From that moment," says Nelson, "not a soldier stayed at his post: it was the devil take the hindmost. Many thousands ran away who had never seen the enemy; some of them thirty miles from the advanced posts. Had I not, though I own, against my inclination, been kept at Genoa, from 8,000 to 10,000 men would have been taken prisoners, and, amongst the number, General de Vins himself; but by this means the pass of the Bocchetta was kept open. The purser of the ship, who was at Vado, ran with the Austrians eighteen miles without stopping; the men without arms, officers without soldiers, women without assistance. The oldest officers say they never heard of so complete a defeat, and certainly without any reason. Thus has ended my campaign. We have established the French republic: which but for us, I verily believe, would never have been settled by such a volatile, changeable people. I hate a Frenchman: they are equally objects of my detestation whether royalists or republicans: in some points, I believe, the latter are the best."

Nelson had a lieutenant and two midshipmen taken at Vado: they told him, in their letter, that few of the French soldiers were more than three or four and twenty years old, a great many not more than fourteen, and all were nearly naked; they were sure, they said, his barge's crew could have beat a hundred of them; and that, had he himself seen them, he would not have thought, if the world had been covered with such people, that they could have beaten the Austrian army.

The defeat of General de Vins gave the enemy possession of the Genoese coast from Savona to Voltri, and it deprived the Austrians of their direct communication with the English fleet. The *Agamemnon*, therefore, could no longer be useful on this station, and Nelson sailed for Leghorn to refit. When his ship went into dock, there was not a mast, yard, sail, or any part of the rigging, but what stood in need of repair, having been cut to pieces with shot. The hull was so damaged that it had for some time been secured by cables, which were served or thrapped round it.

Chapter 4
1796–1797

Sir J. Jervis takes the Command—Genoa joins the French—Bounaparte begins his Career—Evacuation of Corsica—Nelson hoists his broad Pendant in the *Minerve*—Action with the *Sabina*—Battle off Cape St. Vincent—Nelson commands the inner Squadron at the Blockade of Cadiz—Boat Action in the Bay of Cadiz—Expedition against Teneriffe—Nelson loses an Arm—His Sufferings in England, and Recovery.

Sir John Jervis had now arrived to take the command of the Mediterranean fleet. The *Agamemnon* having, as her captain said, been made as fit for sea as a rotten ship could be, Nelson sailed from Leghorn, and joined the admiral in Fiorenzo Bay.

"I found him," said he, "anxious to know many things which I was a good deal surprised to find had not been communicated to him by others in the fleet; and it would appear that he was so well satisfied with my opinion of what is likely to happen, and the means of prevention to be taken, that he had no reserve with me respecting his information and ideas of what is likely to be done."

The manner in which Nelson was received is said to have excited some envy. One captain observed to him: "You did just as you pleased in Lord Hood's time, the same in Admiral Hotham's, and now again with Sir John Jervis: it makes no difference to you who is commander-in-chief."

A higher compliment could not have been paid to any commander-in-chief than to say of him that he understood the merits of Nelson, and left him, as far as possible, to act upon his own judgment.

Sir John Jervis offered him the *St. George*, ninety, or the *Zealous*, seventy-four, and asked if he should have any objection to serve under him with his flag. He replied, that if the *Agamemnon* were ordered home, and his flag were not arrived, he should, on many accounts, wish to return to England; still, if the war continued, he should be very proud of hoisting his flag under Sir John's command.

"We cannot spare you," said Sir John, "either as captain or admiral."

Accordingly, he resumed his station in the Gulf of Genoa.

The French had not followed up their successes in that quarter with their usual celerity. Scherer, who commanded there, owed his advancement to any other cause than his merit: he was a favourite of the directory; but for the present, through the influence of Barras, he was removed from a command for which his incapacity was afterwards clearly proved, and Buonaparte was appointed to succeed him.

Buonaparte had given indications of his military talents at Toulon, and of his remorseless nature at Paris; but the extent either of his ability or his wickedness was at this time known to none, and perhaps not even suspected by himself.

Nelson supposed, from the information which he had obtained, that one column of the French army would take possession of Port Especia; either penetrating through the Genoese territory, or proceeding coast-ways in light vessels; our ships of war not being able to approach the coast, because of the shallowness of the water.

To prevent this, he said; two things were necessary: the possession of Vado Bay, and the taking of Port Especia; if either of these points were secured, Italy would be safe from any attack of the French by sea.

General Beaulieu, who had now superseded De Vins in the command of the allied Austrian and Sardinian army, sent his nephew and *aide-de-camp* to communicate with Nelson, and inquire whether he could anchor in any other place than Vado Bay.

Nelson replied, that Vado was the only place where the British fleet could lie in safety, but all places would suit his squadron; and wherever the general came to the sea-coast, there he should find it.

The Austrian repeatedly asked, if there was not a risk of losing the squadron? and was constantly answered, that if these ships should be lost, the admiral would find others. But all plans of co-operation with the Austrians were soon frustrated by the battle of Montenotte.

Beaulieu ordered an attack to be made upon the post of Voltri. It was made twelve hours before the time which he had fixed, and before he arrived to direct it. In consequence, the French were enabled to effect their retreat, and fall back to Montenotte, thus giving the troops there a decisive superiority in number over the division which attacked them. This drew on the defeat of the Austrians.

Buonaparte, with a celerity which had never before been witnessed in modern war, pursued his advantages; and, in the course of a fortnight, dictated to the court of Turin terms of peace, or rather of submission; by which all the strongest places of Piedmont were put into his bands.

On one occasion, and only on one, Nelson was able to impede the progress of this new conqueror.

Six vessels, laden with cannon and ordnance-stores for the siege of Mantua, sailed from Toulon for St. Pier d'Arena. Assisted by Captain Cockburn, in the *Meleager*, he drove them under a battery; pursued them, silenced the batteries, and captured the whole. Military books, plans and maps of Italy, with the different points marked upon them where former battles had been fought, sent by the directory for Buonaparte's use, were found in the convoy.

The loss of this artillery was one of the chief causes which compelled the French to raise the siege of Mantua; but there was too much treachery, and too much imbecility, both in the councils and armies of the allied powers, for Austria to improve this momentary success.

Buonaparte perceived that the conquest of Italy was within his reach; treaties, and the rights of neutral or of friendly powers, were as little regarded by him as by the government for which he acted. In open contempt of both he entered Tuscany, and took possession of Leghorn.

In consequence of this movement, Nelson blockaded that port, and landed a British force in the Isle of Elba, to secure Porto Ferrajo.

Soon afterwards he took the Island of Capraja, which had formerly belonged to Corsica, being less than forty miles distant from it; a distance, however, short as it was, which enabled the Genoese to retain it, after their infamous sale of Corsica to France.

Genoa had now taken part with France: its government had long covertly assisted the French, and now willingly yielded to the first compulsory menace which required them to exclude the English from their ports. Capraja was seized in consequence; but this act of vigour was not followed up as it ought to have been.

England at that time depended too much upon the feeble governments of the Continent, and too little upon itself. It was determined by the British cabinet to evacuate Corsica, as soon as Spain should form an offensive alliance with France. This event, which, from the moment that Spain had been compelled to make peace, was clearly foreseen, had now taken place; and orders for the evacuation of the island were immediately sent out.

It was impolitic to annex this island to the British dominions; but having done so, it was disgraceful thus to abandon it. The disgrace would have been spared, and every advantage which could have been derived from the possession of the island secured, if the people had at first been left to form a government for themselves, and protected by us in the enjoyment of their independence.

The viceroy, Sir Gilbert Elliott, deeply felt the impolicy and ignominy of this evacuation.

The fleet also was ordered to leave the Mediterranean. This resolution was so contrary to the last instructions which had been received, that Nelson exclaimed, "Do his majesty's ministers know their own minds? They at home," said he, "do not know what this fleet is capable of performing—anything and everything. Much as I shall rejoice to see England, I lament our present orders in sack-cloth and ashes, so dishonourable to the dignity of England, whose fleets are equal to meet the world in arms; and of all the fleets I ever saw, I never beheld one, in point of officers and men, equal to Sir John Jervis's, who is a commander-in-chief able to lead them to glory."

Sir Gilbert Elliott believed that the great body of the Corsicans were perfectly satisfied, as they had good reason to be, with the British Government, sensible of its advantages, and attached to it. However this may have been, when they found that the English intended to evacuate the island, they naturally and necessarily sent to make their peace with the French.

The partisans of France found none to oppose them. A committee of thirty took upon them the government of Bastia, and sequestrated all the British property; armed Corsicans mounted guard at every place, and a plan was laid for seizing the viceroy.

Nelson, who was appointed to superintend the evacuation, frustrated these projects. At a time when every one else despaired of saving stores, cannon, provisions, or property of any kind, and a privateer was moored across the mole-head to prevent all boats from passing, he sent word to the committee, that if the slightest opposition were made to the embarkment and removal of British property, he would batter the town down.

The privateer pointed her guns at the officer who carried this message, and muskets were levelled against his boats from the mole-head. Upon this Captain Sutton, of the *Egmont*, pulling out his watch, gave them a quarter of an hour to deliberate upon their answer. In five minutes after the expiration of that time, the ships, he said, would open their fire.

Upon this the very sentinels scampered off, and every vessel came out of the mole.

A shipowner complained to the commodore that the municipality refused to let him take his goods out of the custom-house. Nelson directed him to say, that unless they were instantly delivered, he would open his fire.

The committee turned pale, and, without answering a word, gave him the keys.

Their last attempt was to levy a duty upon the things that were re-embarked. He sent them word, that he would pay them a disagreeable visit, if there were any more complaints. The committee then finding that they had to deal with a man who knew his own power, and was determined to make the British name respected, desisted from the insolent conduct which they had assumed; and it was acknowledged that Bastia never had been so quiet and orderly since the English were in possession of it.

This was on the 14th of October [1796]; during the five following days the work of embarkation was carried on, the private property was saved, and public stores to the amount of £200,000.

The French, favoured by the Spanish fleet, which was at that time within twelve leagues of Bastia, pushed over troops from Leghorn, who landed near Cape Corse on the 18th; and on the 20th, at one in the morning, entered the citadel, an hour only after the British had spiked the guns and evacuated it.

Nelson embarked at daybreak, being the last person who left the shore; having thus, as he said, seen the first and the last of Corsica.

Provoked at the conduct of the municipality, and the disposition which the populace had shown to profit by the confusion, he turned towards the shore, as he stepped into his boat, and exclaimed: "Now,

John Corse, follow the natural bent of your detestable character—plunder and revenge."

This, however, was not Nelson's deliberate opinion of the people of Corsica; he knew that their vices were the natural consequences of internal anarchy and foreign oppression, such as the same causes would produce in any people; and when he saw, that of all those who took leave of the viceroy there was not one who parted from him without tears, he acknowledged that they manifestly acted not from dislike of the English, but from fear of the French. England then might, with more reason, reproach her own rulers for pusillanimity than the Corsicans for ingratitude.

Having thus ably effected this humiliating service, Nelson was ordered to hoist his broad pendant on board the *Minerve* frigate, Captain George Cockburn, and with the *Blanche* under his command, proceed to Porto Ferrajo, and superintend the evacuation of that place also.

On his way, he fell in with two Spanish frigates, the *Sabina* and the *Ceres*. The *Minerve* engaged the former, which was commanded by D. Jacobo Stuart, a descendent of the Duke of Berwick[49].

After an action of three hours, during which the Spaniards lost 164 men, the *Sabina* struck. The Spanish captain, who was the only surviving officer, had hardly been conveyed on board the *Minerve*, when another enemy's frigate came up, compelled her to cast off the prize, and brought her a second time into action.

After half an hour's trial of strength, this new antagonist wore and hauled off; but a Spanish squadron of two ships of the line and two frigates came in sight.

The *Blanche*, from which the *Ceres* had got off, was far to windward, and the *Minerve* escaped only by the anxiety of the enemy to recover their own ship.

As soon as Nelson reached Porto Ferrajo he sent his prisoner in a flag of truce to Carthagena, having returned him his sword; this he did in honour of the gallantry which D. Jacobo had displayed, and not without some feeling of respect for his ancestry.

"I felt it," said he, "consonant to the dignity of my country and I

49 The first Duke of Berwick was James FitzJames, an illegitimate son of King James II. Don Jacobo was his grand-son. The Berwick title is considered extinct in the U.K., but continues to be claimed by the Spanish branch of the family, who are also dukes in their own right in the Spanish nobility.

always act as I feel right, without regard to custom; he was reputed the best officer in Spain, and his men were worthy of such a commander."

By the same flag of truce he sent back all the Spanish prisoners at Porto Ferrajo; in exchange for whom he received his own men who had been taken in the prize[50].

General de Burgh, who commanded at the Isle of Elba, did not think himself authorised to abandon the place till he had received specific instructions from England to that effect; professing that he was unable to decide between the contradictory orders of government, or to guess at what their present intentions might be; but he said, his only motive for urging delay in this measure arose from a desire that his own conduct might be properly sanctioned, not from any opinion that Porto Ferrajo ought to be retained.

But Naples having made peace, Sir John Jervis considered his business with Italy as concluded; and the protection of Portugal was the point to which he was now instructed to attend.

Nelson, therefore, whose orders were perfectly clear and explicit, withdrew the whole naval establishment from that station, leaving the transports victualled, and so arranged that all the troops and stores could be embarked in three days.

He was now about to leave the Mediterranean. Mr. Drake, who had been our minister at Genoa, expressed to him, on this occasion, the very high opinion which the allies entertained of his conspicuous merit; adding, that it was impossible for any one, who had the honour of co-operating with him, not to admire the activity, talents, and zeal which he had so eminently and constantly displayed.

In fact, during this long course of services in the Mediterranean, the whole of his conduct had exhibited the same zeal, the same indefatigable energy, the same intuitive judgment, the same prompt and unerring decision which characterised his after-career of glory. His name was as yet hardly known to the English public; but it was feared and respected throughout Italy.

A letter came to him, directed "Horatio Nelson, Genoa;" and the

---

50 These included *Minerve*'s first lieutenant, John Culverhouse (–1808), and Lieutenant Thomas Masterman Hardy (1769–1839). Culverhouse was promoted to commander shortly after this action, becoming a captain in 1802. He drowned in 1809. Hardy would go on to serve as Nelson's flag captain at Trafalgar, and ultimately he would serve as First Sea Lord.

writer, when he was asked how he could direct it so vaguely, replied, "Sir, there is but one Horatio Nelson in the world."

At Genoa, in particular, where he had so long been stationed, and where the nature of his duty first led him to continual disputes with the government, and afterwards compelled him to stop the trade of the port, he was equally respected by the Doge and by the people; for, while he maintained the rights and interests of Great Britain with becoming firmness, he tempered the exercise of power with courtesy and humanity wherever duty would permit.

"Had all my actions," said he, writing at this time to his wife, "been gazetted, not one fortnight would have passed, during the whole war, without a letter from me. One day or other I will have a long *Gazette* to myself. I feel that such an opportunity will be given me. I cannot, if I am in the field of glory, be kept out of sight; wherever there is anything to be done, there Providence is sure to direct my steps."

These hopes and anticipations were soon to be fulfilled.

Nelson's mind had long been irritated and depressed by the fear that a general action would take place before he could join the fleet. At length he sailed from Porto Ferrajo with a convoy for Gibraltar; and having reached that place, proceeded to the westward in search of the admiral.

Off the mouth of the Straits he fell in with the Spanish fleet; and on the 13th of February reaching the station off Cape St. Vincent, communicated this intelligence to Sir John Jervis.

He was now directed to shift his broad pendant on board the *Captain*, seventy-four, Captain R.W. Miller; and before sunset the signal was made to prepare for action, and to keep, during the night, in close order.

At daybreak the enemy were in sight. The British force consisted of two ships of one hundred guns, two of ninety-eight, two of ninety, eight of seventy-four, and one sixty-four; fifteen of the line in all; with four frigates, a sloop, and a cutter.

The Spaniards had one four-decker, of one hundred and thirty-six guns; six three-deckers, of one hundred and twelve; two eighty-four, eighteen seventy-four—in all, twenty-seven ships of the line, with ten frigates and a brig.

Their admiral, D. Joseph de Cordova, had learnt from an American on the 5th, that the English had only nine ships, which was indeed the case when his informer had seen them; for a reinforcement of five ships from England, under Admiral Parker, had not then joined, and the *Culloden* had parted company.

Upon this information the Spanish commander, instead of going into Cadiz, as was his intention when he sailed from Carthagena, determined to seek an enemy so inferior in force; and relying, with fatal confidence, upon the American account, he suffered his ships to remain too far dispersed, and in some disorder.

When the morning of the 14th broke, and discovered the English fleet, a fog for some time concealed their number. That fleet had heard their signal-guns during the night, the weather being fine though thick and hazy; soon after daylight they were seen very much scattered, while the British ships were in a compact little body.

The look-out ship of the Spaniards, fancying that her signal was disregarded because so little notice seemed to be taken of it, made another signal, that the English force consisted of forty sail of the line. The captain afterwards said he did this to rouse the admiral; it had the effect of perplexing him and alarming the whole fleet.

The absurdity of such an act shows what was the state of the Spanish navy under that miserable government by which Spain was so long oppressed and degraded, and finally betrayed. In reality, the general incapacity of the naval officers was so well known, that in a *pasquinade*[51], which about this time appeared at Madrid, wherein the different orders of the state were advertised for sale, the greater part of the sea-officers, with all their equipments, were offered as a gift; and it was added, that any person who would please to take them, should receive a handsome gratuity.

When the probability that Spain would take part in the war, as an ally of France, was first contemplated, Nelson said that their fleet, if it were no better than when it acted in alliance with us, would "soon be done for."

Before the enemy could form a regular order of battle, Sir J. Jervis, by carrying a press of sail, came up with them, passed through their fleet, then tacked, and thus cut off nine of their ships from the main body.

51 An anonymous lampoon, sometimes in verse. From the old Roman tradition of pasting these on the base of the statue of "Pasquino." The actual subject of the statue is unknown.

These ships attempted to form on the larboard tack, either with a design of passing through the British line, or to leeward of it, and thus rejoining their friends.

Only one of them succeeded in this attempt; and that only because she was so covered with smoke that her intention was not discovered till she had reached the rear: the others were so warmly received, that they put about, took to flight, and did not appear again in the action to its close.

The admiral was now able to direct his attention to the enemy's main body, which was still superior in number to his whole fleet, and greatly so in weight of metal.

He made signal to tack in succession. Nelson, whose station was in the rear of the British line, perceived that the Spaniards were bearing up before the wind, with an intention of forming their line, going large, and joining their separated ships, or else of getting off without an engagement. To prevent either of these schemes, he disobeyed the signal without a moment's hesitation: and ordered his ship to be wore.

This at once brought him into action with the *Santísima Trinidad*, one hundred and thirty-six; the *San Joseph*, one hundred and twelve; the *Salvador Del Mundo*, one hundred and twelve; the *San Nicolas*, eighty; the *San Isidro*, seventy-four, another seventy-four, and another first-rate.

Troubridge, in the *Culloden*, immediately joined, and most nobly supported him; and for nearly an hour did the *Culloden* and *Captain* maintain what Nelson called "this apparently, but not really unequal contest;"—such was the advantage of skill and discipline, and the confidence which brave men derive from them.

The *Blenheim* then passing between them and the enemy, gave them a respite, and poured in her fire upon the Spaniards. The *Salvador Del Mundo* and *San Isidro* dropped astern, and were fired into in a masterly style by the *Excellent*, Captain Collingwood.

The *San Isidro* struck; and Nelson thought that the *Salvador* struck also. "But Collingwood," says he, "disdaining the parade of taking possession of beaten enemies, most gallantly pushed up, with every sail set, to save his old friend and messmate, who was to appearance in a critical situation;" for the *Captain* was at this time actually fired upon by three first-rates—by the San Nicolas, and by a seventy-four, within about pistol-shot of that vessel.

The *Blenheim* was ahead, the *Culloden* crippled and astern. Collingwood ranged up, and hauling up his mainsail just astern, passed within ten feet of the *San Nicolas*, giving her a most tremendous fire, then passed on for the *Santísima Trinidad.*

The *San Nicolas* luffing up, the San Joseph fell on board her, and Nelson resumed his station abreast of them, and close alongside. The *Captain* was now incapable of further service, either in the line or in chase: she had lost her foretop-mast; not a sail, shroud, or rope was left, and her wheel was shot away. Nelson therefore directed Captain Miller to put the helm a-starboard, and calling for the boarders, ordered them to board.

Captain Berry, who had lately been Nelson's first lieutenant, was the first man who leaped into the enemy's mizen chains. Miller, when in the very act of going, was ordered by Nelson to remain.

Berry was supported from the spritsail-yard, which locked in the *San Nicolas*'s main rigging. A soldier of the 69th broke the upper quarter-gallery window, and jumped in, followed by the commodore himself and by the others as fast as possible.

The cabin doors were fastened, and the Spanish officers fired their pistols at them through the window; the doors were soon forced, and the Spanish brigadier fell while retreating to the quarter-deck.

Nelson pushed on, and found Berry in possession of the poop, and the Spanish ensign hauling down. He passed on to the forecastle, where he met two or three Spanish officers, and received their swords. The English were now in full possession of every part of the ship, when a fire of pistols and musketry opened upon them from the admiral's stern-gallery of the *San Joseph.*

Nelson having placed sentinels at the different ladders, and ordered Captain Miller to send more men into the prize, gave orders for boarding that ship from the San Nicolas[52]. It was done in an instant, he himself leading the way. and exclaiming, "Westminster Abbey or victory!"

Berry assisted him into the main chains; and at that moment a Spanish officer looked over the quarter-deck rail, and said they surrendered. It was not long before he was on the quarter-deck, where the Spanish captain presented to him his sword, and told him the admiral was below dying of his wounds.

---

52 This action, crossing over one captured ship to take a second, would quickly prompt stories of "Nelson's patent boarding bridge."

There, on the quarter-deck of an enemy's first-rate, he received the swords of the officers, giving them, as they were delivered, one by one to William Fearney, one of his old *Agamemnons*, who, with the utmost coolness, put them under his arm, "bundling them up," in the lively expression of Collingwood, "with as much composure as he would have made a faggot, though twenty-two sail of their line were still within gunshot."

One of his sailors came up, and with an Englishman's feeling took him by the hand, saying he might not soon have such another place to do it in, and he was heartily glad to see him there. Twenty-four of the *Captain*'s men were killed, and fifty-six wounded; a fourth part of the loss sustained by the whole squadron falling upon this ship. Nelson received only a few bruises.

The Spaniards had still eighteen or nineteen ships which had suffered little or no injury: that part of the fleet which had been separated from the main body in the morning was now coming up, and Sir John Jervis made signal to bring to.

His ships could not have formed without abandoning those which they had captured, and running to leeward: the *Captain* was lying a perfect wreck on board her two prizes; and many of the other vessels were so shattered in their masts and rigging as to be wholly unmanageable.

The Spanish admiral meantime, according to his official account, being altogether undecided in his own opinion respecting the state of the fleet, inquired of his captains whether it was proper to renew the action; nine of them answered explicitly that it was not; others replied that it was expedient to delay the business. The *Pelayo* and the *Prince Conquistador* were the only ships that were for fighting.

As soon as the action was discontinued, Nelson went on board the admiral's ship. Sir John Jervis received him on the quarter-deck, took him in his arms, and said he could not sufficiently thank him.

For this victory the commander-in-chief was rewarded with the title of Earl St. Vincent.

Nelson, who before the action was known in England had been advanced to the rank of rear-admiral, had the Order of the Bath given him. The sword of the Spanish rear-admiral, which Sir John Jervis insisted upon his keeping, he presented to the Mayor and Corporation of Norwich, saying that he knew no place where it could give him or his family more pleasure to have it kept than in the capital city of the county where he was born. The freedom of that city was voted him on this occasion.

But of all the numerous congratulations which he received, none could have affected him with deeper delight than that which came from his venerable father.

"I thank my God," said this excellent man, "with all the power of a grateful soul, for the mercies He has most graciously bestowed on me in preserving you. Not only my few acquaintance here, but the people in general, met me at every corner with such handsome words, that I was obliged to retire from the public eye. The height of glory to which your professional judgment, united with a proper degree of bravery, guarded by Providence, has raised you, few sons, my dear child, attain to, and fewer fathers live to see. Tears of joy have involuntarily trickled down my furrowed cheeks: who could stand the force of such general congratulation? The name and services of Nelson have sounded through this city of Bath—from the common ballad-singer to the public theatre." The good old man concluded by telling him that the field of glory, in which he had so long been conspicuous, was still open, and by giving him his blessing.

Sir Horatio, who had now hoisted his flag as rear-admiral of the blue, was sent to bring away the troops from Porto Ferrajo; having performed this, he shifted his flag to the *Theseus.*

That ship, had taken part in the mutiny in England[53], and being just arrived from home, some danger was apprehended from the temper of the men. This was one reason why Nelson was removed to her. He had not been on board many weeks before a paper, signed in the name of all the ship's company, was dropped on the quarter-deck, containing these words: "Success attend Admiral Nelson! God bless Captain Miller! We thank them for the officers they have placed over us. We are happy and comfortable, and will shed every drop of blood in our veins to support

53 There were two large-scale mutinies in the British fleet in 1797. The first, from 16 April to 12 May, at Spithead, involved 16 ships, of which *Theseus* was one. This was arguably more in the nature of a strike than a true mutiny, and involved a number of grievances, including pay rates for the seamen, which had not increased in 40 years. The Spithead Mutiny was finally settled after negotiations with Lord Howe, with the major grievances addressed. The second mutiny, which occurred at the Nore from 12 May through 13 June, was not settled so amicably. In the Nore Mutiny, in which the mutineers sent all of the captains ashore, and threatened to sail the ships to France if their conditions were not met, force was ultimately employed and the ring leaders were hanged. Perhaps curiously to modern observers, who have formed their opinions from distorted motion picture portrayals, the one captain at the Nore whose crew *protested* his removal was William Bligh, who was sent ashore only at the demand of the "committee," comprised of men from other ships.

them; and the name of the *Theseus* shall be immortalised as high as her captain's."

Wherever Nelson commanded, the men soon became attached to him; in ten days' time he would have restored the most mutinous ship in the navy to order. Whenever an officer fails to win the affections of those who are under his command, he may be assured that the fault is chiefly in himself.

While Sir Horatio was in the *Theseus*, he was employed in the command of the inner squadron at the blockade of Cadiz. During this service, the most perilous action occurred in which he was ever engaged. Making a night attack upon the Spanish gun-boats, his barge was attacked by an armed launch, under their commander, D. Miguel Tregoyen, carrying 26 men.

Nelson had with him only his ten bargemen, Captain Freemantle, and his coxswain, John Sykes, an old and faithful follower, who twice saved the life of his admiral by parrying the blows that were aimed at him, and at last actually interposed his own head to receive the blow of a Spanish sabre, which he could not by any other means avert; thus dearly was Nelson beloved.

This was a desperate service—hand to hand with swords; and Nelson always considered that his personal courage was more conspicuous on this occasion than on any other during his whole life. Notwithstanding the great disproportion of numbers, 18 of the enemy were killed, all the rest wounded, and their launch taken.

Nelson would have asked for a lieutenancy for Sykes, if he had served long enough; his manner and conduct, he observed, were so entirely above his situation, that Nature certainly intended him for a gentleman; but though he recovered from the dangerous wound which he received in this act of heroic attachment, he did not live to profit by the gratitude and friendship of his commander.

Twelve days after this *rencontre,* Nelson sailed at the head of an expedition against Teneriffe. A report had prevailed a few months before, that the viceroy of Mexico, with the treasure ships, had put into that island. This had led Nelson to meditate the plan of an attack upon it, which he communicated to Earl St. Vincent.

He was perfectly aware of the difficulties of the attempt. "I do not," said he, "reckon myself equal to Blake; but, if I recollect right, he was more obliged to the wind coming off the land than to any exertions of his own. The approach by sea to the anchoring-place is under very high land, passing three valleys; therefore the wind is either in from the sea, or squally with calms from the mountains:" and he perceived that if the Spanish ships were won, the object would still be frustrated if the wind did not come off shore.

The land force, he thought, would render success certain; and there were the troops from Elba, with all necessary stores and artillery, already embarked.

"But here," said he, "soldiers must be consulted; and I know, from experience, they have not the same boldness in undertaking a political measure that we have: we look to the benefit of our country, and risk our own fame every day to serve her; a soldier obeys his orders, and no more."

Nelson's experience at Corsica justified him in this harsh opinion: he did not live to see the glorious days of the British army under Wellington. The army from Elba, consisting of 3,700 men, would do the business, he said, in three days, probably in much less time; and he would undertake, with a very small squadron, to perform the naval part; for though the shore was not easy of access, the transports might run in and land the troops in one day.

The report concerning the viceroy was unfounded: but a homeward-bound Manilla ship put into Santa Cruz at this time, and the expedition was determined upon. It was not fitted out upon the scale which Nelson had proposed. Four ships of the line, three frigates, and the *Fox* cutter, formed the squadron; and he was allowed to choose such ships and officers as he thought proper.

No troops were embarked; the seamen and marines of the squadron being thought sufficient. His orders were, to make a vigorous attack; but on no account to land in person, unless his presence should be absolutely necessary.

The plan was, that the boats should land in the night, between the fort on the N.E. side of Santa Cruz bay and the town, make themselves masters of that fort, and then send a summons to the governor. By midnight, the three frigates, having the force on board which was intended for this debarkation, approached within three miles of the place; but owing to a strong gale of wind in the offing, and a strong current against them in-shore, they were not able to get within a mile of the landing-place before daybreak; and then they were seen, and their intention discovered.

Troubridge and Bowen, with Captain Oldfield, of the marines, went upon this to consult with the admiral what was to be done; and it was resolved that they should attempt to get possession of the heights above the fort.

The frigates accordingly landed their men; and Nelson stood in with the line-of-battle ships, meaning to batter the fort for the purpose of distracting the attention of the garrison.

A calm and contrary current hindered him from getting within a league of the shore; and the heights were by this time so secured, and manned with such a force, as to be judged impracticable. Thus foiled in his plans by circumstances of wind and tide, he still considered it a point of honour that some attempt should be made.

This was on the 22nd of July: he re-embarked his men that night, got the ships on the 24th to anchor about two miles north of the town, and made show as if he intended to attack the heights. At six in the evening signal was made for the boats to prepare to proceed on the service as previously ordered.

When this was done, Nelson addressed a letter to the commander-in-chief—the last which was ever written with his right hand.

"I shall not," said he, "enter on the subject, why we are not in possession of Santa Cruz. Your partiality will give credit, that all has hitherto been done which was possible, but without effect. This night I, humble as I am, command the whole destined to land under the batteries of the town; and to-morrow my head will probably be crowned either with laurel or cypress. I have only to recommend Josiah Nisbet to you and my country. The Duke of Clarence, should I fall, will, I am confident, take a lively interest for my son-in-law[54], on his name being mentioned."

Perfectly aware how desperate a service this was likely to prove, before he left the *Theseus* he called Lieutenant Nisbet, who had the watch on deck, into the cabin, that he might assist in arranging and burning his mother's letters. Perceiving that the young man was armed, he earnestly begged him to remain behind.

54 Josiah Nisbet was the son of Lady Nelson and her deceased first husband, a physician, also named Josiah Nisbet. In modern terminology, then, he would be Nelson's step-son, rather than his son-in-law, which we would now presume to be a daughter's husband. The cordial relations between step-father and step-son spoken of her would not last.

"Should we both fall, Josiah," said he, "what will become of your poor mother! The care of the *Theseus* falls to you: stay, therefore, and take charge of her."

Nisbet replied: "Sir, the ship must take care of herself: I will go with you to-night, if I never go again."

He met his captains at supper on board the *Seahorse,* Captain Freemantle[55], whose wife, whom he had lately married in the Mediterranean, presided at table.

At eleven o'clock the boats, containing between 600 and 700 men, with 180 on board the *Fox* cutter, and from 70 to 80 in a boat which had been taken the day before, proceeded in six divisions toward the town, conducted by all the captains of the squadron, except Freemantle and Bowen, who attended with Nelson to regulate and lead the way to the attack.

They were to land on the mole, and thence hasten as fast as possible into the great square; then form and proceed as should be found expedient. They were not discovered till about half-past one o'clock, when, being within half gun-shot of the landing-place, Nelson directed the boats to cast off from each other, give a huzza, and push for the shore.

But the Spaniards were exceedingly well prepared; the alarm-bells answered the huzza, and a fire of thirty or forty pieces of cannon, with musketry from one end of the town to the other, opened upon the invaders.

Nothing, however, could check the intrepidity with which they advanced. The night was exceedingly dark: most of the boats missed the mole and went on shore through a raging surf, which stove all to the left of it.

The Admiral, Freemantle, Thompson, Bowen, and four or five other boats, found the mole: they stormed it instantly, and carried it, though it was defended, as they imagined, by 400 or 500 men. Its guns, which were six-and-twenty pounders, were spiked[56]; but such a heavy fire

55 Later Vice-Admiral Sir Thomas Francis Fremantle (1765–1819). Fremantle would again serve with Nelson at Copenhagen, where he commanded HMS *Ganges*, and at Trafalgar in command of HMS *Neptune*. Fremantle had recently married Betsey Wynne. The city of Fremantle, Western Australia, is named for their son, Captain Charles Howe Fremantle, who officially established the colony in 1829.

56 Guns (cannon) were spiked by driving a large nail or spike into the touch hole. This was only a temporary hindrance to firing the piece, but would prevent its use until the

of musketry and grape[57] was kept up from the citadel and the houses at the head of the mole, that the assailants could not advance, and nearly all of them were killed or wounded.

In the act of stepping out of the boat, Nelson received a shot through the right elbow, and fell; but as he fell he caught the sword, which he had just drawn, in his left hand, determined never to part with it while he lived, for it had belonged to his uncle, Captain Suckling, and he valued it like a relic.

Nisbet, who was close to him, placed him at the bottom of the boat, and laid his hat over the shattered arm, lest the sight of the blood, which gushed out in great abundance, should increase his faintness. He then examined the wound, and taking some silk handkerchiefs from his neck, bound them round tight above the lacerated vessels. Had it not been for this presence of mind in his son-in-law, Nelson must have perished.

One of his bargemen, by name Level, tore his shirt into shreds, and made a sling with them for the broken limb. They then collected five other seamen, by whose assistance they succeeded at length in getting the boat afloat; for it had grounded with the falling tide. Nisbet took one of the oars and ordered the steersman to go close under the guns of the battery, that they might be safe from its tremendous fire.

Hearing his voice, Nelson roused himself, and desired to be lifted up in the boat that he might look about him. Nisbet raised him up; but nothing could be seen except the firing of the guns on shore, and what could be discerned by their flashes upon a stormy sea.

In a few minutes a general shriek was heard from the crew of the *Fox*, which had received a shot under water, and went down. Ninety-seven men were lost in her: 83 were saved, many by Nelson himself, whose

---

gunners were able to drill out the spikes and re-open the priming vent, so it put the gun out of action long enough to allow an attacker to do whatever other damage he wished and escape. Guns could be put permanently out of action by blowing off the trunions (the stubby cylinders projecting from opposite sides of the gun barrel, upon which it rested in the carriage), or by overloading the gun, driving in wedges to keep the shot from being able to leave the barrel, and firing the gun, blowing it up.

57 Musket balls or small iron balls, fired from a cannon. The could be loaded loose, but the usual practice was to make up bundles of shot held together by light netting or canvas for ease in loading. The name derives from a perceived resemblance of the shot clusters to clusters of grapes. The effect was rather like a giant shotgun. In modern warfare, machine-guns served much the same purpose in breaking up troops advancing in formation.

exertions on this occasion greatly increased the pain and danger of his wound.

The first ship which the boat could reach happened to be the *Seahorse*; but nothing could induce him to go on board, though he was assured that if they attempted to row to another ship it might be at the risk of his life.

"I had rather suffer death," he replied, "than alarm Mrs. Freemantle, by letting her see me in this state, when I can give her no tidings whatever of her husband."

They pushed on for the *Theseus*. When they came alongside he peremptorily refused all assistance in getting on board, so impatient was he that the boat should return, in hopes that it might save a few more from the *Fox*. He desired to have only a single rope thrown over the side, which he twisted round his left hand, saying "Let me alone; I have yet my legs left and one arm. Tell the surgeon to make haste and get his instruments. I know I must lose my right arm, so the sooner it is off the better." The spirit which he displayed in jumping up the ship's side astonished everybody.

Freemantle had been severely wounded in the right arm soon after the admiral. He was fortunate enough to find a boat on the beach, and got instantly to his ship. Thompson was wounded: Bowen killed, to the great regret of Nelson: as was also one of his own officers, Lieutenant Weatherhead, who had followed him from the *Agamemnon*, and whom he greatly and deservedly esteemed.

Troubridge, meantime, fortunately for his party, missed the mole in the darkness, but pushed on shore under the batteries, close to the south end of the citadel. Captain Waller, of the *Emerald*, and two or three other boats, landed at the same time. The surf was so high that many others put back.

The boats were instantly filled with water and stove against the rocks; and most of the ammunition in the men's pouches was wetted.

Having collected a few men they pushed on to the great square, hoping there to find the admiral and the rest of the force. The ladders were all lost, so that they could make no immediate attempt on the citadel; but they sent a sergeant with two of the town's-people to summon it: this messenger never returned; and Troubridge having waited about an hour in painful expectation of his friends, marched to join Captains Hood and Miller, who had effected their landing to the south-west.

They then endeavoured to procure some intelligence of the admiral and the rest of the officers, but without success.

By daybreak they had gathered together about eighty marines, eighty pikemen, and one hundred and eighty small-arm seamen; all the survivors of those who had made good their landing. They obtained some ammunition from the prisoners whom they had taken, and marched on to try what could be done at the citadel without ladders.

They found all the streets commanded by field-pieces, and several thousand Spaniards, with about a hundred French, under arms, approaching by every avenue.

Finding himself without provisions, the powder wet, and no possibility of obtaining either stores or reinforcements from the ships, the boats being lost, Troubridge with great presence of mind, sent Captain Samuel Hood with a flag of truce to the governor to say he was prepared to burn the town, and would instantly set fire to it if the Spaniards approached one inch nearer. This, however, if he were compelled to do it, he should do with regret, for he had no wish to injure the inhabitants; and he was ready to treat upon these terms—that the British troops should re-embark, with all their arms of every kind, and take their own boats, if they were saved, or be provided with such others as might be wanting; they, on their part, engaging that the squadron should not molest the town, or any of the Canary Islands: all prisoners on both sides to be given up.

When these terms were proposed the governor made answer, that the English ought to surrender as prisoners of war; but Captain Hood replied, he was instructed to say, that if the terms were not accepted in five minutes, Captain Troubridge would set the town on fire and attack the Spaniards at the point of the bayonet.

Satisfied with his success, which was indeed sufficiently complete, and respecting, like a brave and honourable man, the gallantry of his enemy, the Spaniard acceded to the proposal, found boats to re-embark them, their own having all been dashed to pieces in landing, and before they parted gave every man a loaf and a pint of wine.

"And here," says Nelson in his journal, "it is right we should notice the noble and generous conduct of Don Juan Antonio Gutierrez, the Spanish governor. The moment the terms were agreed to, he directed our wounded men to be received into the hospitals, and all our people to be supplied with the best provisions that could be procured; and made it known that the ships were at liberty to send on shore and purchase whatever refreshments they were in want of during the time they might be off the island."

A youth, by name Don Bernardo Collagon, stripped himself of his shirt to make bandages for one of those Englishmen against whom, not an hour before, he had been engaged in battle. Nelson wrote to thank the governor for the humanity which he had displayed. Presents were interchanged between them. Sir Horatio offered to take charge of his despatches for the Spanish Government, and thus actually became the first messenger to Spain of his own defeat.

The total loss of the English in killed, wounded, and drowned, amounted to 250. Nelson made no mention of his own wound in his official despatches; but in a private letter to Lord St. Vincent—the first which he wrote with his left hand—he shows himself to have been deeply affected by the failure of this enterprise.

"I am become," he said, "a burthen to my friends, and useless to my country; but by my last letter you will perceive my anxiety for the promotion of my son-in-law, Josiah Nisbet. When I leave your command I become dead to the world—"I go hence, and am no more seen." If from poor Bowen's loss, you think it proper to oblige me, I rest confident you will do it. The boy is under obligations to me, but he repaid me by bringing me from the mole of Santa Cruz. I hope you will be able to give me a frigate to convey the remains of my carcass to England."

"A left-handed admiral," he said in a subsequent letter, "will never again be considered as useful; therefore the sooner I get to a very humble cottage the better, and make room for a sounder man to serve the state."

His first letter to Lady Nelson was written under the same opinion, but in a more cheerful strain. "It was the chance of war," said he, "and I have great reason to be thankful: and I know it will add much to your pleasure to find that Josiah, under God's providence, was principally instrumental in saving my life. I shall not be surprised if I am neglected and forgotten: probably I shall no longer be considered as useful; however, I shall feel rich if I continue to enjoy your affection. I beg neither you nor my father will think much of this mishap; my mind has long been made up to such an event."

His son-in-law, according to his wish, was immediately promoted; and honours enough to heal his wounded spirit awaited him in England. Letters were addressed to him by the first lord of the Admiralty, and by his steady friend the Duke of Clarence, to congratulate him on his return, covered as he was with glory.

He assured the Duke, in his reply, that not a scrap of that ardour with which he had hitherto served his king had been shot away.

The freedom of the cities of Bristol and London were transmitted to him; he was invested with the Order of the Bath, and received a pension of £1000 a year. The memorial which, as a matter of form, he was called upon to present on this occasion, exhibited an extraordinary catalogue of services performed during the war.

It stated that he had been in four actions with the fleets of the enemy, and in three actions with boats employed in cutting out of harbour, in destroying vessels, and in taking three towns. He had served on shore with the army four months, and commanded the batteries at the sieges of Basti and Calvi: he had assisted at the capture of seven sail of the line, six frigates, four corvettes, and eleven privateers: taken and destroyed near fifty sail of merchant vessels, and actually been engaged against the enemy upwards of a hundred and twenty times, in which service he had lost his right eye and right arm, and been severely wounded and bruised in his body.

His sufferings from the lost limb were long and painful. A nerve had been taken up in one of the ligatures at the time of the operation; and the ligature, according to the practice of the French surgeons, was of silk instead of waxed thread; this produced a constant irritation and discharge; and the ends of the ligature being pulled every day, in hopes of bringing it away, occasioned fresh agony.

He had scarcely any intermission of pain, day or night, for three months after his return to England. Lady Nelson, at his earnest request, attended the dressing of his arm, till she had acquired sufficient resolution and skill to dress it herself.

One night, during this state of suffering, after a day of constant pain, Nelson retired early to bed, in hope of obtaining some respite by means of laudanum[58]. He was at that time lodging in Bond Street, and the family were soon disturbed by a mob knocking loudly and violently at the door. The news of Duncan's victory[59] had been made public, and

58 Tincture of opium.

59 A British fleet under Admiral Adam Duncan defeated a Dutch fleet under Admiral DeWinter at Camperdown on 11 October 1797, taking eleven enemy ships and in

the house was not illuminated.

But when the mob were told that Admiral Nelson lay there in bed, badly wounded, the foremost of them made answer: "You shall hear no more from us to-night:" and in fact, the feeling of respect and sympathy was communicated from one to another with such effect that, under the confusion of such a night, the house was not molested again.

About the end of November, after a night of sound sleep, he found the arm nearly free from pain. The surgeon was immediately sent for to examine it; and the ligature came away with the slightest touch. From that time it began to heal. As soon as he thought his health established, he sent the following form of thanksgiving to the minister of St. George's, Hanover Square:—"An officer desires to return thanks to Almighty God for his perfect recovery from a severe wound, and also for the many mercies bestowed on him."

Not having been in England till now, since he lost his eye, he went to receive a year's pay as smart money; but could not obtain payment, because he had neglected to bring a certificate from a surgeon that the sight was actually destroyed.

A little irritated that this form should be insisted upon, because, though the fact was not apparent, he thought it was sufficiently notorious, he procured a certificate at the same time for the loss of his arm; saying, they might just as well doubt one as the other. This put him in good humour with himself, and with the clerk who had offended him.

On his return to the office, the clerk, finding it was only the annual pay of a captain, observed, he thought it had been more.

"Oh!" replied Nelson, "this is only for an eye. In a few days I shall come for an arm; and in a little time longer, God knows, most probably for a leg."

Accordingly he soon afterwards went, and with perfect good humour exhibited the certificate of the loss of his arm.

---

the process ending the threat of invasion from the Continent. Duncan arrived back in England with news of the victory on 18 October, suggesting this incident at Nelson's home would have taken place within the next day or two. In recognition of this victory, Duncan was created Viscount Duncan of Camperdown.

Chapter 5
1798

Nelson rejoins Earl St. Vincent in the *Vanguard*—Sails in Pursuit of the French in Egypt—Returns to Sicily, and sails again to Egypt—Battle of the Nile.

Early in the year 1798, Sir Horatio Nelson hoisted his flag in the *Vanguard,* and was ordered to rejoin Earl St. Vincent.

Upon his departure, his father addressed him with that affectionate solemnity by which all his letters were distinguished. "I trust in the Lord," said he, "that He will prosper your going out and your coming in. I earnestly desired once more to see you, and that wish has been heard. If I should presume to say, I hope to see you again, the question would be readily asked, How old art thou? *Vale! Vale! Domine, vale!*"

It is said that a gloomy foreboding hung on the spirits of Lady Nelson at their parting. This could have arisen only from the dread of losing him by the chance of war. Any apprehension of losing his affections could hardly have existed, for all his correspondence to this time shows that he thought himself happy in his marriage; and his private character had hitherto been as spotless as his public conduct. One of the last things he said to her was, that his own ambition was satisfied, but that he went to raise her to that rank in which he had long wished to see her.

Immediately on his rejoining the fleet, he was despatched to the Mediterranean with a small squadron, in order to ascertain, if possible, the object of the great expedition which at that time was fitting out under Buonaparte at Toulon. The defeat of this armament, whatever might be its destination, was deemed by the British government an object paramount to every other; and Earl St. Vincent was directed, if he thought it necessary, to take his whole force into the Mediterranean, to relinquish, for that purpose, the blockade of the Spanish fleet, as a thing of inferior moment; but if he should deem a detachment sufficient, "I think it almost necessary," said the first lord of the Admiralty in his secret instructions, "to suggest to you the propriety of putting it under Sir Horatio Nelson."

It is to the honour of Earl St. Vincent that he had already made the same choice. This appointment to a service in which so much honour might be acquired, gave great offence to the senior admirals of the fleet.

Sir William Parker, who was a very excellent naval officer, and as gallant a man as any in the navy, and Sir John Orde, who on all occasions of service had acquitted himself with great honour, each wrote to Lord Spencer, complaining that so marked a preference should have been given to a junior of the same fleet.

This resentment is what most men in a like case would feel; and if the preference thus given to Nelson had not originated in a clear perception that (as his friend Collingwood said of him a little while before) his spirit was equal to all undertakings, and his resources fitted to all occasions, an injustice would have been done to them by his appointment. But if the service were conducted with undeviating respect to seniority, the naval and military character would soon be brought down to the dead level of mediocrity.

The armament at Toulon consisted of thirteen ships of the line, seven forty-gun frigates, with twenty-four smaller vessels of war, and nearly 200 transports.

Mr. Udney, our consul at Leghorn, was the first person who procured certain intelligence of the enemy's design against Malta; and, from his own sagacity, foresaw that Egypt must be their after object.

Nelson sailed from Gibraltar on the 9th of May [1798], with the *Vanguard*, *Orion*, and *Alexander*, seventy-fours; the *Caroline*, *Flora*, *Emerald*, and *Terpsichore*, frigates; and the *Bonne Citoyenne*, sloop of war, to watch this formidable armament.

On the 19th, when they were in the Gulf of Lyons, a gale came on from the N.W. It moderated so much on the 20th as to enable them to get their top-gallant masts and yards aloft. After dark it again began to blow strong, but the ships had been prepared for a gale, and therefore Nelson's mind was easy.

Shortly after midnight, however, his main-topmast went over the side, and the mizen-topmast soon afterward. The night was so tempestuous that it was impossible for any signal either to be seen or heard; and Nelson determined, as soon as it should be daybreak, to wear, and scud before the gale; but at half-past three the fore-mast went in three pieces, and the bowsprit was found to be sprung in three places.

When day broke they succeeded in wearing the ship with a remnant of the spritsail. This was hardly to have been expected. The *Vanguard* was at that time twenty-five leagues south of the island of Hieres; with her head lying to the N.E., and if she had not wore, the ship must have drifted to Corsica.

Captain Ball, in the *Alexander*, took her in tow, to carry her into the Sardinian harbour of St. Pietro. Nelson, apprehensive that this attempt might endanger both vessels, ordered him to cast off; but that excellent officer, with a spirit like his commanders, replied, he was confident he could save the *Vanguard*, and, by God's help, he would do it.

There had been a previous coolness between these great men; but from this time Nelson became fully sensible of the extraordinary talents of Captain Ball, and a sincere friendship subsisted between them during the remainder of their lives.

"I ought not," said the admiral, writing to his wife—"I ought not to call what has happened to the *Vanguard* by the cold name of accident: I believe firmly it was the Almighty's goodness, to check my consummate vanity. I hope it has made me a better officer, as I feel confident it has made me a better man. Figure to yourself, on Sunday evening at sunset, a vain man walking in his cabin, with a squadron around him, who looked up to their chief to lead them to glory, and in whom their chief placed the firmest reliance that the proudest ships of equal numbers belonging to France would have lowered their flags; figure to yourself, on Monday morning, when the sun rose, this proud man, his ship dismasted, his fleet dispersed, and himself in such distress that the meanest frigate out of France would have been an unwelcome guest."

Nelson had, indeed, more reason to refuse the cold name of accident to this tempest than he was then aware of, for on that very day the French fleet sailed from Toulon, and must have passed within a few leagues of his little squadron, which was thus preserved by the thick weather that came on.

The British Government at this time, with a becoming spirit, gave orders that any port in the Mediterranean should be considered as hostile where the governor or chief magistrate should refuse to let our ships of war procure supplies of provisions, or of any article which they might require.

In these orders the ports of Sardinia were excepted. The continental possessions of the King of Sardinia were at this time completely at the mercy of the French, and that prince was now discovering, when too late, that the terms to which he had consented, for the purpose of escaping immediate danger, necessarily involved the loss of the dominions which they were intended to preserve.

The citadel of Turin was now occupied by French troops; and his wretched court feared to afford the common rights of humanity to British ships, lest it should give the French occasion to seize on the remainder of his dominions—a measure for which it was certain they would soon make a pretext, if they did not find one. Nelson was informed that he could not be permitted to enter the port of St Pietro.

Regardless of this interdict, which, under his circumstances, it would have been an act of suicidal folly to have regarded, he anchored in the harbour; and, by the exertions of Sir James Saumarez, Captain Ball, and Captain Berry, the *Vanguard* was refitted in four days; months would have been employed in refitting her in England.

Nelson, with that proper sense of merit, wherever it was found, which proved at once the goodness and the greatness of his character, especially recommended to Earl St. Vincent the carpenter of the Alexander, under whose directions the ship had been repaired; stating, that he was an old and faithful servant of the Crown, who had been nearly thirty years a warrant carpenter, and begging most earnestly that the Commander-in-Chief would recommend him to the particular notice of the Board of Admiralty.

He did not leave the harbour without expressing his sense of the treatment which he had received there, in a letter to the Viceroy of Sardinia.

"Sir," it said, "having, by a gale of wind, sustained some trifling damages, I anchored a small part of his Majesty's fleet under my orders off this island, and was surprised to hear, by an officer sent by the governor, that admittance was to be refused to the flag of his Britannic Majesty into this port. When I reflect, that my most gracious sovereign is the oldest, I believe, and certainly the most faithful ally which the King of Sardinia ever had, I could feel the sorrow which it must have been to his majesty to have given such an order; and also for your excellency, who had to direct its execution. I cannot but look at the African shore, where the followers of Mahomet are performing the part of the good Samaritan, which I look for in vain at St. Peter's, where it is said the Christian religion is professed."

The delay which was thus occasioned was useful to him in many respects; it enabled him to complete his supply of water, and to receive a reinforcement which Earl St. Vincent, being himself reinforced from England, was enabled to send him. It consisted of the best ships of his fleet; the *Culloden*, seventy-four, Captain T. Troubridge; *Goliath*, seventy-four, Captain T.Foley; *Minotaur*, seventy-four, Captain T. Louis; *Defence*, seventy-four, Captain John Peyton; *Bellerophon*, seventy-four, Captain H.D.E. Darby; *Majestic*, seventy-four, Captain G. B. Westcott; *Zealous*, seventy-four, Captain S. Hood; *Swiftsure*, seventy-four, Captain B. Hallowell; *Theseus*, seventy-four, Captain R. W. Miller; *Audacious*, seventy-four, Captain Davidge Gould. The *Leander*, fifty, Captain T. E. Thompson, was afterwards added.

These ships were made ready for the service as soon as Earl St. Vincent received advice from England that he was to be reinforced. As soon as the reinforcement was seen from the mast-head of the admiral's ship, off Cadiz Bay, signal was immediately made to Captain Troubridge to put to sea; and he was out of sight before the ships from home cast anchor in the British station. Troubridge took with him no instructions to Nelson as to the course he was to steer, nor any certain account of the enemy's destination; everything was left to his own judgment.

Unfortunately, the frigates had been separated from him in the tempest and had not been able to rejoin: they sought him unsuccessfully in the Bay of Naples, where they obtained no tidings of his course: and he sailed without them.

The first news of the enemy's armament was that it had surprised Malta. Nelson formed a plan for attacking it while at anchor at Gozo; but on the 22nd of June intelligence reached him that the French had left that island on the 16th, the day after their arrival.

It was clear that their destination was eastward—he thought for

Egypt—and for Egypt, therefore, he made all sail. Had the frigates been with him, he could scarcely have failed to gain information of the enemy; for want of them, he only spoke three vessels on the way: two came from Alexandria, one from the Archipelago, and neither of them had seen anything of the French.

He arrived off Alexandria on the 28th, and the enemy were not there, neither was there any account of them; but the governor was endeavouring to put the city in a state of defence, having received advice from Leghorn that the French expedition was intended against Egypt, after it had taken Malta.

Nelson then shaped his course to the northward for Caramania, and steered from thence along the southern side of Candia, carrying a press of sail both night and day, with a contrary wind. It would have been his delight, he said, to have tried Buonaparte on a wind. It would have been the delight of Europe, too, and the blessing of the world, if that fleet had been overtaken with its general on board.

But of the myriads and millions of human beings who would have been preserved by that day's victory, there is not one to whom such essential benefit would have resulted as to Buonaparte himself. It would have spared him his defeat at Acre—his only disgrace[60]; for to have been defeated by Nelson upon the seas would not have been disgraceful; it would have spared him all his after enormities.

Hitherto his career had been glorious; the baneful principles of his heart had never yet passed his lips; history would have represented him as a soldier of fortune, who had faithfully served the cause in which he engaged; and whose career had been distinguished by a series of successes unexampled in modern times. A romantic obscurity would have hung over the expedition to Egypt, and he would have escaped the perpetration of those crimes which have incarnadined his soul with a deeper dye than that of the purple for which he committed them—those acts of perfidy, midnight murder, usurpation, and remorseless tyranny, which

60 At the time Southey published his biography of Nelson in 1813, the French emperor had invaded Russia, with the well known disastrous results, but at the time these words were penned it is likely that the invasion had either not yet begun, or still appeared likely to succeed. In the days of hand-set type, it might take several months to set the type, more to make corrections, and even longer for the finished product—which would have to be hand bound—to finally appear in a book store. The defeat of Napoleon's forces at Leipzig and his first abdication and exile was still a year away; his final defeat at Waterloo in 1815 even farther in the future.

have consigned his name to universal execration, now and for ever[61].

Conceiving that when an officer is not successful in his plans it is absolutely necessary that he should explain the motives upon which they were founded, Nelson wrote at this time an account and vindication of his conduct for having carried the fleet to Egypt. The objection which he anticipated was that he ought not to have made so long a voyage without more certain information.

"My answer," said he, "is ready. Who was I to get it from? The governments of Naples and Sicily either knew not, or chose to keep me in ignorance. Was I to wait patiently until I heard certain accounts? If Egypt were their object, before I could hear of them they would have been in India. To do nothing was disgraceful; therefore I made use of my understanding. I am before your lordships' judgment; and if, under all circumstances, it is decided that I am wrong, I ought, for the sake of our country, to be superseded; for at this moment, when I know the French are not in Alexandria, I hold the same opinion as off Cape Passaro—that, under all circumstances, I was right in steering for Alexandria; and by that opinion I must stand or fall."

Captain Ball, to whom he showed this paper, told him he should recommend a friend never to begin a defence of his conduct before he was accused of error: he might give the fullest reasons for what he had done, expressed in such terms as would evince that he had acted from the strongest conviction of being right; and of course he must expect that the public would view it in the same light. Captain Ball judged rightly of the public, whose first impulses, though, from want of sufficient information, they must frequently be erroneous, are generally founded upon just feelings.

But the public are easily misled, and there are always persons ready to mislead them. Nelson had not yet attained that fame which compels envy to be silent; and when it was known in England that he had returned after an unsuccessful pursuit, it was said that he deserved impeachment; and Earl St. Vincent was severely censured for having sent so young an officer upon so important a service.

Baffled in his pursuit, he returned to Sicily. The Neapolitan ministry had determined to give his squadron no assistance, being resolved to

61 This isn't exactly the way Napoleon is thought of today, but Southey's virulently negative opinion was probably shared by most of his original British readers.

do nothing which could possibly endanger their peace with the French Directory; by means, however, of Lady Hamilton's influence at court, he procured secret orders to the Sicilian governors; and under those orders obtained everything which he wanted at Syracuse—a timely supply; without which, he always said, he could not have recommenced his pursuit with any hope of success.

"It is an old saying," said he in his letter, "that the devil's children have the devil's luck. I cannot to this moment learn, beyond vague conjecture, where the French fleet have gone to; and having gone a round of 600 leagues, at this season of the year, with an expedition incredible, here I am, as ignorant of the situation of the enemy as I was twenty-seven days ago. Every moment I have to regret the frigates having left me; had one-half of them been with me, I could not have wanted information. Should the French be so strongly secured in port that I cannot get at them, I shall immediately shift my flag into some other ship, and send the *Vanguard* to Naples to be refitted; for hardly any person but myself would have continued on service so long in such a wretched state."

Vexed, however, and disappointed as he was, Nelson, with the true spirit of a hero, was still full of hope. "Thanks to your exertions," said he, writing to Sir William and Lady Hamilton, "we have victualled and watered; and surely watering at the fountain of Arethusa[62], we must have victory. We shall sail with the first breeze; and be assured I will return either crowned with laurel or covered with cypress."

Earl St. Vincent he assured, that if the French were above water he would find them out: he still held his opinion that they were bound for Egypt: "but," said he to the First Lord of the Admiralty, "be they bound to the Antipodes[63], your lordship may rely that I will not lose a moment in bringing them to action."

On the 25th of July he sailed from Syracuse for the Morea. Anxious beyond measure, and irritated that the enemy should so long have eluded him, the tediousness of the nights made him impatient; and the officer of the watch was repeatedly called on to let him know the hour, and convince him, who measured time by his own eagerness, that it was not yet daybreak.

62 In Greek mythology, Arethusa was a Nereid nymph who was transformed into a fountain in Sicily.

63 In its most literal meaning, the opposite side of the earth. British usage also employ "antipodes" as a reference to Australia, or to other southern lands.

The squadron made the Gulf of Coron on the 28th. Troubridge entered the port, and returned with intelligence that the French fleet had been seen about four weeks before steering to the S.E. from Candia. Nelson then determined immediately to return to Alexandria; and the British fleet accordingly, with every sail set, stood once more for the coast of Egypt.

On the 1st of August, about 10 in the morning, they came in sight of Alexandria: the port had been vacant and solitary when they saw it last; it was now crowded with ships; and they perceived with exultation that the tri-coloured flag was flying upon the walls. At four in the afternoon, Captain Hood, in the *Zealous*, made the signal for the enemy's fleet.

For many preceding days Nelson had hardly taken either sleep or food: he now ordered his dinner to be served, while preparations were making for battle; and when his officers rose from table, and went to their separate stations, he said to them, "Before this time to-morrow I shall have gained a peerage or Westminster Abbey."

The French, steering direct for Candia, had made an angular passage for Alexandria; whereas Nelson, in pursuit of them, made straight for that place, and thus materially shortened the distance. The comparative smallness of his force made it necessary to sail in close order, and it covered a less space than it would have done if the frigates had been with him: the weather also was constantly hazy.

These circumstances prevented the English from discovering the enemy on the way to Egypt, though it appeared, upon examining the journals of the French officers taken in the action, that the two fleets must actually have crossed on the night of the 22nd of June. During the return to Syracuse, the chances of falling in with them were become fewer.

Why Buonaparte, having effected his landing, should not have suffered the fleet to return, has never yet been explained. This much is certain, that it was detained by his command, though, with his accustomed falsehood, he accused Admiral Brueys, after that officer's death, of having lingered on the coast contrary to orders.

The French fleet arrived at Alexandria on the 1st of July, and Brueys, not being able to enter the port, which time and neglect had ruined, moored his ships in Aboukir Bay, in a strong and compact line of battle; the headmost vessel, according to his own account, being as close as possible to a shoal on the N.W., and the rest of the fleet forming a kind of curve along the line of deep water, so as not to be turned by any means in the S.W.

By Buonaparte's desire he had offered a reward of 10,000 livres to any pilot of the country who would carry the squadron in, but none could be found who would venture to take charge of a single vessel drawing more than twenty feet. He had therefore made the best of his situation, and chosen the strongest position which he could possibly take in an open road.

The commissary of the fleet said they were moored in such a manner as to bid defiance to a force more than double their own. This presumption could not then be thought unreasonable.

Admiral Barrington, when moored in a similar manner off St. Lucia, in the year 1778, beat off the Comte d'Estaing in three several attacks, though his force was inferior by almost one-third to that which assailed it. Here, the advantage in numbers, both in ships, guns, and men, was in favour of the French. They had thirteen ships of the line and four frigates, carrying 1,196 guns and 11,230 men.

The English had the same number of ships of the line and one fifty-gun ship, carrying 1,012 guns and 8,068 men. The English ships were all seventy-fours; the French had three eighty-gun ships, and one three-decker of one hundred and twenty.

During the whole pursuit it had been Nelson's practice, whenever circumstances would permit, to have his captains on board the *Vanguard*, and explain to them his own ideas of the different and best modes of attack, and such plans as he proposed to execute on falling in with the enemy, whatever their situation might be. There is no possible position, it is said, which he did not take into calculation. His officers were thus fully acquainted with his principles of tactics; and such was his confidence in their abilities that the only thing determined upon, in case they should find the French at anchor, was for the ships to form as most convenient for their mutual support, and to anchor by the stern.

"First gain the victory," he said, "and then make the best use of it you can."

The moment he perceived the position of the French, that intuitive genius with which Nelson was endowed displayed itself; and it instantly struck him that where there was room for an enemy's ship to swing, there was room for one of ours to anchor. The plan which he intended to pursue, therefore, was to keep entirely on the outer side of the French line, and station his ships, as far as he was able, one on the outer bow, and another on the outer quarter, of each of the enemy's. This plan of doubling on the enemy's ships was projected by Lord Hood, when he designed to attack the French fleet at their anchorage in Gourjean Road.

Lord Hood found it impossible to make the attempt; but the thought was not lost upon Nelson, who acknowledged himself, on this occasion, indebted for it to his old and excellent commander.

Captain Berry, when he comprehended the scope of the design, exclaimed with transport, "If we succeed, what will the world say?"

"There is no *if* in the case," replied the admiral: "that we shall succeed is certain; who may live to tell the story is a very different question."

As the squadron advanced, they were assailed by a shower of shot and shells from the batteries on the island, and the enemy opened a steady fire from the starboard side of their whole line, within half gunshot distance, full into the bows of our van ships.

It was received in silence: the men on board every ship were employed aloft in furling sails, and below in tending the braces and making ready for anchoring. A miserable sight for the French; who, with all their skill, and all their courage, and all their advantages of numbers and situation, were upon that element on which, when the hour of trial comes, a Frenchman has no hope.

Admiral Brueys was a brave and able man; yet the indelible character of his country broke out in one of his letters, wherein he delivered it as his private opinion, that the English had missed him, because, not being superior in force, they did not think it prudent to try their strength with him. The moment was now come in which he was to be undeceived.

A French brig was instructed to decoy the English by manoeuvring so as to tempt them toward a shoal lying off the island of Bekier; but Nelson either knew the danger or suspected some deceit; and the lure was unsuccessful.

Captain Foley led the way in the *Goliath*, outsailing the *Zealous*, which for some minutes disputed this post of honour with him. He had long conceived that if the enemy were moored in line of battle in with the land, the best plan of attack would be to lead between them and the shore, because the French guns on that side were not likely to be manned, nor even ready for action.

Intending, therefore, to fix himself on the inner bow of the *Guerrier,* he kept as near the edge of the bank as the depth of water would admit; but his anchor hung, and having opened his fire he drifted to the second ship, the *Conquerant,* before it was clear; then anchored by the stern inside of her, and in ten minutes shot away her mast.

Hood, in the *Zealous,* perceiving this, took the station which the *Goliath* intended to have occupied, and totally disabled the *Guerrier* in twelve minutes.

The third ship which doubled the enemy's van was the *Orion,* Sir J. Saumarez; she passed to windward of the *Zealous,* and opened her larboard guns as long as they bore on *Guerrier,* then, passing inside the *Goliath,* sunk a frigate which annoyed her, hauled round toward the French line, and anchoring inside, between the fifth and sixth ships from the *Guerrier,* took her station on the larboard bow of the *Franklin* and the quarter of the *Peuple Souverain,* receiving and returning the fire of both.

The sun was now nearly down. The *Audacious,* Captain Gould, pouring a heavy fire into the *Guerrier* and the *Conquerant,* fixed herself on the larboard bow of the latter, and when that ship struck, passed on to the *Peuple Souverain.* The *Theseus,* Capt Miller, followed, brought down the *Guerrier*'s remaining main and mizzen masts, then anchored inside of the *Spartiate,* the third in the French line.

While these advanced ships doubled the French line, the *Vanguard* was the first that anchored on the outer side of the enemy, within half pistol-shot of their third ship, the *Spartiate.* Nelson had six colours flying in different parts of his rigging, lest they should be shot away; that they should be struck, no British admiral considers as a possibility.

He veered half a cable, and instantly opened a tremendous fire; under cover of which the other four ships of his division, the *Minotaur, Bellerophon, Defence,* and *Majestic,* sailed on ahead of the admiral. In a few minutes, every man stationed at the first six guns in the fore part of the *Vanguard*'s deck was killed or wounded. These guns were three times cleared.

Captain Louis, in the *Minotaur,* anchored just ahead, and took off the fire of the *Aquilon,* the fourth in the enemy's line. The *Bellerophon,* Captain Darby, passed ahead, and dropped her stern anchor on the starboard bow of the *Orient,* seventh in the line, Brueys' own ship, of one hundred and twenty guns, whose difference of force was in proportion of more than seven to three, and whose weight of ball, from the lower deck alone, exceeded that from the whole broadside of the *Bellerophon.*

Captain Peyton, in the *Defence,* took his station ahead of the *Minotaur,* and engaged the *Franklin,* the sixth in the line, by which judicious movement the British line remained unbroken.

The *Majestic,* Captain Westcott, got entangled with the main rigging of one of the French ships astern of the *Orient,* and suffered dreadfully from that three-decker's fire; but she swung clear, and closely engaging the *Heureux,* the ninth ship on the starboard bow, received also the fire of the *Tonnant,* which was the eighth in the line. The other four ships of the British squadron, having been detached previous to the discovery of the French, were at a considerable distance when the action began. It commenced at half after six; about seven night closed, and there was no other light than that from the fire of the contending fleets.

Troubridge, in the *Culloden,* then foremost of the remaining ships, was two leagues astern. He came on sounding, as the others had done: as he advanced, the increasing darkness increased the difficulty of the navigation; and suddenly, after having found eleven fathoms water, before the lead could be hove again he was fast aground; nor could all his own exertions, joined with those of the *Leander* and the *Mutine* brig, which came to his assistance, get him off in time to bear a part in the action.

His ship, however, served as a beacon to the *Alexander* and *Swiftsure,* which would else, from the course which they were holding, have gone considerably further on the reef, and must inevitably have been lost.

These ships entered the bay, and took their stations in the darkness, in a manner still spoken of with admiration by all who remember it. Captain Hallowell, in the *Swiftsure,* as he was bearing down, fell in with what seemed to be a strange sail. Nelson had directed his ships to hoist four lights horizontally at the mizzen peak as soon as it became dark; and this vessel had no such distinction. Hallowell, however, with great judgment, ordered his men not to fire: if she was an enemy, he said, she was in too disabled a state to escape; but from her sails being loose, and the way in which her head was, it was probable she might be an English ship.

It was the *Bellerophon,* overpowered by the huge *Orient:* her lights had gone overboard, nearly 200 of her crew were killed or wounded, all her masts and cables had been shot away; and she was drifting out of the line toward the lee side of the bay. Her station, at this important time, was occupied by the *Swiftsure,* which opened a steady fire on the quarter of the *Franklin* and the bows of the French admiral.

At the same instant, Captain Ball, with the *Alexander*, passed under his stern, and anchored within-side on his larboard quarter, raking; him, and keeping up a severe fire of musketry upon his decks. The last ship which arrived to complete the destruction of the enemy was the *Leander*. Captain Thompson, finding that nothing could be done that night to get off the *Culloden*, advanced with the intention of anchoring athwart-hawse of the *Orient*. The *Franklin* was so near her ahead that there was not room for him to pass clear of the two; he therefore took his station athwart-hawse of the latter in such a position as to rake both.

The two first ships of the French line had been dismasted within a quarter of an hour after the commencement of the action; and the others had in that time suffered so severely that victory was already certain. The third, fourth, and fifth were taken possession of at half-past eight.

Meantime Nelson received a severe wound on the head from a piece of langridge[64] shot. Captain Berry caught him in his arms as he was falling. The great effusion of blood occasioned an apprehension that the wound was mortal: Nelson himself thought so; a large flap of the skin of the forehead, cut from the bone, had fallen over one eye; and the other being blind, he was in total darkness.

When he was carried down, the surgeon—in the midst of a scene scarcely to be conceived by those who have never seen a cockpit in time of action, and the heroism which is displayed amid its horrors,—with a natural and pardonable eagerness, quitted the poor fellow then under his hands, that he might instantly attend the admiral.

"No!" said Nelson, "I will take my turn with my brave fellows."

Nor would he suffer his own wound to be examined till every man who had been previously wounded was properly attended to. Fully believing that the wound was mortal, and that he was about to die, as he had ever desired, in battle, and in victory, he called the chaplain, and desired him to deliver what he supposed to be his dying remembrance to lady Nelson; he then sent for Captain Louis on board from the *Minotaur*, that he might thank him personally for the great assistance which he had rendered to the *Vanguard*; and ever mindful of those who deserved to be his friends, appointed Captain Hardy from the brig to the command of his

64 Langridge was not properly formed shot, but small pieces of scrap metal, old nails, and other small junk loaded into a gun. It was used both as an anti-personnel weapon, and to tear up sails and rigging.

own ship, Captain Berry having to go home with the news of the victory.

When the surgeon came in due time to examine his wound (for it was in vain to entreat him to let it be examined sooner), the most anxious silence prevailed; and the joy of the wounded men, and of the whole crew, when they heard that the hurt was merely superficial, gave Nelson deeper pleasure than the unexpected assurance that his life was in no danger.

The surgeon requested, and as far as he could, ordered him to remain quiet; but Nelson could not rest. He called for his secretary, Mr. Campbell, to write the despatches. Campbell had himself been wounded, and was so affected at the blind and suffering state of the admiral that he was unable to write.

The chaplain was then sent for; but before he came, Nelson with his characteristic eagerness took the pen, and contrived to trace a few words, marking his devout sense of the success which had already been obtained. He was now left alone; when suddenly a cry was heard on the deck that the *Orient* was on fire. In the confusion he found his way up, unassisted and unnoticed; and, to the astonishment of every one, appeared on the quarter-deck where he immediately gave order that the boats should be sent to the relief of the enemy.

It was soon after nine that the fire on, board the *Orient* broke out. Brueys was dead; he had received three wounds, yet would not leave his post: a fourth cut him almost in two. He desired not to be carried below, but to be left to die upon deck.

The flames soon mastered his ship. Her sides had just been painted; and the oil-jars and paint buckets were lying on the poop. By the prodigious light of this conflagration, the situation of the two fleets could now be perceived, the colours of both being clearly distinguishable.

About ten o'clock the ship blew up, with a shock which was felt to the very bottom of every vessel. Many of her officers and men jumped overboard, some clinging to the spars and pieces of wreck with which the sea was strewn, others swimming to escape from the destruction which they momently dreaded.

Some were picked up by our boats; and some even in the heat and fury of the action were dragged into the lower ports of the nearest British ships by the British sailors. The greater part of her crew, however, stood the danger till the last, and continued to fire from the lower deck.

This tremendous explosion was followed by a silence not less awful:

the firing immediately ceased on both sides; and the first sound which broke the silence, was the dash of her shattered masts and yards, falling into the water from the vast height to which they had been exploded. It is upon record that a battle between two armies was once broken off by an earthquake. Such an event would be felt like a miracle; but no incident in war, produced by human means, has ever equalled the sublimity of this co-instantaneous pause, and all its circumstances.

About seventy of the *Orient*'s crew were saved by the English boats. Among the many hundreds who perished were the commodore, Casa-Bianca, and his son, a brave boy, only ten years old. They were seen floating on a shattered mast when the ship blew up. She had money on board (the plunder of Malta) to the amount of £600,000 sterling.

The masses of burning wreck, which were scattered by the explosion, excited for some moments apprehensions in the English which they had never felt from any other danger. Two large pieces fell into the main and fore tops of the *Swiftsure* without injuring any person. A port-fire also fell into the main-royal of the *Alexander*; the fire which it occasioned was speedily extinguished.

Captain Ball had provided, as far as human foresight could provide, against any such danger. All the shrouds and sails of his ship, not absolutely necessary for its immediate management, were thoroughly wetted, and so rolled up that they were as hard and as little inflammable as so many solid cylinders.

The firing recommenced with the ships to leeward of the centre, and continued till about three. At daybreak, the *Guillaume Tell* and the *Genereux*, the two rear ships of the enemy, were the only French ships of the line which had their colours flying; they cut their cables in the forenoon, not having been engaged, and stood out to sea, and two frigates with them.

The *Zealous* pursued; but as there was no other ship in a condition to support Captain Hood, he was recalled.

It was generally believed by the officers that if Nelson had not been wounded, not one of these ships could have escaped. The four certainly could not if the *Culloden* had got into action; and if the frigates belonging to the squadron had been present, not one of the enemy's fleet would have left Aboukir Bay.

These four vessels, however, were all that escaped; and the victory was the most complete and glorious in the annals of naval history.

"Victory," said Nelson, "is not a name strong enough for such a scene:" he called it a conquest.

Of thirteen sail of the line, nine were taken and two burned. Of the four frigates, one was sunk, another, the *Artemise*, was burned in a villainous manner by her captain, M. Estandlet, who, having fired a broadside at the *Theseus*, struck his colours, then set fire to the ship and escaped with most of his crew to shore.

The British loss, in killed and wounded, amounted to 895, Westcott was the only captain who fell; 3,105 of the French, including the wounded, were sent on shore by cartel, and 5,225 perished.

As soon as the conquest was completed, Nelson sent orders through the fleet to return thanksgiving in every ship for the victory with which Almighty God had blessed his majesty's arms.

The French at Rosetta, who with miserable fear beheld the engagement, were at a loss to understand the stillness of the fleet during the performance of this solemn duty; but it seemed to affect many of the prisoners, officers as well as men; and graceless and godless as the officers were, some of them remarked that it was no wonder such order was preserved in the British navy, when the minds of our men could be impressed with such sentiments after so great a victory, and at a moment of such confusion.

The French at Rosetta, seeing their four ships sail out of the bay unmolested, endeavoured to persuade themselves that they were in possession of the place of battle. But it was in vain thus to attempt, against their own secret and certain conviction, to deceive themselves; and even if they could have succeeded in this, the bonfires which the Arabs kindled along the whole coast, and over the country, for the three following nights, would soon have undeceived them. Thousands of Arabs and Egyptians lined the shore, and covered the house tops during the action, rejoicing in the destruction which had overtaken their invaders.

Long after the battle, innumerable bodies were seen floating about the bay, in spite of all the exertions which were made to sink them, as well from fear of pestilence as from the loathing and horror which the sight occasioned. Great numbers were cast up upon the Isle of Bekier (Nelson's Island, as it has since been called), and our sailors raised mounds of sand over them. Even after an interval of nearly three years Dr. Clarke saw them, and assisted in interring heaps of human bodies, which, having been thrown up by the sea where there were no jackals to devour them, presented a sight loathsome to humanity.

The shore, for an extent of four leagues, was covered with wreck; and the Arabs found employment for many days in burning on the beach the fragments which were cast up, for the sake of the iron.

Part of the *Orient*'s main-mast was picked up by the *Swiftsure.* Captain Hallowell ordered his carpenter to make a coffin of it; the iron, as well as the wood, was taken from the wreck of the same ship; it was finished as well and handsomely as the workman's skill and materials would permit; and Hallowell then sent it to the admiral with the following letter:—

"Sir, I have taken the liberty of presenting you a coffin made from the main mast of *L'Orient,* that when you have finished your military career in this world you may be buried in one of your trophies. But that that period may be far distant is the earnest wish of your sincere friend, Benjamin Hallowell."

An offering so strange, and yet so suited to the occasion, was received by Nelson in the spirit with which it was sent. As if he felt it good for him, now that he was at the summit of his wishes, to have death before his eyes, he ordered the coffin to be placed upright in his cabin. Such a piece of furniture, however, was more suitable to his own feelings than to those of his guests and attendants; and an old favourite servant entreated him so earnestly to let it be removed, that at length he consented to have the coffin carried below; but he gave strict orders that it should be safely stowed, and reserved for the purpose for which its brave and worthy donor had designed it[65].

The victory was complete; but Nelson could not pursue it as he would have done for want of means. Had he been provided with small craft, nothing could have prevented the destruction of the store-ships and transports in the port of Alexandria: four bomb-vessels would at that time have burned the whole in a few hours.

"Were I to die this moment." said he in his despatches to the Admiralty, "*Want of frigates* would be found stamped on my heart! No words

65 Nelson was, in fact, interred in this coffin, though the relatively plain pine coffin presented to him by Captain Hallowell was, in turn, placed inside a second, more ornate outer coffin, decorated with gilded devices relating to Nelson's life and career. Thus, Nelson was buried in the *Orient* coffin, as he desired, but the public beheld the elaborate outer coffin, more in keeping with the expectations of a state funeral.

of mine can express what I have suffered, and am suffering, for want of them."

He had also to bear up against great bodily suffering: the blow had so shaken his head, that from its constant and violent aching, and the perpetual sickness which accompanied the pain, he could scarcely persuade himself that the skull was not fractured. Had it not been for Troubridge, Ball, Hood, and Hallowell, he declared that he should have sunk under the fatigue of refitting the squadron.

"All," he said, "had done well; but these officers were his supporters."

But, amidst his sufferings and exertions, Nelson could yet think of all the consequences of his victory; and that no advantage from it might be lost, he despatched an officer overland to India, with letters to the governor of Bombay, informing him of the arrival of the French in Egypt, the total destruction of their fleet, and the consequent preservation of India from any attempt against it on the part of this formidable armament.

"He knew that Bombay," he said, "was their first object, if they could get there; but he trusted that Almighty God would overthrow in Egypt these pests of the human race. Buonaparte had never yet had to contend with an English officer, and he would endeavour to make him respect us."

This despatch he sent upon his own responsibility, with letters of credit upon the East India Company, addressed to the British consuls, vice-consuls, and merchants on his route; Nelson saying, "that if he had done wrong, he hoped the bills would be paid, and he would repay the Company; for, as an Englishman, he should be proud that it had been in his power to put our settlements on their guard."

The information which by this means reached India was of great importance. Orders had just been received for defensive preparations, upon a scale proportionate to the apprehended danger; and the extraordinary expenses which would otherwise have been incurred were thus prevented.

Nelson was now at the summit of glory; congratulations, rewards, and honours were showered upon him by all the states, and princes, and powers to whom his victory gave a respite. The first communication of this nature which he received was from the Turkish sultan, who, as soon as the invasion of Egypt was known, had called upon "all true believers to take arms against those swinish infidels the French[66], that they might deliver these blessed habitations from their accursed hands;" and who had ordered his "pashas to turn night into day in their efforts to take vengeance."

The present of "his imperial majesty, the powerful, formidable, and most magnificent Grand Seignior," was a pelisse of sables, with broad sleeves, valued at 5,000 dols.; and a diamond aigrette, valued at 18,000 dols., the most honourable badge among the Turks; and in this instance more especially honourable, because it was taken from one of the royal turbans.

"If it were worth a million," said Nelson to his wife, "my pleasure would be to see it in your possession."

The sultan also sent, in a spirit worthy of imitation, a purse of 2,000 sequins, to be distributed among the wounded. The mother of the sultan sent him a box, set with diamonds, valued at £1,000.

The Czar Paul, in whom the better part of his strangely compounded nature at this time predominated[67], presented him with his portrait, set in diamonds, in a gold box, accompanied with a letter of congratulation, written by his own hand.

The king of Sardinia also wrote to him, and sent a gold box set with diamonds. Honours in profusion were awaiting him at Naples. In his own country the king granted these honourable augmentations to his armorial ensign: a chief undulated, *argent*: thereon waves of the sea; from which a palm tree issuant, between a disabled ship on the dexter, and a ruinous battery on the sinister all proper; and for his crest, on a

---

66 Presumably the Sultan was diplomatic enough to exclude the British, who were also "infidels" in Islamic eyes, from the "swinish" category on this particular occasion, as they had done him a considerable favor by destroying the French fleet. Too, there was a common misperception at this time that the French were mostly atheists, a misperception strongly abetted by British propagandists (Southey included). This seemed to be based on the post-Revolutionary French notion that the Church should have little or no say in government, and the deposing of their king in contravention to St. Paul's dictum that kings were given their status by God and attempting to depose them was, therefore, a defiance of God. The British, for the most part, would have agreed that the Roman Catholic Church shouldn't be involved in government, but there was an obvious Hanoverian feeling that deposing kings was a bad idea (despite their dynasty owing their sovereignty over England to exactly that action).

67 Tsar Paul I of Russia (1754–1801). The Tsar's sanity was generally considered debatable, often with good reason. His mercurial nature would ultimately be cited as a primary reason for his assassination.

naval crown, *or,* the *chelengk,* or plume, presented to him by the Turk, with the motto, *Palmam Qui Meruit Ferat.* [Let him who has earned it bear the palm.]

And to his supporters, being a sailor on the dexter, and a lion on the sinister, were given these honourable augmentations: a palm branch in the sailor's hand, and another in the paw of the lion, both proper; with a tri-coloured flag and staff in the lion's mouth.

He was created Baron Nelson of the Nile, and of Burnham Thorpe, with a pension of £2,000 for his own life, and those of his two immediate successors.

When the grant was moved in the House of Commons, General Walpole expressed an opinion that a higher degree of rank ought to be conferred. Mr. Pitt made answer, that he thought it needless to enter into that question.

"Admiral Nelson's fame," he said, "would be co-equal with the British name; and it would be remembered that he had obtained the greatest naval victory on record, when no man would think of asking whether he had been created a baron, a viscount, or an earl."

It was strange that, in the very act of conferring a title, the minister should have excused himself for not having conferred a higher one, by representing all titles, on such an occasion, as nugatory and superfluous.

True, indeed, whatever title had been bestowed, whether viscount, earl, marquis, duke, or prince, if our laws had so permitted, he who received it would have been Nelson still. That name he had ennobled beyond all addition of nobility; it was the name by which England loved him, France feared him, Italy, Egypt, and Turkey celebrated him, and by which he will continue to be known while the present kingdoms and languages of the world endure, and as long as their history after them shall be held in remembrance.

It depended upon the degree of rank what should be the fashion of his coronet, in what page of the red book his name was to be inserted, and what precedency should be allowed his lady in the drawing-room and at the ball. That Nelson's honours were affected thus far, and no further, might be conceded to Mr. Pitt and his colleagues in administration; but the degree of rank which they thought proper to allot was the measure of their gratitude, though not of his service.

This Nelson felt, and this he expressed, with indignation, among his friends.

Whatever may have been the motives of the ministry, and whatever the formalities with which they excused their conduct to themselves, the importance and magnitude of the victory were universally acknowledged. A grant of £10,000 was voted to Nelson by the East India Company; the Turkish Company presented him with a piece of plate; the City of London presented a sword to him, and to each of his captains; gold medals were distributed to the captains; and the first lieutenants of all the ships were promoted, as had been done after Lord Howe's victory.

Nelson was exceedingly anxious that the captain and first lieutenant of the *Culloden* should not be passed over because of their misfortune. To Troubridge himself he said, "Let us rejoice that the ship which got on shore was commanded by an officer whose character is so thoroughly established."

To the Admiralty he stated that Captain Troubridge's conduct was as fully entitled to praise as that of any one officer in the squadron, and as highly deserving of reward. "It was Troubridge," said he, "who equipped the squadron so soon at Syracuse; it was Troubridge who exerted himself for me after the action; it was Troubridge who saved the *Culloden*, when none that I know in the service would have attempted it."

The gold medal, therefore, by the king's express desire, was given to Captain Troubridge, "for his services both before and since, and for the great and wonderful exertion which he made at the time of the action in saving and getting off his ship."

The private letter from the Admiralty to Nelson informed him that the first lieutenants of all the ships *engaged* were to be promoted. Nelson instantly wrote to the commander-in-chief: "I sincerely hope," said he, "this is not intended to exclude the first lieutenant of the *Culloden*. For heaven's sake—for my sake, if it be so—get it altered. Our dear friend Troubridge has endured enough. His sufferings were, in every respect, more than any of us."

To the Admiralty he wrote in terms equally warm. "I hope, and believe, the word *engaged* is not intended to exclude the *Culloden*. The merits of that ship, and her gallant Captain, are too well known to benefit by anything I could say. Her misfortune was great in getting aground, while her more fortunate companions were in the full tide of happiness. No: I am confident that my good Lord Spencer will never add misery to misfortune. Captain Troubridge on shore is superior to captains afloat: in the midst of his great misfortunes he made those signals which prevented certainly the *Alexander* and *Swiftsure* from running on the shoals. I beg your pardon for writing on a subject which, I verily believe, has never entered your lordship's head; but my heart, as it ought to be, is warm to my gallant friends."

Thus feelingly alive was Nelson to the claims, and interests, and feelings of others. The Admiralty replied, that the exception was necessary, as the ship had not been in action; but they desired the commander-in-chief to promote the lieutenant upon the first vacancy which should occur.

Nelson, in remembrance of an old and uninterrupted friendship, appointed Alexander Davison sole prize agent for the captured ships: upon which Davison ordered medals to be struck in gold, for the captains; in silver, for the lieutenants and warrant officers; in gilt metal for the petty officers; and in copper for the seamen and marines. The cost of this act of liberality amounted nearly to £2,000.

It is worthy of record on another account;—for some of the gallant men, who received no other honorary badge of their conduct on that memorable day than this copper medal from a private individual, years afterwards, when they died upon a foreign station, made it their last request, that the medals might carefully be sent home to their respective friends. So sensible are brave men of honour, in whatever rank they may be placed.

Three of the frigates, whose presence would have been so essential a few weeks sooner, joined the squadron on the twelfth day after the action. The fourth joined a few days after them. Nelson thus received despatches, which rendered it necessary for him to return to Naples.

Before he left Egypt he burned three of the prizes; they could not have been fitted for a passage to Gibraltar in less than a month, and that at a great expense, and with the loss of the services of at least two sail of the line.

"I rest assured," he said to the Admiralty, "that they will be paid for, and have held out that assurance to the squadron. For if an admiral, after a victory, is to look after the captured ships, and not to the distressing of the enemy, very dearly, indeed, must the nation pay for the prizes. I trust that £60,000 will be deemed a very moderate sum for them: and when the services, time, and men, with the expense of fitting the three ships for a voyage to England, are considered, government will save nearly as much as they are valued at. Paying for prizes," he continued, "is no new idea of mine, and would often prove an amazing saving to the state, even without taking into calculation what the nation loses by the attention of admirals to the property of the captors; an attention absolutely necessary, as a recompence for the exertions of the officers and men. An admiral may be amply rewarded by his own feelings, and by the approbation of his superiors; but what reward have the inferior officers and men but the value of the prizes? If an admiral takes that from them, on any consideration, he cannot expect to be well supported."

To Earl St. Vincent he said, "If he could have been sure that government would have paid a reasonable value for them, he would have ordered two of the other prizes to be burnt, for they would cost more in refitting, and by the loss of ships attending them, than they were worth."

Having sent the six remaining prizes forward, under Sir James Saumarez, Nelson left Captain Hood, in the *Zealous* off Alexandria, with the *Swiftsure, Goliath, Alcmene,* and *Emerald,* and stood out to sea himself on the seventeenth day after the battle.

Chapter 6
1798–1800

Nelson returns to Naples—State of that Court and Kingdom—General Mack—The French approach Naples—Flight of the Royal Family—Successes of the Allies in Italy—Transactions in the Bay of Naples—Expulsion of the French from the Neapolitan and Roman States—Nelson is made Duke of Bronte—He leaves the Mediterranean and returns to England.

Nelson's health had suffered greatly while he was in the *Agamemnon.* "My complaint," he said, "is as if a girth were buckled taut over my breast, and my endeavour in the night is to get it loose."

After the battle of Cape St. Vincent he felt a little rest to be so essential to his recovery, that he declared he would not continue to serve longer than the ensuing summer, unless it should be absolutely necessary; for in his own strong language, he had then been four years and nine months without one moment's repose for body or mind. A few months' intermission of labour he had obtained—not of rest, for it was purchased with the loss of a limb; and the greater part of the time had been a season of constant pain. As soon as his shattered frame had sufficiently recovered for him to resume his duties, he was called to services of greater importance than any on which he had hitherto been employed, which brought with them commensurate fatigue and care.

The anxiety which he endured during his long pursuit of the enemy, was rather changed in its direction than abated by their defeat; and this constant wakefulness of thought, added to the effect of his wound, and the exertions from which it was not possible for one of so ardent and wide-reaching a mind to spare himself, nearly proved fatal.

On his way back to Italy he was seized with fever. For eighteen hours his life was despaired of; and even when the disorder took a favourable turn, and he was so far recovered as again to appear on deck, he himself thought that his end was approaching—such was the weakness to which the fever and cough had reduced him.

Writing to Earl St. Vincent on the passage, he said to him, "I never expect, my dear lord, to see your face again. It may please God that this will be the finish to that fever of anxiety which I have endured from the middle of June; but be that as it pleases his goodness. I am resigned to his will."

The kindest attentions of the warmest friendship were awaiting him at Naples.

"Come here," said Sir William Hamilton, "for God's sake, my dear friend, as soon as the service will permit you. A pleasant apartment is ready for you in my house, and Emma is looking out for the softest pillows to repose the few wearied limbs you have left."

Happy would it have been for Nelson if warm and careful friendship had been all that waited him there. He himself saw at that time the character of the Neapolitan court, as it first struck an Englishman, in its true light; and when he was on the way, he declared that he detested the voyage to Naples, and that nothing but necessity could have forced him to it.

But never was any hero, on his return from victory, welcomed with more heartfelt joy.

Before the battle of Aboukir the Court at Naples had been trembling for its existence. The language which the Directory held towards it was well described by Sir William Hamilton as being exactly the language of a highwayman. The Neapolitans were told that Benevento might be added to their dominions, provided they would pay a large sum, sufficient to satisfy the Directory; and they were warned, that if the proposal were refused, or even if there were any delay in accepting it, the French would revolutionise all Italy.

The joy, therefore, of the Court at Nelson's success was in proportion to the dismay from which that success relieved them. The queen was a daughter of Maria Theresa, and sister of Maria Antoinette. Had she been the wisest and gentlest of her sex, it would not have been possible for her to have regarded the French without hatred and horror; and the progress of revolutionary opinions, while it perpetually reminded her of her sister's fate, excited no unreasonable apprehensions for her own. Her feelings, naturally ardent, and little accustomed to restraint, were excited to the highest pitch when the news of the victory arrived.

Lady Hamilton, her constant friend and favourite, who was present, says, "It is not possible to describe her transports; she wept, she kissed her husband, her children, walked frantically about the room, burst into tears again, and again kissed and embraced every person near her; exclaiming, 'O brave Nelson! O God! bless and protect our brave deliverer! O Nelson! Nelson! what do we not owe you! O conqueror—saviour of Italy! O that my swollen heart could now tell him personally what we owe to him!'

"She herself wrote to the Neapolitan ambassador at London upon the occasion, in terms which show the fullness of her joy, and the height of the hopes which it had excited. 'I wish I could give wings,' said she, 'to the bearer of the news, and at the same time to our most sincere gratitude. The whole of the sea-coast of Italy saved; and this is owing alone to the generous English. This battle, or, to speak more correctly, this total defeat of the regicide squadron, was obtained by the valour of this brave admiral, seconded by a navy which is the terror of its enemies. The victory is so complete that I can still scarcely believe it; and if it were not the brave English nation, which is accustomed to perform prodigies by sea, I could not persuade myself that it had happened. It would have moved you to have seen all my children, boys and girls, hanging on my neck, and crying for joy at the happy news. Recommend the hero to his master: he has filled the whole of Italy with admiration of the English. Great hopes were entertained of some advantages being gained by his bravery, but no one could look for so total a destruction. All here are drunk with joy.'"

Such being the feelings of the royal family, it may well be supposed with what delight, and with what honours Nelson would be welcomed.

Early on the 22nd of September the poor wretched *Vanguard*, as he called his shattered vessel, appeared in sight of Naples. The *Culloden* and *Alexander* had preceded her by some days, and given notice of her approach. Many hundred boats and barges were ready to go forth and meet him, with music and streamers and every demonstration of joy and triumph.

Sir William and Lady Hamilton led the way in their state barge. They had seen Nelson only for a few days, four years ago, but they then perceived in him that heroic spirit which was now so fully and gloriously manifested to the world.

Emma Lady Hamilton, who from this time so greatly influenced his future life, was a woman whose personal accomplishments have seldom been equalled, and whose powers of mind were not less fascinating than her person. She was passionately attached to the queen; and by her influence the British fleet had obtained those supplies at Syracuse, without which, Nelson always asserted, the battle of Aboukir could not have been fought.

During the long interval which passed before any tidings were received, her anxiety had been hardly less than that of Nelson himself, while pursuing an enemy of whom he could obtain no information; and when the tidings were brought her by a joyful bearer, open-mouthed, its effect was such that she fell like one who had been shot.

She and Sir William had literally been made ill by their hopes and fears, and joy at a catastrophe so far exceeding all that they had dared to hope for. Their admiration for the hero necessarily produced a degree of proportionate gratitude and affection; and when their barge came alongside the *Vanguard*, at the sight of Nelson, Lady Hamilton sprang up the ship's side, and exclaiming, "O God! is it possible!" fell into his arms more, he says, like one dead than alive.

He described the meeting as "terribly affecting."

These friends had scarcely recovered from their tears, when the king, who went out to meet him three leagues in the royal barge, came on board and took him by the hand, calling him his deliverer and preserver.

From all the boats around he was saluted with the same appellations: the multitude who surrounded him when he landed repeated the same enthusiastic cries; and the *lazzaroni* displayed their joy by holding up birds in cages, and giving them their liberty as he passed.

His birth-day, which occurred a week after his arrival, was celebrated with one of the most splendid fêtes ever beheld at Naples. But, notwithstanding the splendour with which he was encircled, and the flattering honours with which all ranks welcomed him, Nelson was fully sensible of the depravity, as well as weakness, of those by whom he was surrounded.

"What precious moments," said he, "the courts of Naples and Vienna are losing! Three months would liberate Italy! but this court is so enervated that the happy moment will be lost. I am very unwell; and their miserable conduct is not likely to cool my irritable temper. It is a country of fiddlers and poets, whores and scoundrels."

This sense of their ruinous weakness he always retained; nor was he ever blind to the mingled folly and treachery of the Neapolitan ministers, and the complication in iniquities under which the country groaned; but he insensibly, under the influence of Lady Hamilton, formed an affection for the court, to whose misgovernment the miserable condition of the country was so greatly to be imputed. By the kindness of her nature, as well as by her attractions, she had won his heart.

Earl St. Vincent, writing to her at this time, says, "Pray do not let your fascinating Neapolitan dames approach too near our invaluable friend Nelson, for he is made of flesh and blood, and cannot resist their temptations." But this was addressed to the very person from whom he was in danger.

The state of Naples may be described in few words. The king was one of the Spanish Bourbons. As the Cæsars have shown us to what wickedness the moral nature of princes may be perverted, so in this family, the degradation to which their intellectual nature can be reduced has been not less conspicuously evinced.

Ferdinand, like the rest of his race, was passionately fond of field sports, and cared for nothing else. His queen had all the vices of the house of Austria, with little to mitigate, and nothing to ennoble them—provided she could have her pleasures, and the king his sports, they cared not in what manner the revenue was raised or administered.

Of course a system of favouritism existed at court, and the vilest and most impudent corruption prevailed in every department of state, and in every branch of administration, from the highest to the lowest. It is only the institutions of Christianity, and the vicinity of better-regulated states, which prevent kingdoms, under such circumstances of misrule, from sinking into a barbarism like that of Turkey.

A sense of better things was kept alive in some of the Neapolitans by literature, and by their intercourse with happier countries. These persons naturally looked to France, at the commencement of the Revolution, and during all the horrors of that Revolution still cherished a hope that, by the aid of France, they might be enabled to establish a new order of things in Naples.

They were grievously mistaken in supposing that the principles of liberty would ever be supported by France, but they were not mistaken in believing that no government could be worse than their own; and therefore they considered any change as desirable. In this opinion men of the most different characters agreed. Many of the nobles, who were not in favour, wished for a revolution, that they might obtain the ascendancy to which they thought themselves entitled; men of desperate fortunes desired it, in the hope of enriching themselves; knaves and intriguers sold themselves to the French to promote it; and a few enlightened men, and true lovers of their country, joined in the same cause, from the purest and noblest motives.

All these were confounded under the common name of Jacobins; and the Jacobins of the continental kingdoms were regarded by the English with more hatred than they deserved. They were classed with Phillippe Egalité, Marat, and Hebert; whereas they deserved rather to be ranked, if not with Locke, and Sydney, and Russell, at least with Argyle and Monmouth, and those who, having the same object as the prime movers of our own Revolution, failed in their premature but not unworthy attempt.

No circumstances could be more unfavourable to the best interests of Europe, than those which placed England in strict alliance with the superannuated and abominable governments of the continent. The subjects of those governments who wished for freedom thus became enemies to England, and dupes and agents of France.

They looked to their own grinding grievances, and did not see the danger with which the liberties of the world were threatened.

England, on the other hand, saw the danger in its true magnitude, but was blind to these grievances, and found herself compelled to support systems which had formerly been equally the object of her abhorrence and her contempt. This was the state of Nelson's mind; he knew that there could be no peace for Europe till the pride of France was humbled, and her strength broken; and he regarded all those who were the friends of France as traitors to the common cause, as well as to their own individual sovereigns.

There are situations in which the most opposite and hostile parties may mean equally well, and yet act equally wrong. The court of Naples, unconscious of committing any crime by continuing the system of misrule to which they had succeeded, conceived that, in maintaining things as they were, they were maintaining their own rights, and preserving the people from such horrors as had been perpetrated in France.

The Neapolitan revolutionists thought that without a total change of system, any relief from the present evils was impossible, and they believed themselves justified in bringing about that change by any means.

Both parties knew that it was the fixed intention of the French to revolutionise Naples. The revolutionists supposed that it was for the purpose of establishing a free government; the court, and all disinterested persons, were perfectly aware that the enemy had no other object than conquest and plunder.

The battle of the Nile shook the power of France. Her most successful general, and her finest army, were blocked up in Egypt—hopeless, as it appeared, of return; and the government was in the hands of men without talents, without character, and divided among themselves.

Austria, whom Buonaparte had terrified into a peace, at a time when constancy on her part would probably have led to his destruction, took advantage of the crisis to renew the war.

Russia also was preparing to enter the field with unbroken forces, led by a general, whose extraordinary military genius would have entitled him to a high and honourable rank in history, if it had not been sullied by all the ferocity of a barbarian[68].

Naples, seeing its destruction at hand, and thinking that the only means of averting it was by meeting the danger, after long vacillations, which were produced by the fears and treachery of its council, agreed at last to join this new coalition with a numerical force of 80,000 men.

Nelson told the king, in plain terms, that he had his choice, either to advance, trusting to God for his blessing on a just cause, and prepared to die sword in hand, or to remain quiet, and be kicked out of his kingdom; one of these things must happen.

The king made answer he would go on, and trust in God and Nelson; and Nelson, who would else have returned to Egypt, for the purpose of destroying the French shipping in Alexandria, gave up his intention at the desire of the Neapolitan court, and resolved to remain on that station, in the hope that he might be useful to the movements of the army.

He suspected also, with reason, that the continuance of his fleet was so earnestly requested, because the royal family thought their per-

---

68 Count Alexander Suvorov (1729–1800). Suvorov achieved notable victories for Russia against the Ottoman Turks and Poland, but both were marred by massacres of civilians.

sons would be safer, in case of any mishap, under the British flag, than under their own.

His first object was the recovery of Malta—an island which the King of Naples pretended to claim.

The Maltese, whom the villainous knights of their order had betrayed to France, had taken up arms against their rapacious invaders, with a spirit and unanimity worthy of the highest praise. They blockaded the French garrison by land, and a small squadron, under Captain Ball, began to blockade them by sea, on the 12th of October. Twelve days afterwards Nelson arrived.

"It is as I suspected," he says: "the ministers at Naples know nothing of the situation of the island. Not a house or bastion of the town is in possession of the islanders: and the Marquis de Niza tells us they want arms, victuals, and support. He does not know that any Neapolitan officers are on the island; perhaps, although I have their names, none are arrived; and it is very certain, by the marquis's account, that no supplies have been sent by the governors of Syracuse and Messina."

The little island of Gozo, dependent upon Malta, which had also been seized and garrisoned by the French, capitulated soon after his arrival, and was taken possession of by the British, in the name of his Sicilian Majesty—a power who had no better claim to it than France.

Having seen this effected, and reinforced Captain Ball, he left that able officer to perform a most arduous and important part, and returned himself to co-operate with the intended movements of the Neapolitans.

General Mack[69] was at the head of the Neapolitan troops. All that is now doubtful concerning this man is, whether he was a coward or a traitor. At that time he was assiduously extolled as a most consummate commander, to whom Europe might look for deliverance. And when he was introduced by the king and queen to the British admiral, the queen said to him, "Be to us by land, general, what my hero Nelson has been by sea."

Mack, on his part, did not fail to praise the force which he was appointed to command. "It was," he said, "the finest army in Europe."

Nelson agreed with him that there could not be finer men; but when the general, at a review, so directed the operations of a mock fight, that by an unhappy blunder his own troops were surrounded, instead of

69 General Freiherr Karl Mack von Leiberich (1752–1828), Austrian general.

those of the enemy, he turned to his friends and exclaimed with bitterness, that the fellow did not understand his business.

Another circumstance, not less characteristic, confirmed Nelson in his judgment. "General Mack:" said he, in one of his letters, "cannot move without five carriages! I have formed my opinion. I heartily pray I may be mistaken."

While Mack, at the head of 32,000 men, marched into the Roman state, 5,000 Neapolitans were embarked on board the British and Portuguese squadron, to take possession of Leghorn. This was effected without opposition; and the Grand Duke of Tuscany, whose neutrality had been so outrageously violated by the French, was better satisfied with the measure than some of the Neapolitans themselves.

Nasseli, their general, refused to seize the French vessels at Leghorn, because he and the Duke di Sangro, who was ambassador at the Tuscan court, maintained that the king of Naples was not at war with France.

"What!" said Nelson, "has not the king received, as a conquest made by him, the republican flag taken at Gozo? Is not his own flag flying there, and at Malta, not only by his permission, but by his order? Is not his flag shot at every day by the French, and their shot returned from batteries which bear that flag? Are not two frigates and a corvette placed under my orders ready to fight the French, meet them where they may? Has not the king sent publicly from Naples guns, mortars, &c., with officers and artillery, against the French in Malta? If these acts are not tantamount to any written paper, I give up all knowledge of what is war."

This reasoning was of less avail than argument addressed to the general's fears. Nelson told him that, if he permitted the many hundred French who were then in the mole to remain neutral, till they had a fair opportunity of being active, they had one sure resource, if all other schemes failed, which was to set one vessel on fire; the mole would be destroyed, probably the town also, and the port ruined for twenty years.

This representation made Naselli agree to the half measure of laying an embargo on the vessels; among them were a great number of French privateers, some of which were of such force as to threaten the greatest mischief to our commerce, and about seventy sail of vessels belonging to the Ligurian republic, as Genoa was now called, laden with corn, and ready to sail for Genoa and France; where their arrival would have expedited the entrance of more French troops into Italy.

"The general," said Nelson, "saw, I believe, the consequence of permitting these vessels to depart, in the same light as myself; but there is this difference between us: he prudently, and certainly safely, waits the orders of his court, taking no responsibility upon himself; I act from the circumstances of the moment, as I feel may be most advantageous for the cause which I serve, taking all responsibility on myself."

It was in vain to hope for anything vigorous or manly from such men as Nelson was compelled to act with. The crews of the French ships and their allies were ordered to depart in two days.

Four days elapsed and nobody obeyed the order; nor, in spite of the representations of the British minister, Mr. Wyndham, were any means taken to enforce it: the true Neapolitan shuffle, as Nelson called it, took place on all occasions.

After an absence of ten days he returned to Naples; and receiving intelligence there from Mr. Wyndham that the privateers were at last to be disarmed, the corn landed, and the crews sent away, he expressed his satisfaction at the news in characteristic language, saying, "So far I am content. The enemy will be distressed; and, thank God, I shall get no money. The world, I know, think that money is our god; and now they will be undeceived as far as relates to us. Down, down with the French! is my constant prayer."

Odes, sonnets, and congratulatory poems of every description were poured in upon Nelson on his arrival at Naples. An Irish Franciscan, who was one of the poets, not being content with panegyric upon this occasion, ventured on a flight of prophecy, and predicted that Lord Nelson would take Rome with his ships.

His lordship reminded Father M'Cormick that ships could not ascend the Tiber; but the father, who had probably forgotten this circumstance, met the objection with a bold front, and declared he saw that it would come to pass notwithstanding.

Rejoicings of this kind were of short duration. The King of Naples was with the army which had entered Rome; but the castle of St. Angelo was held by the French, and 13,000 French were strongly posted in the Roman states at Castallana.

Mack had marched against them with 20,000 men. Nelson saw that the event was doubtful, or rather that there could be very little hope of the result. But the immediate fate of Naples, as he well knew, hung upon the issue.

"If Mack is defeated," said he, "in fourteen days this country is lost; for the emperor has not yet moved his army, and Naples has not the power of resisting the enemy. It was not a case for choice, but of necessity, which induced the king to march out of his kingdom, and not wait till the French had collected a force sufficient to drive him out of it in a week."

He had no reliance upon the Neapolitan officers, who, as he described them, seemed frightened at a drawn sword or a loaded gun; and he was perfectly aware of the consequences which the sluggish movements and deceitful policy of the Austrians were likely to bring down upon themselves and all their continental allies.

"A delayed war on the part of the emperor," said he, writing to the British minister at Vienna, "will be destructive to this monarchy of Naples; and, of course, to the newly-acquired dominions of the Emperor in Italy. Had the war commenced in September or October, all Italy would, at this moment, have been liberated. This month is worse than the last; the next will render the contest doubtful; and, in six months, when the Neapolitan republic will be organised, armed, and with its numerous resources called forth, the emperor will not only be defeated in Italy, but will totter on his throne at Vienna. *Down, down with the French!* ought to be written in the council-room of every country in the world; and may Almighty God give right thoughts to every sovereign, is my constant prayer!"

His perfect foresight of the immediate event was clearly shown in this letter, when he desired the ambassador to assure the empress (who was a daughter of the house of Naples) that, notwithstanding the councils which had shaken the throne of her father and mother, he would remain there, ready to save their persons, and her brothers and sisters; and that he had also left ships at Leghorn to save the lives of the grand duke and her sister: "For all," said he, "must be a republic, if the emperor does not act with expedition and vigour."

His fears were soon verified. "The Neapolitan officers," said Nelson, "did not lose much honour, for, God knows, they had not much to lose; but they lost all they had."

General St. Philip commanded the right wing, of 19,000 men. He fell in with 3,000 of the enemy; and, as soon as he came near enough, deserted to them. One of his men had virtue enough to level a musket at him, and shot him through the arm; but the wound was not sufficient to prevent him from joining with the French in pursuit of his own countrymen.

Cannon, tents, baggage, and military chest, were all forsaken by the runaways, though they lost only forty men; for the French having put them to flight and got possession of everything, did not pursue an army of more than three times their own number.

The main body of the Neapolitans, under Mack, did not behave better.

The king returned to Naples, where every day brought with it tidings of some new disgrace from the army and the discovery of some new treachery at home; till, four days after his return, the general sent him advice that there was no prospect of stopping the progress of the enemy, and that the royal family must look to their own personal safety.

The state of the public mind at Naples was such, at this time, that neither the British minister nor the British Admiral thought it prudent to appear at court. Their motions were watched; and the revolutionists had even formed a plan for seizing and detaining them as hostages, to prevent an attack on the city after the French should have taken possession of it.

A letter which Nelson addressed at this time to the First Lord of the Admiralty, shows in what manner he contemplated the possible issue of the storm. It was in these words:—

"My dear lord, there is an old saying, that when things are at the worst they must mend: now the mind of man cannot fancy things worse than they are here. But, thank God! my health is better, my mind never firmer, and my heart in the right trim to comfort, relieve, and protect those whom it is my duty to afford assistance to. Pray, my lord, assure our gracious sovereign that while I live, I will support his glory; and that if I fall, it shall be in a manner worthy of your lordship's faithful and obliged Nelson. I must not write more. Every word may be a text for a long letter."

Meantime Lady Hamilton arranged every thing for the removal of the royal family. This was conducted on her part with the greatest address, and without suspicion, because she had been in habits of constant correspondence with the queen.

It was known that the removal could not be effected without danger; for the mob, and especially the *lazzaroni*, were attached to the king; and as at this time they felt a natural presumption in their own numbers and strength, they insisted that he should not leave Naples.

Several persons fell victims to their fury; among others was a messenger from Vienna, whose body was dragged under the windows of the palace in the king's sight.

The king and queen spoke to the mob, and pacified them; but it would not have been safe, while they were in this agitated state, to have embarked the effects of the royal family openly.

Lady Hamilton, like a heroine of modern romance, explored with no little danger a subterraneous passage leading from the palace to the sea-side: through this passage the royal treasures, the choicest pieces of painting and sculpture, and other property to the amount of two millions and a half, were conveyed to the shore, and stowed safely on board the English ships.

On the night of the 21st, at half-past eight, Nelson landed, brought out the whole royal family, embarked them in three barges, and carried them safely, through a tremendous sea, to the *Vanguard*.

Notice was then immediately given to the British merchants, that they would be received on board any ships in the squadron. Their property had previously been embarked in transports.

Two days were passed in the bay, for the purpose of taking such persons on board as required an asylum; and, on the night of the 23rd, the fleet sailed.

The next day a more violent storm arose than Nelson had ever before encountered. On the 25th, the youngest of the princes was taken ill, and died in Lady Hamilton's arms. During this whole trying season, Lady Hamilton waited upon the royal family with the zeal of the most devoted servant, at a time when, except one man, no person belonging to the court assisted them.

On the morning of the 26th the royal family were landed at Palermo. It was soon seen that their flight had not been premature.

Prince Pignatelli, who had been left as vicar-general and viceroy, with orders to defend the kingdom to the last rock in Calabria, sent plenipotentiaries to the French camp before Capua; and they, for the sake of saving the capital, signed an armistice, by which the greater part of the kingdom was given up to the enemy: a cession that necessarily led to the loss of the whole.

This was on the 10th of January. The French advanced towards Naples. Mack, under pretext of taking shelter from the fury of the *lazzaroni*, fled to the French General Championet, who sent him under an escort to Milan; but as France hoped for further services from this wretched traitor, it was thought prudent to treat him apparently as a prisoner of war.

The Neapolitan army disappeared in a few days: of the men, some, following their officers, deserted to the enemy; the greater part took the opportunity of disbanding themselves.

The *lazzaroni* proved true to their country; they attacked the enemy's advanced posts, drove them in, and were not dispirited by the murderous defeat which they suffered from the main body. Flying into the city, they continued to defend it, even after the French had planted their artillery in the principal streets. Had there been a man of genius to have directed their enthusiasm, or had there been any correspondent feelings in the higher ranks, Naples might have set a glorious example to Europe, and have proved the grave of every Frenchman who entered it.

But the vices of the government had extinguished all other patriotism than that of the rabble, who had no other than that sort of loyalty which was like the fidelity of a dog to its master. This fidelity the French and their adherents counteracted by another kind of devotion: the priests affirmed that St. Januarius had declared in favour of the revolution. The miracle of his blood was performed with the usual success[70], and more than usual effect, on the very evening when, after two days of desperate fighting, the French obtained possession of Naples.

A French guard of honour was stationed at his church. Championet gave, "Respect for St. Januarius!" as the word for the army; and the next day *Te Deum* was sung by the archbishop in the cathedral; and the inhabitants were invited to attend the ceremony, and join in thanksgiving for the glorious entry of the French; who, it was said, being under the peculiar protection of Providence, had regenerated the Neapolitans, and were come to establish and consolidate their happiness.

It seems to have been Nelson's opinion that the Austrian cabinet regarded the conquest of Naples with complacency, and that its measures were directed so as designedly not to prevent the French from overrunning it. That cabinet was assuredly capable of any folly, and of any baseness; and it is not improbable that at this time, calculating upon the success of the new coalition, it indulged a dream of adding extensively

70 Saint Januarius (c.275– c.305), was the Bishop of Naples at the time he was martyred. Relics of his supposed blood are kept in Naples. The "miracle" involves displaying the vials containing the dried blood, which then becomes liquid again.

to its former Italian possessions; and, therefore, left the few remaining powers of Italy to be overthrown, as a means which would facilitate its own ambitious views.

The King of Sardinia, finding it impossible longer to endure the exactions of France and the insults of the French commissary, went to Leghorn, embarked on board a Danish frigate, and sailed, under British protection, to Sardinia—that part of his dominions which the maritime supremacy of England rendered a secure asylum.

On his arrival he published a protest against the conduct of France, declaring, upon the faith and word of a king, that he had never infringed, even in the slightest degree, the treaties which he had made with the French republic.

Tuscany was soon occupied by French troops—a fate which bolder policy might, perhaps, have failed to avert, but which its weak and timid neutrality rendered inevitable. Nelson began to fear even for Sicily.

"Oh, my dear sir," said he, writing to Commodore Duckworth, "one thousand English troops would save Messina; and I fear General Stuart cannot give me men to save this most important island!"

But his representations were not lost upon Sir Charles Stuart. This officer hastened immediately from Minorca with 1,000 men, assisted in the measures of defence which were taken, and did not return before he had satisfied himself that, if the Neapolitans were excluded from the management of affairs, and the spirit of the peasantry properly directed, Sicily was safe.

Before his coming, Nelson had offered the king, if no resources should arrive, to defend Messina with the ship's company of an English man-of-war.

Russia had now entered into the war. Corfu, surrendered to a Russian and Turkish fleet, acting now, for the first time, in strange confederacy yet against a power which was certainly the common and worst enemy of both.

Troubridge having given up the blockade of Alexandria to Sir Sidney Smith, joined Nelson, bringing with him a considerable addition of strength; and in himself what Nelson valued more, a man, upon whose sagacity, indefatigable zeal, and inexhaustible resources, he could place full reliance.

Troubridge was intrusted to commence the operations against the French in the bay of Naples. Meantime Cardinal Ruffo, a man of questionable character, but of a temper fitted for such times, having landed in Calabria, raised what he called a Christian army, composed of the best and the vilest materials—loyal peasants, enthusiastic priests and friars, galley slaves, the emptying of the jails, and *banditti*.

The islands in the bay of Naples were joyfully delivered up by the inhabitants, who were in a state of famine already, from the effect of this baleful revolution. Troubridge distributed among them all his flour, and Nelson pressed the Sicilian court incessantly for supplies; telling them that £10,000 given away in provisions would, at this time, purchase a kingdom.

Money, he was told, they had not to give; and the wisdom and integrity which might have supplied its wants were not to be found.

"There is nothing," said he, "which I propose, that is not, so far as orders go, implicitly complied with; but the execution is dreadful, and almost makes me mad. My desire to serve their majesties faithfully, as is my duty, has been such that I am almost blind and worn out; and cannot in my present state hold out much longer."

Before any government can be overthrown by the consent of the people, the government must be intolerably oppressive, or the people thoroughly corrupted. Bad as the misrule at Naples had been, its consequences had been felt far less there than in Sicily; and the peasantry had that attachment to the soil which gives birth to so many of the noblest as well as of the happiest feelings. In all the islands the people were perfectly frantic with joy when they saw the Neapolitan colours hoisted.

At Procida, Troubridge could not procure even a rag of the tricoloured flag to lay at the king's feet: it was rent into ten thousand pieces by the inhabitants, and entirely destroyed.

"The horrid treatment of the French," he said, "had made them mad."

It exasperated the ferocity of a character which neither the laws nor the religion under which they lived tended to mitigate. Their hatred was especially directed against the Neapolitan revolutionists; and the fishermen, in concert among themselves, chose each his own victim, whom he would stiletto when the day of vengeance should arrive.

The head of one was sent off one morning to Troubridge, with his basket of grapes for breakfast; and a note from the Italian who had, what he called, the glory of presenting it, saying, he had killed the man as he was running away, and begging his excellency to accept the head, and consider it as a proof of the writer's attachment to the crown.

With the first successes of the court the work of punishment began. The judge at Ischia said it was necessary to have a bishop to degrade the traitorous priests before he could execute them; upon which Troubridge advised him to hang them first, and send them to him afterwards, if he did not think that degradation sufficient.

This was said with the straightforward feeling of a sailor, who cared as little for canon-law as he knew about it; but when he discovered that the judge's orders were to go through the business in a summary manner, under his sanction, he told him at once that could not be, for the prisoners were not British subjects; and he declined having anything to do with it.

There were manifestly persons about the court, who, while they thirsted for the pleasure of vengeance, were devising how to throw the odium of it upon the English. They wanted to employ an English man-of-war to carry the priests to Palermo for degradation, and then bring them back for execution; and they applied to Troubridge for a hangman, which he indignantly refused.

He, meantime, was almost heart-broken by the situation in which he found himself. He had promised relief to the islanders, relying upon the queen's promise to him. He had distributed the whole of his private stock,—there was plenty of grain at Palermo, and in its neighbourhood, and yet none was sent him: the enemy, he complained, had more interest there than the king; and the distress for bread which he witnessed was such, he said, that it would move even a Frenchman to pity.

Nelson's heart, too, was at this time ashore. "To tell you," he says, writing to Lady Hamilton, "how dreary and uncomfortable the *Vanguard* appears, is only telling you what it is to go from the pleasantest society to a solitary cell, or from the dearest friends to no friends. I am now perfectly the *great man*—not a creature near me. From my heart I wish myself the little man again. You and good Sir William have spoiled me for any place but with you.—

His mind was not in a happier state respecting public affairs.

"As to politics," said he, "at this time they are my abomination: the ministers of kings and princes are as great scoundrels as ever lived. The brother of the emperor is just going to marry the great Something of

Russia, and it is more than expected that a kingdom is to be found for him in Italy, and that the king of Naples will be sacrificed."

Had there been a wise and manly spirit in the Italian states, or had the conduct of Austria been directed by anything like a principle of honour, a more favourable opportunity could not have been desired for restoring order and prosperity in Europe, than the misconduct of the French Directory at this time afforded. But Nelson perceived selfishness and knavery wherever he looked; and even the pleasure of seeing a cause prosper, in which he was so zealously engaged, was poisoned by his sense of the rascality of those with whom he was compelled to act.

At this juncture intelligence arrived that the French fleet had escaped from Brest, under cover of a fog, passed Cadiz unseen by Lord Keith's squadron, in hazy weather, and entered the Mediterranean. It was said to consist of twenty-four sail of the line, six frigates, and three sloops.

The object of the French was to liberate the Spanish fleet, form a junction with them, act against Minorca and Sicily, and overpower our naval force in the Mediterranean, by falling in with detached squadrons, and thus destroying it in detail. When they arrived off Carthagena, they requested the Spanish ships to make sail and join; but the Spaniards replied they had not men to man them.

To this it was answered that the French had men enough on board for that purpose.

But the Spaniards seem to have been apprehensive of delivering up their ships thus entirely into the power of such allies, and refused to come out. The fleet from Cadiz, however, consisting of from seventeen to twenty sail of the line, got out, under Masaredo, a man who then bore an honourable name, which he has since rendered infamous by betraying his country. They met with a violent storm off the coast of Oran, which dismasted many of their ships, and so effectually disabled them as to prevent the junction, and frustrate a well-planned expedition.

Before this occurred, and while the junction was as probable as it would have been formidable, Nelson was in a state of the greatest anxiety.

"What a state am I in!" said he to Earl St. Vincent. "If I go, I risk, and more than risk, Sicily; for we know, from experience, that more depends upon opinion than upon acts themselves; and, as I stay, my heart is breaking."

His first business was to summon Troubridge to join him, with all the ships of the line under his command, and a frigate, if possible. Then hearing that the French had entered the Mediterranean, and expecting them at Palermo, where he had only his own ship—with that single ship he prepared to make all the resistance possible.

Troubridge having joined him, he left Captain E. J. Foote, of the *Seahorse*, to command the smaller vessels in the bay of Naples, and sailed with six ships—one a Portuguese, and a Portuguese corvette—telling Earl St. Vincent that the squadron should never fall into the hands of the enemy.

"And before we are destroyed," said he, "I have little doubt but they will have their wings so completely clipped that they may be easily overtaken."

It was just at this time that he received from Captain Hallowell the present of the coffin. Such a present was regarded by the men with natural astonishment. One of his old shipmates in the *Agamemnon* said, "We shall have hot work of it indeed! You see the admiral intends to fight till he is killed; and there he is to be buried."

Nelson placed it upright against the bulkhead of his cabin, behind his chair, where he sat at dinner. The gift suited him at this time. It is said that he was disappointed in the step-son whom he had loved so dearly from his childhood, and who had saved his life at Teneriffe; and it is certain that he had now formed an infatuated attachment for Lady Hamilton, which totally weaned his affections from his wife. Farther than this, there is no reason to believe that this most unfortunate attachment was criminal; but this was criminality enough, and it brought with it its punishment.

Nelson was dissatisfied with himself, and therefore weary of the world. This feeling he now frequently expressed.

"There is no true happiness in this life," said he, "and in my present state I could quit it with a smile."

And in a letter to his old friend Davison he said, "Believe me, my only wish is to sink with honour into the grave; and when that shall please God, I shall meet death with a smile. Not that I am insensible to the honours and riches my king and country have heaped upon me—so much more than any officer could deserve; yet am I ready to quit this world of trouble, and envy none but those of the estate six feet by two."

Well had it been for Nelson if he had made no other sacrifices to this unhappy attachment than his peace of mind; but it led to the only blot upon his public character.

While he sailed from Palermo, with the intention of collecting his whole force, and keeping off Maretimo, either to receive reinforcements there if the French were bound upwards, or to hasten to Minorca if that should be their destination, Captain Foote, in the *Seahorse*, with the Neapolitan frigates, and some small vessels, under his command, was left to act with a land force consisting of a few regular troops, of four different nations, and with the armed rabble which Cardinal Ruffo called the Christian army. His directions were to co-operate to the utmost of his power with the royalists, at whose head Ruffo had been placed, and he had no other instructions whatever.

Ruffo advancing without any plan, but relying upon the enemy's want of numbers, which prevented them from attempting to act upon the offensive, and ready to take advantage of any accident which might occur, approached Naples.

Fort St. Elmo, which commands the town, was wholly garrisoned by the French troops; the castles of Uovo and Nuovo, which commanded the anchorage, were chiefly defended by Neapolitan revolutionists, the powerful men among them having taken shelter there. If these castles were taken, the reduction of Fort St. Elmo would be greatly expedited. They were strong places, and there was reason to apprehend that the French fleet might arrive to relieve them.

Ruffo proposed to the garrison to capitulate, on condition that their persons and property should be guaranteed, and that they should, at their own option, either be sent to Toulon or remain at Naples, without being molested either in their persons or families. This capitulation was accepted: it was signed by the cardinal, and the Russian and Turkish commanders; and lastly, by Captain Foote, as commander of the British force.

About six-and-thirty hours afterwards Nelson arrived in the bay with a force which had joined him during his cruise, consisting of seventeen sail of the line, with 1,700 troops on board, and the Prince Royal of Naples in the admiral's ship. A flag of truce was flying on the castles, and on board the *Seahorse*.

Nelson made a signal to annul the treaty; declaring that he would grant rebels no other terms than those of unconditional submission. The cardinal objected to this: nor could all the arguments of Nelson, Sir W. Hamilton, and Lady Hamilton, who took an active part in the conference, convince him that a treaty of such a nature, solemnly concluded, could honourably be set aside. He retired at last, silenced by Nelson's authority, but not convinced.

Captain Foote was sent out of the bay; and the garrisons, taken out of the castles under pretence of carrying the treaty into effect, were delivered over as rebels to the vengeance of the Sicilian court. A deplorable transaction! a stain upon the memory of Nelson and the honour of England! To palliate it would be in vain; to justify it would be wicked: there is no alternative, for one who will not make himself a participator in guilt, but to record the disgraceful story with sorrow and with shame.

Prince Francesco Caraccioli, a younger branch of one of the noblest Neapolitan families, escaped from one of these castles before it capitulated. He was at the head of the marine, and was nearly seventy years of age, bearing a high character, both for professional and personal merit. He had accompanied the court to Sicily; but when the revolutionary government, or Parthenopean Republic, as it was called, issued an edict, ordering all absent Neapolitans to return on pain of confiscation of their property, he solicited and obtained permission of the king to return, his estates being very great.

It is said that the king, when he granted him this permission, warned him not to take any part in politics; expressing at the same time his own persuasion that he should recover his kingdom. But neither the king, nor he himself, ought to have imagined that, in such times, a man of such reputation would be permitted to remain inactive; and it soon appeared that Caraccioli was again in command of the navy, and serving under the republic against his late sovereign.

The sailors reported that he was forced to act thus; and this was believed, till it was seen that he directed ably the offensive operations of the revolutionists, and did not avail himself of opportunities for escaping when they offered.

When the recovery of Naples was evidently near, he applied to Cardinal Ruffo, and to the Duke of Calvirrano, for protection; expressing his hope that the few days during which he had been forced to obey the French would not outweigh forty years of faithful services; but perhaps not receiving such assurances as he wished, and knowing too well the temper of the Sicilian court, he endeavoured to secrete himself, and a price was set upon his head. More unfortunately for others than for himself, he was brought in alive, having been discovered in the disguise of a peasant, and carried one morning on board Lord Nelson's ship, with his hands tied behind him.

Caraccioli was well known to the British officers, and had been ever highly esteemed by all who knew him. Captain Hardy ordered him immediately to be unbound, and to be treated with all those attentions which he felt due to a man who, when last on board the *Foudroyant*, had been received as an admiral and a prince.

Sir William and Lady Hamilton were in the ship; but Nelson, it is affirmed, saw no one except his own officers during the tragedy which ensued. His own determination was made; and he issued an order to the Neapolitan commodore, Count Thurn, to assemble a court-martial of Neapolitan officers, on board the British flag-ship, proceed immediately to try the prisoner, and report to him, if the charges were proved, what punishment he ought to suffer.

These proceedings were as rapid as possible; Caraccioli was brought on board at nine in the forenoon, and the trial began at ten. It lasted two hours: he averred in his defence that he had acted under compulsion, having been compelled to serve as a common soldier, till he consented to take command of the fleet.

This, the apologists of Lord Nelson say, he failed in proving. They forget that the possibility of proving it was not allowed him, for he was brought to trial within an hour after he was legally in arrest; and how, in that time, was he to collect his witnesses?

He was found guilty, and sentenced to death; and Nelson gave orders that the sentence should be carried into effect that evening, at five o'clock, on board the Sicilian frigate, *La Minerva*, by hanging him at the fore-yard-arm till sunset; when the body was to be cut down and thrown into the sea.

Caraccioli requested Lieut. Parkinson, under whose custody he was placed, to intercede with Lord Nelson for a second trial—for this, among other reasons, that Count Thurn, who presided at the court-martial, was notoriously his personal enemy.

Nelson made answer, that the prisoner had been fairly tried by the officers of his own country, and he could not interfere; forgetting that, if he felt himself justified in ordering the trial and the execution, no human being could ever have questioned the propriety of his interfering on the side of mercy. Caraccioli then entreated that he might be shot.

"I am an old man, sir," said he: "I leave no family to lament me, and therefore cannot be supposed to be very anxious about prolonging my life; but the disgrace of being hanged is dreadful to me."

When this was repeated to Nelson, he only told the lieutenant, with much agitation, to go and attend his duty.

As a last hope, Caraccioli asked the lieutenant if he thought an application to Lady Hamilton would be beneficial? Parkinson went to seek her; she was not to be seen on this occasion; but she was present at the execution.

She had the most devoted attachment to the Neapolitan court; and the hatred which she felt against those whom she regarded as its enemies, made her at this time forget what was due to the character of her sex as well as of her country.

Here, also, a faithful historian is called upon to pronounce a severe and unqualified condemnation of Nelson's conduct. Had he the authority of his Sicilian majesty for proceeding as he did? If so, why was not that authority produced? If not, why were the proceedings hurried on without it? Why was the trial precipitated, so that it was impossible for the prisoner, if he had been innocent, to provide the witnesses, who might have proved him so? Why was a second trial refused, when the known animosity of the president of the court against the prisoner was considered? Why was the execution hastened, so as to preclude any appeal for mercy, and render the prerogative of mercy useless?

Doubtless, the British Admiral seemed to himself to be acting under a rigid sense of justice; but to all other persons it was obvious that he was influenced by an infatuated attachment—a baneful passion, which destroyed his domestic happiness, and now, in a second instance, stained ineffaceably his public character.

The body was carried out to a considerable distance, and sunk in the bay, with three double-headed shot, weighing 250 lbs., tied to its legs.

Between two or three weeks afterward, when the king was on board the *Foudroyant*, a Neapolitan fisherman came to the ship, and solemnly declared that Caraccioli had risen from the bottom of the sea, and was coming as fast as he could to Naples, swimming half out of the water. Such an account was listened to like a tale of idle credulity.

The day being fair, Nelson, to please the king, stood out to sea; but the ship had not proceeded far before a body was distinctly seen, upright in the water, and approaching them. It was soon recognised to be indeed the corpse of Caraccioli, which had risen and floated, while the great weights attached to the legs kept the body in a position like that of a living man.

A fact so extraordinary astonished the king, and perhaps excited some feeling of superstitious fear, akin to regret. He gave permission for the body to be taken on shore and receive Christian burial.

It produced no better effect.

Naples exhibited more dreadful scenes than it had witnessed in the days of Massaniello[71]. After the mob had had their fill of blood and plunder, the reins were given to justice—if that can be called justice which annuls its own stipulations, looks to the naked facts alone, disregarding all motives and all circumstances; and without considering character, or science, or sex, or youth, sacrifices its victims, not for the public weal, but for the gratification of greedy vengeance.

The castles of St. Elmo, Gaieta, and Capua remained to be subdued.

On the land side there was no danger that the French in these garrisons should be relieved, for Suvarof was now beginning to drive the enemy before him; but Nelson thought his presence necessary in the bay of Naples: and when Lord Keith, having received intelligence that the French and Spanish fleets had formed a junction, and sailed for Carthagena, ordered him to repair to Minorca with the whole or the greater part of his force, he sent Admiral Duckworth with a small part only. This was a dilemma which he had foreseen.

"Should such an order come at this moment," he said, in a letter previously written to the Admiralty, "it would be a case for some consideration, whether Minorca is to be risked, or the two kingdoms of Naples and Sicily; I rather think my decision would be to risk the former."

And after he had acted upon this opinion, he wrote in these terms to the Duke of Clarence, with whose high notions of obedience he was

71 Tommaso Aniello (1622–1647), called Masaniello, was a Neapolitan fisherman. In 1647 he led a revolt against the Hapsburg rulers of Naples. Starting with peasant complaints about a new tax on fruit, it quickly degenerated into a general revolt characterized by the violent settling of old grudges and the judicial murder of a number of citizens. Aniello was murdered near the end of the revolt.

well acquainted: "I am well aware of the consequences of disobeying my orders; but as I have often before risked my life for the good cause, so I with cheerfulness did my commission; for although a military tribunal may think me criminal, the world will approve of my conduct; and I regard not my own safety when the honour of my king is at stake."

Nelson was right in his judgment: no attempt was made on Minorca: and the expulsion of the French from Naples may rather be said to have been effected than accelerated by the English and Portuguese of the allied fleet, acting upon shore, under Troubridge.

The French commandant at St. Elmo, relying upon the strength of the place, and the nature of the force which attacked it, had insulted Captain Foote in the grossest terms; but *Citoyen* Mejan was soon taught better manners, when Troubridge, in spite of every obstacle, opened five batteries upon the fort.

He was informed that none of his letters, with the insolent printed words at the top, *Liberte Eqalite, Guerre aux Tyrans*, &c. would be received; but that if he wrote like a soldier and a gentleman he would be answered in the same style. The Frenchman then began to flatter his antagonist upon the *bienfaisance* and *humanité* which, he said, were the least of the many virtues which distinguished *Monsieur* Troubridge.

Monsieur Troubridge's *bienfaisance* was at this time thinking of mining the fort. "If we can accomplish that," said he, "I am a strong advocate to send them, hostages and all, to Old Nick, and surprise him with a group of nobility and republicans. Meantime," he added, "it was some satisfaction to perceive that the shells fell well, and broke some of their shins."

Finally, to complete his character, Mejan offered to surrender for 150,000 ducats. Great Britain, perhaps, has made but too little use of this kind of artillery, which France has found so effectual towards subjugating the continent: but Troubridge had the prey within his reach; and in the course of a few days, his last battery, "after much trouble and palaver," as he said, "brought the vagabonds to their senses."

Troubridge had more difficulties to overcome this siege, from the character of the Neapolitans who pretended to assist him, and whom he made useful, than even from the strength of the place and the skill of the French.

"Such damned cowards and villains," he declared, "he had never seen before." The men at the advanced posts carried on, what he called, "a diabolical good understanding" with the enemy, and the workmen would sometimes take fright and run away. "I make the best I can," said he, "of the degenerate race I have to deal with; the whole means of guns, ammunition, pioneers, &c., with all materials, rest with them. With fair promises to the men, and threats of instant death if I find any one erring, a little spur has been given."

Nelson said of him with truth, upon this occasion, that he was a first-rate general. "I find, sir," said he afterwards in a letter to the Duke of Clarence, "that General Koehler does not approve of such irregular proceedings as naval officers attacking and defending fortifications. We have but one idea—to get close alongside. None but a sailor would have placed a battery only 180 yards from the Castle of St. Elmo; a soldier must have gone according to art, and the /\/\/\/\/\/ way. My brave Troubridge went straight on, for we had no time to spare."

Troubridge then proceeded to Capua, and took the command of the motley besieging force. One thousand of the best men in the fleet were sent to assist in the siege.

Just at this time Nelson received a peremptory order from Lord Keith to sail with the whole of his force for the protection of Minorca; or, at least, to retain no more than was absolutely necessary at Sicily.

"You will easily conceive my feelings," said he in communicating this to Earl St. Vincent; "but my mind, as your lordship knows, was perfectly prepared for this order; and it is now, more than ever, made up. At this moment I will not part with a single ship; as I cannot do that without drawing a hundred and twenty men from each ship, now at the siege of Capua. I am fully aware of the act I have committed; but I am prepared for any fate which may await my disobedience. Capua and Gaieta will soon fall; and the moment the scoundrels of French are out of this kingdom I shall send eight or nine ships of the line to Minorca. I have done what I thought right—others may think differently; but it will be my consolation that I have gained a kingdom, seated a faithful ally of his Majesty firmly on his throne, and restored happiness to millions."

At Capua, Troubridge had the same difficulties as at St. Elmo; and being farther from Naples, and from the fleet, was less able to overcome them. The powder was so bad that he suspected treachery; and when he asked Nelson to spare him forty casks from the ships, he told him it would be necessary that some Englishmen should accompany it, or they would steal one-half, and change the other.

"All the men you see," said he, "gentle and simple, are such notorious villains, that it is misery to be with them."

Capua, however, soon fell; Gaieta immediately afterwards surrendered to Captain Louis of the *Minotaur.* Here the commanding officer acted more unlike a Frenchman, Captain Louis said, than any one he had ever met; meaning that he acted like a man of honour.

He required, however, that the garrison should carry away their horses, and other pillaged property: to which Nelson replied, "That no property which they did not bring with them into the country could be theirs: and that the greatest care should be taken to prevent them from carrying it away."

"I am sorry," said he to Captain Louis, "that you have entered into any altercation. There is no way of dealing with a Frenchman but to knock him down; to be civil to them is only to be laughed at, when they are enemies."

The whole kingdom of Naples was thus delivered by Nelson from the French.

The Admiralty, however, thought it expedient to censure him for disobeying Lord Keith's orders, and thus hazarding Minorca, without, as it appeared to them, any sufficient reason; and also for having landed seamen for the siege of Capua, to form part of an army employed in operations at a distance from the coast; where, in case of defeat, they might have been prevented from returning to their ships; and they enjoined him, "not to employ the seamen in like manner in future." This reprimand was issued before the event was known; though, indeed, the event would not affect the principle upon which it proceeded.

When Nelson communicated the tidings of his complete success, he said, in his public letter, "that it would not be the less acceptable for having been principally brought about by British sailors." His judgment in thus employing them had been justified by the result; and his joy was evidently heightened by the gratification of a professional and becoming pride.

To the first lord he said, at the same time, "I certainly, from having only a left hand, cannot enter into details which may explain the motives that actuated my conduct. My principle is, to assist in driving the French to the devil, and in restoring peace and happiness to mankind. I feel that I am fitter to do the action than to describe it." He then added that he would take care of Minorca.

In expelling the French from Naples, Nelson had, with characteristic zeal and ability, discharged his duty; but he deceived himself when he imagined that he had seated Ferdinand firmly on his throne, and that he had restored happiness to millions. These objects might have been accomplished if it had been possible to inspire virtue and wisdom into a vicious and infatuated court; and if Nelson's eyes had not been, as it were, spell-bound by that unhappy attachment, which had now completely mastered him, he would have seen things as they were; and might, perhaps, have awakened the Sicilian court to a sense of their interest, if not of their duty.

That court employed itself in a miserable round of folly and festivity, while the prisons of Naples were filled with groans, and the scaffolds streamed with blood. St. Januarius was solemnly removed from his rank as patron saint of the kingdom, having been convicted of Jacobinism; and St. Antonio as solemnly installed in his place.

The king, instead of re-establishing order at Naples by his presence, speedily returned to Palermo, to indulge in his favourite amusements. Nelson, and the ambassador's family, accompanied the court; and Troubridge remained, groaning over the villainy and frivolity of those with whom he was compelled to deal.

A party of officers applied to him for a passage to Palermo, to see the procession of St. Rosalia: he recommended them to exercise their troops, and not behave like children. It was grief enough for him that the court should be busied in these follies, and Nelson involved in them. "I dread, my lord," said he, "all the feasting, &c. at Palermo. I am sure your health will be hurt. If so, all their saints will be damned by the navy. The king would be better employed digesting a good government; everything gives way to their pleasures. The money spent at Palermo gives discontent here; fifty thousand people are unemployed, trade discouraged, manufactures at a stand. It is the interest of many here to keep the king away: they all dread reform. Their villainies are so deeply rooted, that if some method is not taken to dig them out, this government cannot hold together. Out of twenty millions of ducats, collected as the revenue, only thirteen millions reach the treasury; and the king pays four ducats where he should pay one. He is surrounded by thieves; and none of them have honour or honesty enough to tell him the real and true state of things."

In another letter he expressed his sense of the miserable state of Naples. "There are upwards of forty thousand families," said he, "who have relations confined. If some act of oblivion is not passed, there will be no end of persecution; for the people of this country have no idea of anything but revenge, and to gain a point would swear ten thousand false oaths. Constant efforts are made to get a man taken up, in order to rob him. The confiscated property does not reach the king's treasury. All thieves! It is selling for nothing. His own people, whom he employs, are buying it up, and the vagabonds pocket the whole. I should not be surprised to hear that they brought a bill of expenses against him for the sale."

The Sicilian court, however, were at this time duly sensible of the services which had been rendered them by the British fleet, and their gratitude to Nelson was shown with proper and princely munificence. They gave him the dukedom and domain of Bronte, worth about £3,000 a year.

It was some days before he could be persuaded to accept it; the argument which finally prevailed is said to have been suggested by the queen, and urged, at her request, by Lady Hamilton upon her knees.

"He considered his own honour too much," she said, "if he persisted in refusing what the king and queen felt to be absolutely necessary for the preservation of theirs."

The king himself, also, is said to have addressed him in words, which show that the sense of rank will sometimes confer a virtue upon those who seem to be most unworthy of the lot to which they have been born: "Lord Nelson, do you wish that your name alone should pass with honour to posterity; and that I, Ferdinand Bourbon, should appear ungrateful?"

He gave him also, when the dukedom was accepted, a diamond-hilted sword, which his father, Charles III of Spain, had given him on his accession to the throne of the two Sicilies.

Nelson said, "the reward was magnificent, and worthy of a king, and he was determined that the inhabitants on the domain should be the happiest in all his Sicilian majesty's dominions. Yet," said he, speaking of these and the other remunerations which were made him for his services, "these presents, rich as they are, do not elevate me. My pride is, that at Constantinople, from the grand seignior to the lowest Turk, the name of Nelson is familiar in their mouths; and in this country I am everything which a grateful monarch and people can call me."

Nelson, however, had a pardonable pride in the outward and visible signs of honour which he had so fairly won. He was fond of his Sicilian title; the signification, perhaps, pleased him; Duke of Thunder[72] was what in Dahomy would be called a *strong name*; it was to a sailor's taste; and certainly, to no man could it ever be more applicable.

But a simple offering, which he received not long afterwards, from the island of Zante, affected him with a deeper and finer feeling. The Greeks of that little community sent him a golden-headed sword and a truncheon, set round with all the diamonds that the island could furnish, in a single row. They thanked him "for having, by his victory, preserved that part of Greece from the horrors of anarchy; and prayed that his exploits might accelerate the day, in which, amidst the glory and peace of thrones, the miseries of the human race would cease."

This unexpected tribute touched Nelson to the heart. "No officer," he said, "had ever received from any country a higher acknowledgment of his services."

The French still occupied the Roman states; from which, according to their own admission, they had extorted in jewels, plate, specie, and requisitions of every kind, to the enormous amount of eight millions sterling; yet they affected to appear as deliverers among the people whom they were thus cruelly plundering; and they distributed portraits of Buonaparte, with the blasphemous inscription, "This is the true likeness of the holy saviour of the world!"

The people, detesting the impiety, and groaning beneath the exactions of these perfidious robbers, were ready to join any regular force that should come to their assistance; but they dreaded Cardinal Ruffo's rabble, and declared they would resist him as a *banditti* [*sic*], who came only for the purpose of pillage.

Nelson perceived that no object was now so essential for the tranquillity of Naples as the recovery of Rome; which in the present state of things, when Suvarof was driving the French before him, would complete the deliverance of Italy. He applied, therefore, to Sir James St. Clair Erskine, who in the absence of General Fox commanded at Minorca, to assist in this great object with 1,200 men.

"The field of glory," said he, "is a large one, and was never more open to any one than at this moment to you. Rome would throw open her gates and receive you as her deliverer; and the pope would owe his restoration to a heretic."

---

72 "Bronte" means "thunder" in classical Greek.

But Sir James Erskine looked only at the difficulties of the undertaking. "Twelve hundred men," he thought, "would be too small a force to be committed in such an enterprise; for Civita Vecchia was a regular fortress; the local situation and climate also were such, that even if this force were adequate, it would be proper to delay the expedition till October. General Fox, too, was soon expected; and during his absence, and under existing circumstances, he did not feel justified in sending away such a detachment."

What this general thought it imprudent to attempt, Nelson and Troubridge effected without his assistance, by a small detachment from the fleet.

Troubridge first sent Captain Hallowell to Civita Vecchia[73] to offer the garrison there and at Castle St. Angelo the same terms which had been granted to Gaieta. Hallowell perceived, by the overstrained civility of the officers who came off to him, and the compliments which they paid to the English nation, that they were sensible of their own weakness and their inability to offer any effectual resistance; but the French know, that while they are in a condition to serve their government, they can rely upon it for every possible exertion in their support; and this reliance gives them hope and confidence to the last.

Upon Hallowell's report, Troubridge, who had now been made Sir Thomas for his services, sent Captain Louis with a squadron to enforce the terms which he had offered; and, as soon as he could leave Naples, he himself followed.

The French, who had no longer any hope from the fate of arms, relied upon their skill in negotiation, and proposed terms to Troubridge with that effrontery which characterises their public proceedings; but which is as often successful as it is impudent.

They had a man of the right stamp to deal with. Their ambassador at Rome began by saying, that the Roman territory was the property of the French by right of conquest.

The British commodore settled that point, by replying, "It is mine by reconquest."

A capitulation was soon concluded for all the Roman states, and Captain Louis rowed up the Tiber in his barge, hoisted English colours

---

73 More correctly, Civitavecchia, the primary port of Rome, and located about 49 miles WNW of that city. The name translates as "old" or "ancient" city.

on the capitol, and acted for the time as governor of Rome. The prophecy of the Irish poet was thus accomplished, and the friar reaped the fruits; for Nelson, who was struck with the oddity of the circumstance, and not a little pleased with it, obtained preferment for him from the King of Sicily, and recommended him to the Pope.

Having thus completed his work upon the continent of Italy, Nelson's whole attention was directed towards Malta; where Captain Ball, with most inadequate means, was besieging the French garrison.

Never was any officer engaged in more anxious and painful service: the smallest reinforcement from France would, at any moment, have turned the scale against him; and had it not been for his consummate ability, and the love and veneration with which the Maltese regarded him, Malta must have remained in the hands of the enemy.

Men, money, food—all things were wanting. The garrison consisted of 5,000 troops; the besieging force of 500 English and Portuguese marines, and about 1,500 armed peasants.

Long and repeatedly did Nelson solicit troops to effect the reduction of this important place. "It has been no fault of the navy," said he, "that Malta has not been attacked by land; but we have neither the means ourselves nor influence with those who have."

The same causes of demurral existed which prevented British troops from assisting in the expulsion of the French from Rome. Sir James Erskine was expecting General Fox; he could not act without orders; and not having, like Nelson, that lively spring of hope within him, which partakes enough of the nature of faith to work miracles in war, he thought it "evident that unless a respectable land force, in numbers sufficient to undertake the siege of such a garrison, in one of the strongest places of Europe, and supplied with proportionate artillery and stores, were sent against it, no reasonable hope could be entertained of its surrender."

Nelson groaned over the spirit of over-reasoning caution and unreasoning obedience. "My heart," said he, "is almost broken. If the enemy gets supplies in, we may bid adieu to Malta; all the force we can collect would then be of little use against the strongest place in Europe. To say that an officer is never, for any object, to alter his orders, is what I cannot comprehend. The circumstances of this war so often vary, that an officer has almost every moment to consider, what would my superiors direct, did they know what was passing under my nose?"

"But, sir," said he writing to the Duke of Clarence, "I find few think as I do. To obey orders is all perfection. To serve my king, and to destroy the French, I consider as the great order of all, from which little ones spring; and if one of these militate against it (for who can tell exactly at a distance?) I go back and obey the great order and object, to down—down with the damned French villains!—my blood boils at the name of Frenchmen!"

At length, General Fox arrived at Minorca—and at length permitted Col. Graham to go to Malta, but with means miserably limited. In fact, the expedition was at a stand for want of money; when Troubridge arriving at Messina to co-operate in it, and finding this fresh delay, immediately offered all that he could command of his own.

"I procured him, my lord," said he to Nelson, "1,500 of my cobs—every farthing and every atom of me shall be devoted to the cause."

"What can this mean?" said Nelson, when he learned that Col. Graham was ordered not to incur any expenses for stores, or any articles except provisions!—"the cause cannot stand still for want of a little money. If nobody will pay it, I will sell Bronte and the Emperor of Russia's box."

And he actually pledged Bronte for £6,600 if there should be any difficulty about paying the bills. The long-delayed expedition was thus, at last, sent forth; but Troubridge little imagined in what scenes of misery he was to bear his part.

He looked to Sicily for supplies: it was the interest, as well as the duty of the Sicilian government to use every exertion for furnishing them; and Nelson and the British ambassador were on the spot to press upon them the necessity of exertion. But, though Nelson saw with what a knavish crew the Sicilian court was surrounded, he was blind to the vices of the court itself; and resigning himself wholly to Lady Hamilton's influence, never even suspected the crooked policy which it was remorselessly pursuing.

The Maltese and the British in Malta severely felt it. Troubridge, who had the truest affection for Nelson, knew his infatuation, and feared that it might prove injurious to his character, as well as fatal to an enterprise which had begun so well, and been carried on so patiently.

"My lord," said he, writing to him from the siege, "we are dying off fast for want. I learn that Sir William Hamilton says Prince Luzzi refused corn some time ago, and Sir William does not think it worth while making another application. If that be the case, I wish he commanded this distressing scene instead of me. Puglia had an immense harvest; near thirty sail left Messina before I did, to load corn. Will they let us have any? If not, a short time will decide the business. The German interest prevails. I wish I was at your Lordship's elbow for an hour. *All, all,* will be thrown on you!" I will parry the blow as much as in my power: I foresee much mischief brewing. God bless your Lordship; I am miserable I cannot assist your operations more. Many happy returns of the day to you—(it was the first of the new year)—I never spent so miserable a one. I am not very tender-hearted; but really the distress here would even move a Neapolitan."

Soon afterwards he wrote, "I have this day saved thirty thousand people from starving; but with this day my ability ceases. As the government are bent on starving us, I see no alternative but to leave these poor unhappy people to perish, without our being witnesses of their distress. I curse the day I ever served the Neapolitan government. We have characters, my lord, to lose; these people have none. Do not suffer their infamous conduct to fall on us. Our country is just, but severe. Such is the fever of my brain this minute, that I assure you, on my honour, if the Palermo traitors were here, I would shoot them first, and then myself.

"Girgenti is full of corn; the money is ready to pay for it; we do not ask it as a gift. Oh! could you see the horrid distress I daily experience, something would be done. Some engine is at work against us at Naples; and I believe I hit on the proper person. If you complain he will be immediately promoted, agreeably to the Neapolitan custom. All I write to you is known at the queen's. For my own part, I look upon the Neapolitans as the worst of intriguing enemies: every hour shows me their infamy and duplicity. I pray your lordship be cautious: your honest, open manner of acting will be made a handle of. When I see you, and tell of their infamous tricks, you will be as much surprised as I am. The whole will fall on you."

Nelson was not, and could not be, insensible to the distress which his friend so earnestly represented. He begged, almost on his knees, he said, small supplies of money and corn, to keep the Maltese from starving. And when the court granted a small supply, protesting their poverty, he believed their protestations, and was satisfied with their professions, instead of insisting that the restrictions upon the exportation of corn should be withdrawn.

The anxiety, however, which he endured, affected him so deeply that he said it had broken his spirit for ever. Happily, all that Troubridge with so much reason foreboded, did not come to pass. For Captain Ball, with more decision than Nelson himself would have shown at that time and upon that occasion, ventured upon a resolute measure, for which his name would deserve always to be held in veneration by the Maltese, even if it had no other claims to the love and reverence of a grateful people.

Finding it hopeless longer to look for succour or common humanity from the deceitful and infatuated court of Sicily, which persisted in prohibiting by sanguinary edicts the exportation of supplies, at his own risk, he sent his first lieutenant to the port of Girgenti, with orders to seize and bring with him to Malta the ships which were there lying laden with corn; of the numbers of which he had received accurate information.

These orders were executed to the great delight and advantage of the shipowners and proprietors: the necessity of raising the siege was removed, and Captain Ball waited in calmness for the consequences to himself.

The Neapolitan government complained to the English ambassador, and the complaint was communicated to Nelson, who, in return, requested Sir William Hamilton would fully and plainly state, that the act ought not to be considered as any intended disrespect to his Sicilian Majesty, but as of the most absolute and imperious necessity; the alternative being either of abandoning Malta to the French, or of anticipating the king's orders for carrying the corn in those vessels to Malta.

"I trust," he added, "that the government of the country will never again force any of our royal master's servants to so unpleasant an alternative."

Thus ended the complaint of the Neapolitan court. "The sole result was," says Mr. Coleridge, "that the governor of Malta became an especial object of its hatred, its fears, and its respect."

Nelson himself, at the beginning of February, sailed for that island. On the way he fell in with a French squadron bound for its relief, and consisting of the *Genereux* seventy-four, three frigates, and a corvette. One of these frigates and the line-of-battle ship were taken; the others escaped, but failed in their purpose of reaching La Valette. This success was peculiarly gratifying to Nelson, for many reasons.

During some months he had acted as commander-in-chief in the Mediterranean, while Lord Keith was in England. Lord Keith was now returned; and Nelson had, upon his own plan, and at his own risk, left him to sail for Malta, "for which," said he, "if I had not succeeded, I might have been broke: and if I had not acted thus, the *Genereux* never would have been taken."

This ship was one of those which had escaped from Aboukir. Two frigates, and the *Guillaume Tell*, eighty-six were all that now remained of the fleet which Buonaparte had conducted to Egypt. The *Guillaume Tell* was at this time closely watched in the harbour of La Valette; and shortly afterwards, attempting to make her escape from thence, was taken after an action, in which greater skill was never displayed by British ships, nor greater gallantry by an enemy.

She was taken by the *Foudroyant*, *Lion*, and *Penelope* frigate. Nelson, rejoicing at what he called this glorious finish to the whole French Mediterranean fleet, rejoiced also that he was not present to have taken a sprig of these brave men's laurels.

"They are," said he, "and I glory in them, my children; they served in my school; and all of us caught our professional zeal and fire from the great and good Earl St. Vincent. What a pleasure, what happiness, to have the Nile fleet all taken, under my orders and regulations!"

The two frigates still remained in La Valette; before its surrender they stole out; one was taken in the attempt; the other was the only ship of the whole fleet which escaped capture or destruction.

Letters were found on board the *Guillaume Tell* showing that the French were now become hopeless of preserving the conquest which they had so foully acquired. Troubridge and his brother officers were anxious that Nelson should have the honour of signing the capitulation. They told him that they absolutely, as far as they dared, insisted on his staying to do this; but their earnest and affectionate entreaties were vain.

Sir William Hamilton had just been superseded: Nelson had no feeling of cordiality towards Lord Keith; and thinking that after Earl St. Vincent no man had so good a claim to the command in the Mediterranean as himself, he applied for permission to return to England; telling the First Lord of the Admiralty that his spirit could not submit patiently, and that he was a broken-hearted man.

From the time of his return from Egypt, amid all the honours which were showered upon him, he had suffered many mortifications.

Sir Sidney Smith had been sent to Egypt with orders to take under his command the squadron which Nelson had left there. Sir Sidney appears to have thought that this command was to be independent of Nelson; and Nelson himself thinking so, determined to return, saying to Earl St. Vincent, "I do feel, for I am a man, that it is impossible for me to serve in these seas with a squadron under a junior officer."

Earl St. Vincent seems to have dissuaded him from this resolution: some heart-burnings, however, still remained, and some incautious expressions of Sir Sidney's were noticed by him in terms of evident displeasure. But this did not continue long, as no man bore more willing testimony than Nelson to the admirable defence of Acre.

He differed from Sir Sidney as to the policy which ought to be pursued toward the French in Egypt; and strictly commanded him, in the strongest language, not, on any pretence, to permit a single Frenchman to leave the country, saying that he considered it nothing short of madness to permit that band of thieves to return to Europe.

"No," said he, "to Egypt they went with their own consent, and there they shall remain while Nelson commands this squadron; for never, never, will he consent to the return of one ship or Frenchman. I wish them to perish in Egypt, and give an awful lesson to the world of the justice of the Almighty."

If Nelson had not thoroughly understood the character of the enemy against whom he was engaged, their conduct in Egypt would have disclosed it. After the battle of the Nile he had landed all his prisoners, upon a solemn engagement made between Troubridge on one side and Captain Barre on the other, that none of them should serve until regularly exchanged.

They were no sooner on shore than part of them were drafted into the different regiments, and the remainder formed into a corps, called the Nautic Legion. This occasioned Captain Hallowell to say that the French had forfeited all claim to respect from us.

"The army of Buonaparte," said he, "are entirely destitute of every principle of honour: they have always acted like licentious thieves."

Buonaparte's escape was the more regretted by Nelson, because, if he had had sufficient force, he thought it would certainly have been prevented. He wished to keep ships upon the watch to intercept anything coming from Egypt; but the Admiralty calculated upon the assistance of the Russian fleet, which failed when it was most wanted. The ships which should have been thus employed were then required for more pressing services; and the bloody Corsican was thus enabled to reach Europe in safety; there to become the guilty instrument of a wider-spreading destruction than any with which the world had ever before been visited.

Nelson had other causes of chagrin. Earl St. Vincent, for whom he felt such high respect, and whom Sir John Orde had challenged for having nominated Nelson instead of himself to the command of the Nile squadron, laid claim to prize money, as commander-in-chief, after he had quitted the station. The point was contested, and decided against him.

Nelson, perhaps, felt this the more, because his own feelings, with regard to money, were so different. An opinion had been given by Dr. Lawrence, which would have excluded the junior flag-officers from prize-money. When this was made known to him, his reply was in these words: "Notwithstanding Dr. Lawrence's opinion, I do not believe I have any right to exclude the junior flag-officers; and if I have, I desire that no such claim may be made: no, not if it were sixty times the sum—and, poor as I am, I were never to see prize-money."

A ship could not be spared to convey him to England; he therefore travelled through Germany to Hamburgh, in company with his inseparable friends, Sir William and Lady Hamilton. The Queen of Naples went with them to Vienna.

While they were at Leghorn, upon a report that the French were approaching (for, through the folly of weak courts and the treachery of venal cabinets, they had now recovered their ascendancy in Italy), the people rose tumultuously, and would fain have persuaded Nelson to lead them against the enemy.

Public honours, and yet more gratifying testimonials of public admiration, awaited Nelson wherever he went. The Prince of Esterhazy entertained him in a style of Hungarian magnificence—a hundred grenadiers, each six feet in height, constantly waiting at table[74].

At Madgeburgh, the master of the hotel where he was entertained contrived to show him for money—admitting the curious to mount a ladder, and peep at him through a small window.

A wine merchant at Hamburgh, who was above seventy years of age, requested to speak with Lady Hamilton; and told her he had some Rhenish wine, of the vintage of 1625, which had been in his own possession more than half-a-century: he had preserved it for some extraordi-

74 Height and physical strength being primary selection criteria for grenadier regiments, finding troops of this height to serve at table would not have been that difficult.

nary occasion; and that which had now arrived was far beyond any that he could ever have expected. His request was, that her ladyship would prevail upon Lord Nelson to accept six dozen of this incomparable wine: part of it would then have the honour to flow into the heart's blood of that immortal hero; and this thought would make him happy during the remainder of his life.

Nelson, when this singular request was reported to him, went into the room, and taking the worthy old gentleman kindly by the hand, consented to receive six bottles, provided the donor would dine with him next day. Twelve were sent; and Nelson, saying that he hoped yet to win half-a-dozen more great victories, promised to lay by six bottles of his Hamburgh friend's wine, for the purpose of drinking one after each.

A German pastor, between seventy and eighty years of age, travelled forty miles, with the Bible of his parish church, to request that Nelson would write his name on the first leaf of it. He called him the Saviour of the Christian world. The old man's hope deceived him. There was no Nelson upon shore, or Europe would have been saved; but in his foresight of the horrors with which all Germany and all Christendom were threatened by France, the pastor could not possibly have apprehended more than has actually taken place.

Chapter 7

1800–1801

Nelson separates himself from his Wife—Northern Confederacy—He goes to the Baltic, under Sir Hyde Parker—Battle of Copenhagen, and subsequent Negotiation—Nelson is made a Viscount.

Nelson was welcomed in England with every mark of popular honour. At Yarmouth, where he landed, every ship in the harbour hoisted her colours. The mayor and corporation waited upon him with the freedom of the town, and accompanied him in procession to church, with all the naval officers on shore, and the principal inhabitants. Bonfires and illuminations concluded the day; and on the morrow, the volunteer cavalry drew up, and saluted him as he departed, and followed the carriage to the borders of the county.

At Ipswich, the people came out to meet him, drew him a mile into the town, and three miles out[75]. When he was in the *Agamemnon*, he wished to represent this place in parliament, and some of his friends had consulted the leading men of the corporation—the result was not successful; and Nelson, observing that he would endeavour to find out a preferable path into parliament, said there might come a time when the people of Ipswich would think it an honour to have had him for their representative.

In London, he was feasted by the City, drawn by the populace from Ludgate-hill to Guildhall, and received the thanks of the common-council for his great victory, and a golden-hilted sword studded with diamonds.

---

75 That is, they unhitched the horses from Nelson's carriage, attached ropes to the draw bars, and the people of the town then pulled it themselves.

Nelson had every earthly blessing except domestic happiness; he had forfeited that for ever. Before he had been three months in England he separated from Lady Nelson. Some of his last words to her were—

"I call God to witness, there is nothing in you, or your conduct, that I wish otherwise."

This was the consequence of his infatuated attachment to Lady Hamilton. It had before caused a quarrel with his son-in-law, and occasioned remonstrances from his truest friends, which produced no other effect than that of making him displeased with them, and more dissatisfied with himself.

The Addington[76] administration was just at this time formed; and Nelson, who had solicited employment, and been made vice-admiral of the blue, was sent to the Baltic, as second in command, under Sir Hyde Parker, by Earl St. Vincent, the new First Lord of the Admiralty.

The three Northern courts had formed a confederacy for making England resign her naval rights. Of these courts, Russia was guided by the passions of its emperor, Paul, a man not without fits of generosity, and some natural goodness, but subject to the wildest humours of caprice, and erased by the possession of greater power than can ever be safely, or perhaps innocently, possessed by weak humanity.

Denmark was French at heart: ready to co-operate in all the views of France, to recognise all her usurpations, and obey all her injunctions. Sweden, under a king whose principles were right, and whose feelings were generous, but who had a taint of hereditary insanity, acted in acquiescence with the dictates of two powers whom it feared to offend.

The Danish navy, at this time, consisted of 23 ships of the line, with about 31 frigates and smaller vessels, exclusive of guard-ships. The Swedes had 18 ships of the line, 14 frigates and sloops, seventy-four galleys and smaller vessels, besides gun-boats; and this force was in a far better state of equipment than the Danish. The Russians had 82 sail of the line and 40 frigates. Of these there were 47 sail of the line at Cronstadt, Revel, Petersburgh, and Archangel; but the Russian fleet was ill-manned, ill-officered, and ill-equipped.

Such a combination under the influence of France would soon have become formidable; and never did the British Cabinet display more

76 Henry Addington (1757–1844) was Prime Minister from 1801 to 1804. He was created Viscount Sidmouth after leaving office, serving in subsequent governments as a cabinet member.

decision than in instantly preparing to crush it. They erred, however, in permitting any petty consideration to prevent them from appointing Nelson to the command.

The public properly murmured at seeing it intrusted to another; and he himself said to Earl St. Vincent that, circumstanced as he was, this expedition would probably be the last service that he should ever perform. The earl, in reply, besought him, for God's sake, not to suffer himself to be carried away by any sudden impulse.

The season happened to be unusually favourable; so mild a winter had not been known in the Baltic for many years. When Nelson joined the fleet at Yarmouth, he found the admiral "a little nervous about dark nights and fields of ice."

"But we must brace up," said he; "these are not times for nervous systems. I hope we shall give our northern enemies that hailstorm of bullets which gives our dear country the dominion of the sea. We have it, and all the devils in the north cannot take it from us, if our wooden walls have fair play."

Before the fleet left Yarmouth, it was sufficiently known that its destination was against Denmark. Some Danes, who belonged to the *Amazon* frigate, went to Captain Riou, and telling him what they had heard, begged that he would get them exchanged into a ship bound on some other destination.

"They had no wish," they said, "to quit the British service; but they entreated that they might not be forced to fight against their own country."

There was not in our whole navy a man who had a higher and more chivalrous sense of duty than Riou. Tears came into his eyes while the men were speaking. Without making any reply, he instantly ordered his boat, and did not return to the *Amazon* till he could tell them that their wish was effected.

The fleet sailed on the 12th of March. Mr. Vansittart[77] sailed in it; the British Cabinet still hoping to attain its end by negotiation.

It was well for England that Sir Hyde Parker placed a fuller confidence in Nelson than the government seems to have done at this most

77 Nicholas Vansittart (1766–1851), 1st Baron Bexley. In addition to his diplomatic duties, Vansittart would go on to serve as Chancellor of the Exchequer in the administration of the Earl of Liverpool starting in 1812.

important crisis. Her enemies might well have been astonished at learning that any other man should for a moment have been thought of for the command. But so little deference was paid, even at this time, to his intuitive and all-commanding genius, that when the fleet had reached its first rendezvous, at the entrance of the Cattegat, he had received no official communication whatever of the intended operations.

His own mind had been made up upon them with its accustomed decision. "All I have gathered of our first plans," said he, "I disapprove most exceedingly. Honour may arise from them; good cannot. I hear we are likely to anchor outside of Cronenburgh Castle, instead of Copenhagen, which would give weight to our negotiation. A Danish minister would think twice before he would put his name to war with England, when the next moment he would probably see his master's fleet in flames, and his capital in ruins. The Dane should see our flag every moment he lifted up his head."

Mr Vansittart left the fleet at the Scaw, and preceded it in a frigate with a flag of truce. Precious time was lost by this delay, which was to be purchased by the dearest blood of Britain and Denmark: according to the Danes themselves, the intelligence that a British fleet was seen off the Sound produced a much more general alarm in Copenhagen than its actual arrival in the Roads; for the means of defence were at that time in such a state that they could hardly hope to resist, still less to repel an enemy.

On the 21st Nelson had a long conference with Sir Hyde; and the next day addressed a letter to him, worthy of himself and of the occasion. Mr. Vansittart's report had then been received. It represented the Danish government as in the highest degree hostile, and their state of preparation as exceeding what our cabinet had supposed possible; for Denmark had profited with all activity of the leisure which had so impoliticly been given her.

"The more I have reflected," said Nelson to his commander, "the more I am confirmed in opinion, that not a moment should be lost in attacking the enemy. They will every day and every hour be stronger; we shall never be so good a match for them as at this moment. The only consideration is, how to get at them with the least risk to our ships. Here you are, with almost the safety, certainly with the honour of England, more entrusted to you than ever yet fell to the lot of any British officer. On your decision depends whether our country shall be degraded in the eyes of

Europe, or whether she shall rear her head higher than ever. Again, I do repeat, never did our country depend so much upon the success of any fleet as on this. How best to honour her and abate the pride of her enemies, must be the subject of your deepest consideration."

Supposing him to force the passage of the Sound, Nelson thought some damage might be done among the masts and yards; though, perhaps, not one of them but would be serviceable again. "If the wind be fair," said he, "and you determined to attack the ships and Crown Islands, you must expect the natural issue of such a battle—ships crippled, and perhaps one or two lost for the wind which carries you in will most probably not bring out a crippled ship. This mode I call taking the bull by the horns. It, however, will not prevent the Revel ships, or the Swedes, from joining the Danes and to prevent this is, in my humble opinion, a measure absolutely necessary, and still to attack Copenhagen."

For this he proposed two modes. One was to pass Cronenburg, taking the risk of danger; take the deepest and straightest channel along the middle grounds, and then coming down to Garbar, or King's Channel, attack the Danish line of floating batteries and ships as might be found convenient. This would prevent a junction, and might give an opportunity of bombarding Copenhagen. Or to take the passage of the Belt, which might be accomplished in four or five days; and then the attack by Draco might be made, and the junction of the Russians prevented.

Supposing them through the Belt, he proposed that a detachment of the fleet should be sent to destroy the Russian squadron at Revel; and that the business at Copenhagen should be attempted with the remainder. "The measure," he said, "might be thought bold; but the boldest measures are the safest."

The pilots, as men who had nothing but safety to think of, were terrified by the formidable report of the batteries of Elsinore, and the tremendous preparations which our negotiators, who were now returned from their fruitless mission, had witnessed. They, therefore, persuaded Sir Hyde to prefer the passage of the Belt.

"Let it be by the Sound, by the Belt, or anyhow," cried Nelson, "only lose not an hour!"

On the 26th they sailed for the Belt. Such was the habitual reserve of Sir Hyde that his own captain, the captain of the fleet, did not know which course he had resolved to take till the fleet were getting under weigh. When Captain Domett was thus apprised of it, he felt it his duty to represent to the admiral his belief that if that course were persevered in, the ultimate object would be totally defeated: it was liable to long delays, and to accidents of ships grounding; in the whole fleet there were only one captain and one pilot who knew anything of this formidable passage (as it was then deemed), and their knowledge was very slight—their instructions did not authorise them to attempt it.

Supposing them safe through the Belts, the heavy ships could not come over the *grounds* to attack Copenhagen; and light vessels would have no effect on such a line of defence as had been prepared against them. Domett urged these reasons so forcibly that Sir Hyde's opinion was shaken, and he consented to bring the fleet to and send for Nelson on board. There can be little doubt but that the expedition would have failed if Captain Domett had not thus timeously and earnestly given his advice. Nelson entirely agreed with him; and it was finally determined to take the passage of the Sound, and the fleet returned to its former anchorage.

The next day was more idly expended in despatching a flag of truce to the governor of Cronenburg Castle, to ask whether he had received orders to fire at the British fleet; as the admiral must consider the first gun to be a declaration of war on the part of Denmark.

A soldier-like and becoming answer was returned to this formality. The governor said that the British minister had not been sent away from Copenhagen, but had obtained a passport at his own demand. He himself, as a soldier, could not meddle with politics; but he was not at liberty to suffer a fleet, of which the intention was not yet known, to approach the guns of the castle which he had the honour to command: and he requested, "if the British admiral should think proper to make any proposals to the King of Denmark, that he might be apprised of it before the fleet approached nearer."

During this intercourse, a Dane, who came on board the commander's ship, having occasion to express his business in writing, found the pen blunt; and, holding it up, sarcastically said, "If your guns are not better pointed than your pens, you will make little impression on Copenhagen!"

On that day intelligence reached the admiral of the loss of one of his fleet, the *Invincible*, seventy-four, wrecked on a sand-bank, as she was coming out of Yarmouth: four hundred of her men perished in her.

Nelson, who was now appointed to lead the van, shifted his flag to the *Elephant*, Captain Foley—a lighter ship than the *St. George*, and, therefore, fitter for the expected operations. The two following days were calm. Orders had been given to pass the Sound as soon as the wind would permit; and, on the afternoon of the 29th, the ships were cleared for action, with an alacrity characteristic of British seamen.

At daybreak on the 30th it blew a topsail breeze from N.W. The signal was made, and the fleet moved on in order of battle; Nelson's division in the van, Sir Hyde's in the centre, and Admiral Graves' in the rear.

Great actions, whether military or naval, have generally given celebrity to the scenes from whence they are denominated; and thus petty villages, and capes and bays known only to the coasting trader, become associated with mighty deeds, and their names are made conspicuous in the history of the world. Here, however, the scene was every way worthy of the drama. The political importance of the Sound is such, that grand objects are not needed there to impress the imagination; yet is the channel full of grand and interesting objects, both of art and nature.

This passage, which Denmark had so long considered as the key of the Baltic, is, in its narrowest part, about three miles wide; and here the city of Elsinore is situated; except Copenhagen, the most flourishing of the Danish towns. Every vessel which passes lowers her top-gallant sails and pays toll at Elsinore; a toll which is believed to have had its origin in the consent of the traders to that sea, Denmark taking upon itself the charge of constructing lighthouses, and erecting signals, to mark the shoals and rocks from the Cattegat to the Baltic; and they, on their part, agreeing that all ships should pass this way in order that all might pay their shares: none from that time using the passage of the Belt, because it was not fitting that they who enjoyed the benefit of the beacons in dark and stormy weather, should evade contributing to them in fair seasons and summer nights. Of late years about ten thousand vessels had annually paid this contribution in time of peace.

Adjoining Elsinore, and at the edge of the peninsular promontory, upon the nearest point of land to the Swedish coast, stands Cronenburgh Castle, built after Tycho Brahe's design; a magnificent pile—at once a palace, and fortress, and state-prison, with its spires, and towers, and battlements, and batteries.

On the left of the strait is the old Swedish city of Helsinburg, at the foot, and on the side of a hill. To the north of Helsinburg the shores are steep and rocky; they lower to the south; and the distant spires of Lanscrona, Lund, and Malmoe are seen in the flat country.

The Danish shores consist partly of ridges of sand; but more frequently they are diversified with cornfields, meadows, slopes, and are covered with rich wood, and villages, and villas, and summer palaces belonging to the king and the nobility, and denoting the vicinity of a great capital. The isles of Huen, Statholm, and Amak, appear in the widening channel; and at the distance of twenty miles from Elsinore stands Copenhagen in full view; the best city of the north, and one of the finest capitals of Europe, visible, with its stately spires, far off.

Amid these magnificent objects there are some which possess a peculiar interest for the recollections which they call forth. The isle of Huen, a lovely domain, about six miles in circumference, had been the munificent gift of Frederick the Second to Tycho Brahe. It has higher shores than the near coast of Zealand, or than the Swedish coast in that part. Here most of his discoveries were made; and here the ruins are to be seen of his observatory, and of the mansion where he was visited by princes; and where, with a princely spirit, he received and entertained all comers from all parts, and promoted science by his liberality as well as by his labours.

Elsinore is a name familiar to English ears, being inseparably associated with *Hamlet*, and one of the noblest works of human genius.

Cronenburgh had been the scene of deeper tragedy: here Queen Matilda[78] was confined, the victim of a foul and murderous court intrigue. Here, amid heart-breaking griefs, she found consolation in nursing her infant. Here she took her everlasting leave of that infant, when, by the interference of England, her own deliverance was obtained; and as the ship bore her away from a country where the venial indiscretions of youth and unsuspicious gaiety had been so cruelly punished, upon these towers she fixed her eyes, and stood upon the deck, obstinately gazing toward them till the last speck had disappeared.

---

78 Caroline Matilda (1751–1775), Queen of Denmark from 1766 to 1772. Matilda was the youngest sister of King George III of England. She married Christian VII of Denmark in November 1766. Her first child, who would become King Frederick VI of Denmark, was born to 1768, and a daughter, Princess Louise Auguste, in 1771. Historians are generally agreed that her daughter was most likely fathered not by her husband, but by his personal physician. Eventually the two were found out, and Matilda was confined in Cronenberg, while her lover was executed. Deported to Celle, Germany in May 1772, she died of scarlet fever while still in exile.

The Sound being the only frequented entrance to the Baltic, the great Mediterranean of the North, few parts of the sea display so frequent a navigation. In the height of the season not fewer than a hundred vessels pass every four-and-twenty hours for many weeks in succession; but never had so busy or so splendid a scene been exhibited there as on this day, when the British fleet prepared to force that passage where, till now, all ships had vailed their topsails to the flag of Denmark.

The whole force consisted of fifty-one sail of various descriptions, of which sixteen were of the line. The greater part of the bomb and gun vessels took their stations off Cronenburgh Castle, to cover the fleet; while others on the larboard were ready to engage the Swedish shore.

The Danes, having improved every moment which ill-timed negotiation and baffling weather gave them, had lined their shores with batteries; and as soon as the *Monarch*, which was the leading ship, came abreast of them, a fire was opened from about a hundred pieces of cannon and mortars; our light vessels immediately, in return, opened their fire upon the castle.

Here was all the pompous circumstance and exciting reality of war, without its effects; for this ostentatious display was but a bloodless prelude to the wide and sweeping destruction which was soon to follow. The enemy's shot fell near enough to splash the water on board our ships: not relying upon any forbearance of the Swedes, they meant to have kept the mid channel; but when they perceived that not a shot was fired from Helsinburg, and that no batteries were to be seen on the Swedish shore, they inclined to that side, so as completely to get out of reach of the Danish guns.

The uninterrupted blaze which was kept up from them till the fleet had passed, served only to exhilarate our sailors, and afford them matter for jest, as the shot fell in showers a full cable's length short of its destined aim. A few rounds were returned from some of our leading ships, till they perceived its in-utility: this, however, occasioned the only bloodshed of the day, some of our men being killed and wounded by the bursting of a gun.

As soon as the main body had passed, the gun vessels followed, desisting from their bombardment, which had been as innocent as that of the enemy; and, about mid-day, the whole fleet anchored between the island of Huen and Copenhagen. Sir Hyde, with Nelson, Admiral Graves, some of the senior captains, and the commanding officers of the artillery and the troops, then proceeded in a lugger to reconnoitre the enemy's means of defence; a formidable line of ships, radeaus, pontoons, galleys, fire-ships and gun-boats, flanked and supported by extensive batteries, and occupying, from one extreme point to the other, an extent of nearly four miles.

A council of war was held in the afternoon. It was apparent that the Danes could not be attacked without great difficulty and risk; and some of the members of the council spoke of the number of the Swedes and the Russians whom they should afterwards have to engage, as a consideration which ought to be borne in mind.

Nelson, who kept pacing the cabin, impatient as he ever was of anything which savoured of irresolution, repeatedly said, "The more numerous the better: I wish they were twice as many,—the easier the victory, depend on it."

The plan upon which he had determined; if ever it should be his fortune to bring a Baltic fleet to action, was, to attack the head of their line and confuse their movements. "Close with a Frenchman," he used to say, "but out manoeuvre a Russian."

He offered his services for the attack, requiring ten sail of the line and the whole of the smaller craft. Sir Hyde gave him two more line-of-battle ships than he asked, and left everything to his judgment.

The enemy's force was not the only, nor the greatest, obstacle with which the British fleet had to contend: there was another to be overcome before they could come in contact with it. The channel was little known and extremely intricate: all the buoys had been removed; and the Danes considered this difficulty as almost insuperable, thinking the channel impracticable for so large a fleet.

Nelson himself saw the soundings made and the buoys laid down, boating it upon this exhausting service, day and night, till it was effected. When this was done he thanked God for having enabled him to get through this difficult part of his duty. "It had worn him down," he said, "and was infinitely more grievous to him than any resistance which he could experience from the enemy."

At the first council of war, opinions inclined to an attack from the eastward; but the next day, the wind being southerly, after a second examination of the Danish position, it was determined to attack from the south, approaching in the manner which Nelson had suggested in his first thoughts.

On the morning of the 1st of April the whole fleet removed to an anchorage within two leagues of the town, and off the N.W. end of the Middle Ground; a shoal lying exactly before the town, at about three quarters of a mile distance, and extending along its whole sea-front. The King's Channel, where there is deep water, is between this shoal and the town; and here the Danes had arranged their line of defence, as near the shore as possible: nineteen ships and floating batteries, flanked, at the end nearest the town, by the Crown Batteries, which were two artificial islands, at the mouth of the harbour—most formidable works; the larger one having, by the Danish account, 66 guns; but, as Nelson believed, 88.

The fleet having anchored, Nelson, with Riou, in the *Amazon,* made his last examination of the ground; and about one o'clock, returning to his own ship, threw out the signal to weigh. It was received with a shout throughout the whole division; they weighed with a light and favourable wind: the narrow channel between the island of Saltholm and the Middle Ground had been accurately buoyed; the small craft pointed out the course distinctly; Riou led the way: the whole division coasted along the outer edge of the shoal, doubled its further extremity, and anchored there off Draco Point, just as the darkness closed—the headmost of the enemy's line not being more than two miles distant.

The signal to prepare for action had been made early in the evening; and as his own anchor dropt, Nelson called out, "I will fight them the moment I have a fair wind!"

It had been agreed that Sir Hyde, with the remaining ships, should weigh on the following morning, at the same time as Nelson, to menace the Crown Batteries on his side, and the four ships of the line which lay at the entrance of the arsenal; and to cover our own disabled ships as they came out of action.

The Danes, meantime, had not been idle: no sooner did the guns of Cronenburgh make it known to the whole city that all negotiation was at an end, that the British fleet was passing the Sound, and that the dispute between the two crowns must now be decided by arms, than a spirit displayed itself most honourable to the Danish character. All ranks offered themselves to the service of their country; the university furnished a corps of 1,200 youth, the flower of Denmark—it was one of those emergencies in which little drilling or discipline is necessary to render courage available: they had nothing to learn but how to manage the guns, and day and night were employed in practising them.

When the movements of Nelson's squadron were perceived, it was known when and where the attack was to be expected, and the line of defence was manned indiscriminately by soldiers, sailors, and citizens.

Had not the whole attention of the Danes been directed to strengthen their own means of defence, they might most materially have annoyed the invading squadron, and perhaps frustrated the impending attack; for the British ships were crowded in an anchoring ground of little extent:—it was calm, so that mortar-boats might have acted against them to the utmost advantage; and they were within range of shells from Amak Island. A few fell among them; but the enemy soon ceased to fire. It was learned afterwards, that, fortunately for the fleet, the bed of the mortar had given way; and the Danes either could not get it replaced, or, in the darkness, lost the direction.

This was an awful night for Copenhagen—far more so than for the British fleet, where the men were accustomed to battle and victory, and had none of those objects before their eyes which rendered death terrible. Nelson sat down to table with a large party of his officers: he was, as he was ever wont to be when on the eve of action, in high spirits, and drank to a leading wind, and to the success of the morrow.

After supper they returned to their respective ships, except Riou, who remained to arrange the order of battle with Nelson and Foley, and to draw up instructions.

Hardy, meantime, went in a small boat to examine the channel between them and the enemy; approaching so near that he sounded round their leading ship with a pole, lest the noise of throwing the lead should discover him.

The incessant fatigue of body, as well as mind, which Nelson had undergone during the last three days, had so exhausted him that he was earnestly urged to go to his cot; and his old servant, Allen, using that kind of authority which long and affectionate services entitled and enabled him to assume on such occasions, insisted upon his complying. The cot was placed on the floor, and he continued to dictate from it.

About eleven Hardy returned, and reported the practicability of the channel, and the depth of water up to the enemy's line. About one the orders were completed; and half-a-dozen clerks, in the foremost cabin, proceeded to transcribe them, Nelson frequently calling out to them from his cot to hasten their work, for the wind was becoming fair.

Instead of attempting to get a few hours' sleep, he was constantly receiving reports on this important point.

At daybreak it was announced as becoming perfectly fair. The clerks finished their work about six. Nelson, who was already up, breakfasted, and made signal for all captains.

The land forces and five hundred seamen, under Captain Freemantle and the Hon. Colonel Stewart, were to storm the Crown Battery as soon as its fire should be silenced: and Riou—whom Nelson had never seen till this expedition, but whose worth he had instantly perceived, and appreciated as it deserved—had the *Blanche* and *Alcmene* frigates, the *Dart* and *Arrow* sloops, and the *Zephyr* and *Otter* fire-ships, given him, with a special command to act as circumstances might require—every other ship had its station appointed.

Between eight and nine, the pilots and masters were ordered on board the admirals' ships. The pilots were mostly men who had been mates in Baltic traders; and their hesitation about the bearing of the east end of the shoal, and the exact line of deep water, gave ominous warning of how little their knowledge was to be trusted.

The signal for action had been made, the wind was fair—not a moment to be lost. Nelson urged them to be steady, to be resolute, and to decide; but they wanted the only ground for steadiness and decision in such cases; and Nelson had reason to regret that he had not trusted to Hardy's single report. This was one of the most painful moments of his life; and he always spoke of it with bitterness.

"I experienced in the Sound," said he, "the misery of having the honour of our country entrusted to a set of pilots, who have no other thought than to keep the ships clear of danger, and their own silly heads clear of shot. Everybody knows what I must have suffered; and if any merit attaches itself to me, it was for combating the dangers of the shallows in defiance of them."

At length Mr. Bryerly, the master of the *Bellona*, declared that he was prepared to lead the fleet; his judgment was acceded to by the rest; they returned to their ships; and at half-past nine the signal was made to weigh in succession.

Captain Murray, in the *Edgar*, led the way; the *Agamemnon* was next in order; but on the first attempt to leave her anchorage, she could not weather the edge of the shoal; and Nelson had the grief to see his old ship, in which he had performed so many years' gallant services, immovably aground at a moment when her help was so greatly required.

Signal was then made for the *Polythemus*; and this change in the order of sailing was executed with the utmost promptitude: yet so much delay had thus been unavoidably occasioned, that the *Edgar* was for some time unsupported, and the *Polythemus*, whose place should have been at the end of the enemy's line, where their strength was the greatest, could get no further than the beginning, owing to the difficulty of the channel: there she occupied, indeed, an efficient station, but one where her presence was less required.

The *Isis* followed with better fortune, and took her own berth. The *Bellona*, Sir Thomas Boulden Thompson, kept too close on the starboard shoal, and grounded abreast of the outer ship of the enemy: this was the more vexatious, inasmuch as the wind was fair, the room ample, and three ships had led the way. The *Russell*, following the *Bellona*, grounded in like manner: both were within reach of shot; but their absence from their intended stations was severely felt.

Each ship had been ordered to pass her leader on the starboard side, because the water was supposed to shoal on the larboard shore. Nelson, who came next after these two ships, thought they had kept too far on the starboard direction, and made signal for them to close with the enemy, not knowing that they were aground; but when he perceived that they did not obey the signal, he ordered the *Elephant*'s helm to starboard, and went within these ships: thus quitting the appointed order of sailing, and guiding those which were to follow.

The greater part of the fleet were probably, by this act of promptitude on his part, saved from going on shore. Each ship, as she arrived nearly opposite to her appointed station, let her anchor go by the stern, and presented her broadside to the Danes. The distance between each was about half a cable. The action was fought nearly at the distance of a cable's length from the enemy.

This, which rendered its continuance so long, was owing to the ignorance and consequent indecision of the pilots. In pursuance of the same error which had led the *Bellona* and the *Russell* aground, they, when the lead was at a quarter less five [28' 6"], refused to approach nearer, in dread of shoaling their water on the larboard shore: a fear altogether erroneous, for the water deepened up to the very side of the enemy's line of battle.

At five minutes after ten the action began. The first half of our fleet was engaged in about half an hour; and by half-past eleven the battle became general. The plan of the attack had been complete: but seldom has any plan been more disconcerted by untoward accidents.

Of twelve ships of the line, one was entirely useless, and two others in a situation where they could not render half the service which was required of them. Of the squadron of gun-brigs, only one could get into action; the rest were prevented, by baffling currents, from weathering the eastern end of the shoal; and only two of the bomb-vessels could reach their station on the Middle Ground, and open their mortars on the arsenal, firing over both fleets.

Riou took the vacant station against the Crown Battery, with his frigates: attempting, with that unequal force, a service in which three sail of the line had been directed to assist.

Nelson's agitation had been extreme when he saw himself, before the action began, deprived of a fourth part of his ships of the line; but no sooner was he in battle, where his squadron was received with the fire of more than a thousand guns, than, as if that artillery, like music, had driven away all care and painful thoughts, his countenance brightened; and, as a bystander describes him, his conversation became joyous, animated, elevated, and delightful.

The Commander-in-Chief meantime, near enough to the scene of action to know the unfavourable accidents which had so materially weakened Nelson, and yet too distant to know the real state of the contending parties, suffered the most dreadful anxiety. To get to his assistance was impossible; both wind and current were against him. Fear for the event, in such circumstances, would naturally preponderate in the bravest mind; and at one o'clock, perceiving that, after three hours' endurance, the enemy's fire was unslackened, he began to despair of success.

"I will make the signal of recall," said he to his captain, "for Nelson's sake. If he is in a condition to continue the action successfully, he will disregard it; if he is not, it will be an excuse for his retreat, and no blame can be imputed to him."

Captain Domett urged him at least to delay the signal till he could communicate with Nelson; but in Sir Hyde's opinion the danger was too pressing for delay.

"The fire," he said, "was too hot for Nelson to oppose; a retreat he thought must be made; he was aware of the consequences to his own personal reputation, but it would be cowardly in him to leave Nelson to bear the whole shame of the failure, if shame it should be deemed." Under, a mistaken judgment, therefore, but with this disinterested and generous feeling, he made the signal for retreat.

Nelson was at this time, in all the excitement of action, pacing the quarter-deck. A shot through the mainmast knocked the splinters about; and he observed to one of his officers with a smile, "It is warm work, and this day may be the last to any of us at a moment:"—and then stopping short at the gangway, added, with emotion—"But mark you! I would not be elsewhere for thousands."

About this time the signal-lieutenant called out that number Thirty-nine (the signal for discontinuing the action) was thrown out by the Commander-in-Chief.

He continued to walk the deck, and appeared to take no notice of it. The signal officer met him at the next turn, and asked if he should repeat it.

"No," he replied, "acknowledge it."

Presently he called after him to know if the signal for close action was still hoisted; and being answered in the affirmative, said, "Mind you keep it so." He now paced the deck, moving the stump of his lost arm in a manner which always indicated great emotion.

"Do you know," said he to Mr. Ferguson, "what is shown on board the Commander-in-Chief? Number Thirty-nine!"

Mr. Ferguson asked what that meant.

"Why, to leave off action!" Then shrugging up his shoulders, he repeated the words—"Leave off action? Now, damn me if I do! You know, Foley," turning to the captain, "I have only one eye,—I have a right to be blind sometimes:" and then putting the glass to his blind eye, in that mood of mind which sports with bitterness, he exclaimed, "I really do not see the signal!"

Presently he exclaimed, "Damn the signal! Keep mine for closer battle flying! That's the way I answer signals! Nail mine to the mast!" Admiral Graves, who was so situated that he could not discern what was done on board the *Elephant*, disobeyed Sir Hyde's signal in like manner; whether by fortunate mistake, or by a like brave intention, has not been made known. The other ships of the line, looking only to Nelson, continued the action[79].

The signal, however, saved Riou's little squadron, but did not save its heroic leader. This squadron, which was nearest the Commander-in-Chief, obeyed and hauled off. It had suffered severely in its most unequal contest. For a long time the *Amazon* had been firing, enveloped in smoke, when Riou desired his men to stand fast, and let the smoke clear off, that they might see what they were about.

A fatal order—for the Danes then got clear sight of her from the batteries, and pointed their guns with such tremendous effect that nothing but the signal for retreat saved this frigate from destruction.

"What will Nelson think of us?" was Riou's mournful exclamation when he unwillingly drew off. He had been wounded in the head by a splinter, and was sitting on a gun, encouraging his men, when, just as the *Amazon* showed her stern to the Trekroner battery, his clerk was killed by his side; and another shot swept away several marines who were hauling in the main-brace.

"Come, then, my boys!" cried Riou; "let us die all together!" The words had scarcely been uttered before a raking shot cut him in two. Except it had been Nelson himself, the British navy could not have suffered a severer loss.

The action continued along the line with unabated vigour on our side, and with the most determined resolution on the part of the Danes. They fought to great advantage, because most of the vessels in their line of defence were without masts; the few which had any standing had their top-masts struck, and the hulls could not be seen at intervals.

The *Isis* must have been destroyed by the superior weight of her enemy's fire, if Captain Inman, in the *Desiree* frigate, had not judiciously taken a situation which enabled him to rake the Dane, if the *Polythemus* had not also relieved her.

Both in the *Bellona* and the *Isis* many men were lost by the bursting of their guns. The former ship was about forty years old, and these guns were believed to be the same which she had first taken to sea: they were, probably, originally faulty, for the fragments were full of little air-holes.

79 *Glatton*, immediately following *Elephant*, was the only ship in that column that could also see Parker's signal, and could have repeated it, following normal protocol. Like his admiral, Captain William Bligh chose to ignore Parker's signal and kept Nelson's hoisted. The rest of the squadron saw only that signal.

The *Bellona* lost 75 men; the *Isis*, 110; the *Monarch*, 210. She was, more than any other line-of-battle ship, exposed to the great battery; and supporting, at the same time, the united fire of the *Holstein* and the *Zealand*, her loss this day exceeded that of any single ship during the whole war. Amid the tremendous carnage in this vessel, some of the men displayed a singular instance of coolness: the pork and peas happened to be in the kettle; a shot knocked its contents about; they picked up the pieces, and ate and fought at the same time.

The Prince-Royal [later King Frederick VI, Ed.] had taken his station upon one of the batteries, from [*sic*] whence he beheld the action and issued his orders. Denmark had never been engaged in so arduous a contest, and never did the Danes more nobly display their national courage—a courage not more unhappily than impolitically exerted in subserviency to the interests of France.

Captain Thura, of the *Indfoedsretten*, fell early in the action; and all his officers, except one lieutenant and one marine officer, were either killed or wounded. In the confusion, the colours were either struck or shot away; but she was moored athwart one of the batteries in such a situation that the British made no attempt to board her; and a boat was despatched to the prince, to inform him of her situation.

He turned to those about him, and said, "Gentlemen, Thura is killed; which of you will take the command?"

Schroedersee, a captain who had lately resigned on account of extreme ill-health, answered in a feeble voice, "I will!" and hastened on board.

The crew, perceiving a new commander coming alongside, hoisted their colours again, and fired a broadside. Schroedersee, when he came on deck, found himself surrounded by the dead and wounded, and called to those in the boat to get quickly on board: a ball struck him at that moment.

A lieutenant, who had accompanied him, then took the command, and continued to fight the ship.

A youth of seventeen, by name Villemoes, particularly distinguished himself on this memorable day. He had volunteered to take the command of a floating battery, which was a raft, consisting merely of a number of beams nailed together, with a flooring to support the guns: it was square, with a breast-work full of port-holes, and without masts— carrying twenty-four guns, and one hundred and twenty men. With this he got under the stern of the *Elephant*, below the reach of the stern-chasers; and under a heavy fire of small-arms from the marines, fought his raft, till the truce was announced, with such skill as well as courage, as to excite Nelson's warmest admiration.

Between one and two the fire of the Danes slackened; about two it ceased from the greater part of their line, and some of their lighter ships were adrift. It was, however, difficult to take possession of those which struck, because the batteries on Amak Island protected them; and because an irregular fire was kept up from the ships themselves as the boats approached.

This arose from the nature of the action: the crews were continually reinforced from the shore; and fresh men coming on board, did not inquire whether the flag had been struck, or, perhaps, did not heed it; many or most of them never having been engaged in war before—knowing nothing, therefore, of its laws, and thinking only of defending their country to the last extremity.

The *Danbrog* fired upon the *Elephant*'s boats in this manner, though her commodore had removed her pendant and deserted her, though she had struck, and though she was in flames. After she had been abandoned by the commodore, Braun fought her till he lost his right hand, and then Captain Lemming took the command. This unexpected renewal of her fire made the *Elephant* and *Glatton* renew theirs, till she was not only silenced, but nearly every man in the praams, ahead and astern of her, was killed.

When the smoke of their guns died away, she was seen drifting in flames before the wind: those of her crew who remained alive, and able to exert themselves, throwing themselves out at her port-holes. Captain Bertie of the *Ardent* sent his launch to their assistance, and saved three-and-twenty of them.

Captain Rothe commanded the *Nyeborg* praam; and perceiving that she could not much longer be kept afloat, made for the inner road. As he passed the line, he found the *Aggershuus* praam in a more miserable condition than his own; her masts had all gone by the board, and she was on the point of sinking. Rothe made fast a cable to her stern, and towed her off; but he could get her no further than a shoal called Stubben, when she sunk, and soon after he had worked the *Nyeborg* up to the landing-place, that vessel also sunk to her gunwale. Never did any vessel come out of action in a more dreadful plight. The stump of her foremast was the only stick standing; her cabin had been stove in; every gun, except a single one, was dismounted; and her deck was covered with shattered limbs and dead bodies.

By half-past two the action had ceased along that part of the line which was astern of the *Elephant*, but not with the ships ahead and the Crown Batteries. Nelson, seeing the manner in which his boats were fired upon when they went to take possession of the prizes, became angry, and said he must either send ashore to have this irregular proceeding stopped, or send a fire-ship and burn them.

Half the shot from the Trekroner, and from the batteries at Amak, at this time, struck the surrendered ships, four of which had got close together; and the fire of the English, in return, was equally or even more destructive to these poor devoted Danes.

Nelson, who was as humane as he was brave, was shocked at the massacre—for such he called it; and with a presence of mind peculiar to himself, and never more signally displayed than now, he retired into the stern gallery, and wrote thus to the Crown Prince:—

"Vice-Admiral Lord Nelson has been commanded to spare Denmark when she no longer resists. The line of defence which covered her shores has struck to the British flag; but if the firing is continued on the part of Denmark, he must set on fire all the prizes that he has taken, without having the power of saving the men who have so nobly defended them. The brave Danes are the brothers, and should never be the enemies, of the English."

A wafer was given him, but he ordered a candle to be brought from the cockpit, and sealed the letter with wax, affixing a larger seal than he ordinarily used. "This," said he, "is no time to appear hurried and informal[80]."

Captain Sir Frederick Thesiger, who acted as his *aide-de-camp*, carried this letter with a flag of truce. Meantime the fire of the ships ahead, and the approach of the *Ramillies* and *Defence* from Sir Hyde's division, which had now worked near enough to alarm the enemy, though not to injure them, silenced the remainder of the Danish line to the eastward of

80 At this time, letters were normally folded in a manner that allowed the sheet to serve as its own envelope. Informal letters were sealed with a gummed paper wafer, similar to those circular seals still sold today. More formal missives would be sealed with melted wax, impressed with an embossed seal.

the Trekroner. That battery, however, continued its fire. This formidable work, owing to the want of the ships which had been destined to attack it, and the inadequate force of Riou's little squadron, was comparatively uninjured. Towards the close of the action it had been manned with nearly fifteen hundred men; and the intention of storming it, for which every preparation had been made, was abandoned as impracticable.

During Thesiger's absence, Nelson sent for Freemantle, from the *Ganges,* and consulted with him and Foley whether it was advisable to advance, with those ships which had sustained least damage, against the yet uninjured part of the Danish line.

They were decidedly of opinion that the best thing which could be done was, while the wind continued fair, to remove the fleet out of the intricate channel from which it had to retreat.

In somewhat more than half an hour after Thesiger had been despatched, the Danish adjutant-general, Lindholm came, bearing a flag of truce, upon which the Trekroner ceased to fire, and the action closed, after four hours' continuance. He brought an inquiry from the prince,—What was the object of Nelson's note? The British admiral wrote in reply:—

"Lord Nelson's object in sending the flag of truce was humanity; he therefore consents that hostilities shall cease, and that the wounded Danes may be taken on shore. And Lord Nelson will take his prisoners out of the vessels, and burn or carry off his prizes as he shall think fit. Lord Nelson, with humble duty to his royal highness the prince, will consider this the greatest victory he has ever gained, if it may be the cause of a happy reconciliation and union between his own most gracious sovereign and his majesty the King of Denmark."

Sir Frederick Thesiger was despatched a second time with the reply; and the Danish adjutant-general was referred to the commander-in-chief for a conference upon this overture. Lindholm assenting to this, proceeded to the *London,* which was riding at anchor full four miles off and Nelson, losing not one of the critical moments which he had thus gained, made signal for his leading ships to weigh in succession; they had the shoal to clear, they were much crippled, and their course was immediately under the guns of the Trekroner.

The *Monarch* led the way. This ship had received six-and-twenty shot between wind and water. She had not a shroud standing; there was a double-headed shot in the heart of her foremast, and the slightest wind would have sent every mast over her side.

The imminent danger from which Nelson had extricated himself soon became apparent: the *Monarch* touched immediately upon a shoal, over which she was pushed by the *Ganges* taking her amidships; the *Glatton* went clear; but the other two, the *Defiance* and the *Elephant*, grounded about a mile from the Trekroner, and there remained fixed for many hours, in spite of all the exertions of their wearied crews.

The *Desiree* frigate also, at the other end of the line, having gone toward the close of the action to assist the *Bellona*, became fast on the same shoal. Nelson left the *Elephant* soon after she took the ground, to follow Lindholm.

The heat of the action was over, and that kind of feeling which the surrounding scene of havoc was so well fitted to produce, pressed heavily upon his exhausted spirits. The sky had suddenly become overcast; white flags were waving from the mast-heads of so many shattered ships; the slaughter had ceased, but the grief was to come; for the account of the dead was not yet made up, and no man could tell for what friends he might have to mourn.

The very silence which follows the cessation of such a battle becomes a weight upon the heart at first, rather than a relief; and though the work of mutual destruction was at an end, the *Danbrog* was at this time drifting about in flames; presently she blew up; while our boats, which had put off in all directions to assist her, were endeavouring to pick up her devoted crew, few of whom could be saved.

The fate of these men, after the gallantry which they had displayed, particularly affected Nelson; for there was nothing in this action of that indignation against the enemy, and that impression of retributive justice, which at the Nile had given a sterner temper to his mind, and a sense of austere delight in beholding the vengeance of which he was the appointed minister. The Danes were an honourable foe; they were of English mould as well as English blood; and now that the battle had ceased, he regarded them rather as brethren than as enemies.

There was another reflection also which mingled with these melancholy thoughts, and predisposed him to receive them. He was not here master of his own movements, as at Egypt; he had won the day by disobeying his orders; and in so far as he had been successful, had convicted the commander-in-chief of an error in judgment.

"Well," said he, as he left the *Elephant*, "I have fought contrary to orders, and I shall perhaps be hanged. Never mind: let them!"

This was the language of a man who, while he is giving utterance to uneasy thought, clothes it half in jest, because he half repents that it has been disclosed. His services had been too eminent on that day, his judgment too conspicuous, his success too signal, for any commander, however jealous of his own authority, or envious of another's merits, to express anything but satisfaction and gratitude: which Sir Hyde heartily felt, and sincerely expressed.

It was speedily agreed that there should be a suspension of hostilities for four-and-twenty hours; that all the prizes should be surrendered, and the wounded Danes carried on shore. There was a pressing necessity for this, for the Danes, either from too much confidence in the strength of their position and the difficulty of the channel, or supposing that the wounded might be carried on shore during the action, which was found totally impracticable, or perhaps from the confusion which the attack excited, had provided no surgeons; so that, when our men boarded the captured ships, they found many of the mangled and mutilated Danes bleeding to death for want of proper assistance—a scene, of all others, the most shocking to a brave man's feelings.

The boats of Sir Hyde's division were actively employed all night in bringing out the prizes, and in getting afloat the ships which were on shore.

At daybreak, Nelson, who had slept in his own ship, the *St. George*, rowed to the *Elephant*; and his delight at finding her afloat seemed to give him new life. There he took a hasty breakfast, praising the men for their exertions, and then pushed off to the prizes, which had not yet been removed.

The *Zealand*, seventy-four, the last which struck, had drifted on the shoal under the Trekroner; and relying, as it seems, upon the protection which that battery might have afforded, refused to acknowledge herself captured; saying, that though it was true her flag was not to be seen, her pendant was still flying.

Nelson ordered one of our brigs and three long-boats to approach her, and rowed up himself to one of the enemy's ships, to communicate with the commodore. This officer proved to be an old acquaintance, whom he had known in the West Indies; so he invited himself on board, and with that urbanity as well as decision which always characterised him, urged his claim to the *Zealand* so well that it was admitted.

The men from the boats lashed a cable round her bowsprit, and the gun-vessel towed her away. It is affirmed, and probably with truth, that the Danes felt more pain at beholding this than at all their misfortunes on the preceding day; and one of the officers, Commodore Steen Rille, went to the Trekroner battery, and asked the commander why he had not sunk the *Zealand*, rather than suffer her thus to be carried off by the enemy?

This was, indeed, a mournful day for Copenhagen! It was Good Friday; but the general agitation, and the mourning which was in every house, made all distinction of days be forgotten. There were, at that hour, thousands in that city who felt, and more perhaps who needed, the consolations of Christianity, but few or none who could be calm enough to think of its observances.

The English were actively employed in refitting their own ships, securing the prizes, and distributing the prisoners; the Danes, in carrying on shore and disposing of the wounded and the dead.

It had been a murderous action. Our loss, in killed and wounded, was 953. Part of this slaughter might have been spared.

The commanding officer of the troops on board one of our ships asked where his men should be stationed? He was told that they could be of no use! that they were not near enough for musketry, and were not wanted at the guns; they had, therefore, better go below.

This, he said, was impossible; it would be a disgrace that could never be wiped away. They were, therefore, drawn up upon the gangway, to satisfy this cruel point of honour; and there, without the possibility of annoying the enemy, they were mowed down!

The loss of the Danes, including prisoners, amounted to about six thousand.

The negotiations, meantime, went on; and it was agreed that Nelson should have an interview with the prince the following day.

Hardy and Freemantle landed with him. This was a thing as unexampled as the other circumstances of the battle. A strong guard was appointed to escort him to the palace, as much for the purpose of security as of honour. The populace, according to the British account, showed a mixture of admiration, curiosity, and displeasure, at beholding that man in the midst of them who had inflicted such wounds upon Denmark.

But there were neither acclamations nor murmurs. "The people," says a Dane, "did not degrade themselves with the former, nor disgrace themselves with the latter: the admiral was received as one brave enemy ever ought to receive another—he was received with respect."

The preliminaries of the negotiation were adjusted at this interview. During the repast which followed, Nelson, with all the sincerity of his character, bore willing testimony to the valour of his foes. He told the prince that he had been in a hundred and five engagements, but that this was the most tremendous of all.

"The French," he said, "fought bravely; but they could not have stood for one hour the fight which the Danes had supported for four."

He requested that Villemoes might be introduced to him; and, shaking hands with the youth, told the prince that he ought to be made an admiral. The prince replied: "If, my lord, I am to make all my brave officers admirals, I should have no captains or lieutenants in my service."

The sympathy of the Danes for their countrymen who had bled in their defence, was not weakened by distance of time or place in this instance. Things needful for the service, or the comfort of the wounded, were sent in profusion to the hospitals, till the superintendents gave public notice that they could receive no more.

On the third day after the action, the dead were buried in the naval churchyard: the ceremony was made as public and as solemn as the occasion required; such a procession had never before been seen in that, or perhaps in any other city. A public monument was erected upon the spot where the slain were gathered together.

A subscription was opened on the day of the funeral for the relief of the sufferers, and collections in aid of it made throughout all the churches in the kingdom. This appeal to the feelings of the people was made with circumstances which gave it full effect. A monument was raised in the midst of the church, surmounted by the Danish colours: young maidens, dressed in white, stood round it, with either one who had been wounded in the battle, or the widow and orphans of some one who had fallen: a suitable oration was delivered from the pulpit, and patriotic hymns and songs were afterwards performed.

Medals were distributed to all the officers, and to the men who had distinguished themselves. Poets and painters vied with each other in celebrating a battle which, disastrous as it was, had yet been honourable to their country: some, with pardonable sophistry, represented the advantage of the day as on their own side. One writer discovered a more curious, but less disputable ground of satisfaction, in the reflection that Nelson, as may be inferred from his name, was of Danish descent, and his actions therefore, the Dane argued, were attributable to Danish valour.

The negotiation was continued during the five following days; and in that interval the prizes were disposed of, in a manner which was little approved by Nelson.

Six line-of-battle ships and eight praams had been taken. Of these the *Holstein*, sixty-four, was the only one which was sent home. The *Zealand* was a finer ship; but the *Zealand* and all the others were burned, and their brass battering cannon sunk with the hulls in such shoal water, that, when the fleet returned from Revel, they found the Danes, with craft over the wrecks, employed in getting the guns up again.

Nelson, though he forbore from any public expression of displeasure at seeing the proofs and trophies of his victory destroyed, did not forget to represent to the Admiralty the case of those who were thus deprived of their prize-money.

"Whether," said he to Earl St. Vincent, "Sir Hyde Parker may mention the subject to you, I know not; for he is rich, and does not want it: nor is it, you will believe me, any desire to get a few hundred pounds that actuates me to address this letter to you; but justice to the brave officers and men who fought on that day. It is true our opponents were in hulks and floats, only adapted for the position they were in; but that made our battle so much the harder, and victory so much the more difficult to obtain. Believe me, I have weighed all circumstances; and, in my conscience, I think that the king should send a gracious message to the House of Commons for a gift to this fleet; for what must be the natural feelings of the officers and men belonging to it, to see their rich commander-in-chief burn all the fruits of their victory, which, if fitted up and sent to England (as many of them might have been by dismantling part of our fleet), would have sold for a good round sum."

On the 9th, Nelson landed again, to conclude the terms of the armistice. During its continuance the armed ships and vessels of Denmark were to remain in their actual situation, as to armament, equipment, and hostile position; and the treaty of armed neutrality, as far as related to the co-operation of Denmark, was suspended. The prisoners were to be sent on shore; an acknowledgment being given for them, and for the wounded also, that they might be carried to Great Britain's credit in the account of war, in case hostilities should be renewed. The British fleet was allowed to provide itself with all things requisite for the health and comfort of its men.

A difficulty arose respecting the duration of the armistice. The Danish commissioners fairly stated their fears of Russia; and Nelson, with that frankness which sound policy and the sense of power seem often to require as well as justify in diplomacy, told them his reason for demanding a long term was, that he might have time to act against the Russian fleet, and then return to Copenhagen.

Neither party would yield upon this point; and one of the Danes hinted at the renewal of hostilities.

"Renew hostilities!" cried Nelson to one of his friends—for he understood French enough to comprehend what was said, though not to answer it in the same language—

"Tell him we are ready at a moment! ready to bombard this very night!"

The conference, however, proceeded amicably on both sides; and as the commissioners could not agree on this head, they broke up, leaving Nelson to settle it with the prince.

A levee was held forthwith in one of the state-rooms, a scene well suited for such a consultation; for all these rooms had been stripped of their furniture, in fear of a bombardment. To a bombardment also Nelson was looking at this time: fatigue and anxiety, and vexation at the dilatory measures of the commander-in-chief, combined to make him irritable; and as he was on his way to the prince's dining-room, he whispered to the officer on whose arm he was leaning, "Though I have only one eye, I can see that all this will burn well."

After dinner he was closeted with the prince; and they agreed that the armistice should continue fourteen weeks; and that, at its termination, fourteen days' notice should be given before the recommencement of hostilities.

An official account of the battle was published by Olfert Fischer, the Danish commander-in-chief, in which it was asserted that our force was greatly superior; nevertheless, that two of our ships of the line had struck; that the others were so weakened, and especially Lord Nelson's own ship, as to fire only single shots for an hour before the end of the action; and that this hero himself, in the middle and very heat of the conflict, sent a flag of truce on shore, to propose a cessation of hostilities. For the truth of this account the Dane appealed to the prince, and all those who, like him, had been eyewitnesses of the scene.

Nelson was exceedingly indignant at such a statement, and addressed a letter in confutation of it to the Adjutant-General Lindholm; thinking this incumbent on him for the information of the prince, since His Royal Highness had been appealed to as a witness: "Otherwise," said he, "had Commodore Fischer confined himself to his own veracity, I should have treated his official letter with the contempt it deserved, and allowed the world to appreciate the merits of the two commanding officers."

After pointing out and detecting some of the misstatements in the account, he proceeds: "As to his nonsense about victory, His Royal Highness will not much credit him. I sunk, burnt, captured, or drove into the harbour, the whole line of defence to the southward of the Crown Islands. He says he is told that two British ships struck. Why did he not take possession of them? I took possession of his as fast as they struck. The reason is clear, that he did not believe it: he must have known the falsity of the report. He states that the ship in which I had the honour to hoist my flag fired latterly only single guns. It is true; for steady and cool were my brave fellows, and did not wish to throw away a single shot. He seems to exult that I sent on shore a flag of truce. You know, and His Royal Highness knows, that the guns fired from the shore could only fire through the Danish ships which had surrendered; and that, if I fired at the shore, it could only be in the same manner. God forbid that I should destroy an unresisting Dane! When they become my prisoners, I become their protector."

This letter was written in terms of great asperity to the Danish commander. Lindholm replied in a manner every way honourable to himself. He vindicated the commodore in some points, and excused him in others; reminding Nelson that every commander-in-chief was liable to receive incorrect reports. With a natural desire to represent the action in the most favourable light to Denmark, he took into the comparative strength of the two parties the ships which were aground, and which could not get into action; and omitted the Trekroner and the batteries upon Amak Island.

He disclaimed all idea of claiming as a victory, "what, to every intent and purpose," said he, "was a defeat—but not an inglorious one. As to your lordship's motive for sending a flag of truce, it never can be misconstrued and your subsequent conduct has sufficiently shown that humanity is always the companion of true valour. You have done more: you have shown yourself a friend to the re-establishment of peace and good harmony between this country and Great Britain. It is, therefore, with the sincerest esteem I shall always feel myself attached to your lordship."

Thus handsomely winding up his reply, he soothed and contented Nelson; who drawing up a memorandum of the comparative force of the two parties for his own satisfaction, assured Lindholm that, if the commodore's statement had been in the same manly and honourable strain, he would have been the last man to have noticed any little inaccuracies which might get into a commander-in-chief's public letter.

For the battle of Copenhagen Nelson was raised to the rank of viscount—an inadequate mark of reward for services so splendid, and of such paramount importance to the dearest interests of England. There was, however, some prudence in dealing out honours to him step by step: had he lived long enough, he would have fought his way up to a dukedom.

Chapter 8
1801–1805

Sir Hyde Parker is recalled and Nelson appointed Commander—He goes to Revel—Settlement of Affairs in the Baltic—Unsuccessful Attempt upon the Flotilla at Boulogne—Peace of Amiens—Nelson takes Command in the Mediterranean on the Renewal of the War—Escape of the Toulon Fleet—Nelson chases them to the West Indies and back—Delivers up his Squadron to Admiral Cornwallis and lands in England.

When Nelson informed Earl St. Vincent that the armistice had been concluded, he told him also, without reserve, his own discontent at the dilatoriness and indecision which he witnessed, and could not remedy.

"No man," said he, "but those who are on the spot, can tell what I have gone through, and do suffer. I make no scruple in saying, that I would have been at Revel fourteen days ago! that, without this armistice, the fleet would never have gone, but by order of the Admiralty; and with it, I daresay, we shall not go this week. I wanted Sir Hyde to let me, at least, go and cruise off Carlscrona, to prevent the Revel ships from getting in. I said I would not go to Revel to take any of those laurels which I was sure he would reap there. Think for me, my dear lord: and if I have deserved well, let me return; if ill, for Heaven's sake supersede me, for I cannot exist in this state."

Fatigue, incessant anxiety, and a climate little suited to one of a tender constitution, which had now for many years been accustomed to more genial latitudes, made him at this time seriously determine upon returning home. "If the northern business were not settled," he said, "they must send more admirals; for the keen air of the north had cut him to the heart." He felt the want of activity and decision in the commander-in-chief more keenly; and this affected his spirits, and, consequently, his health, more than the inclemency of the Baltic.

Soon after the armistice was signed, Sir Hyde proceeded to the eastward with such ships as were fit for service, leaving Nelson to follow with the rest, as soon as those which had received slight damages should be repaired, and the rest sent to England. In passing between the isles of Amak and Saltholm, most of the ships touched the ground, and some of them stuck fast for a while: no serious injury, however, was sustained.

It was intended to act against the Russians first, before the breaking up of the frost should enable them to leave Revel; but learning on the way that the Swedes had put to sea to effect a junction with them, Sir Hyde altered his course, in hopes of intercepting this part of the enemy's force.

Nelson had, at this time, provided for the more pressing emergencies of the service, and prepared on the 18th to follow the fleet.

The *St. George* drew too much water to pass the channel between the isles without being lightened; the guns were therefore taken out, and put on board an American vessel; a contrary wind, however, prevented Nelson from moving; and on that same evening, while he was thus delayed, information reached him of the relative situation of the Swedish and British fleets, and the probability of an action.

The fleet was nearly ten leagues distant, and both wind and current contrary, but it was not possible that Nelson could wait for a favourable season under such an expectation. He ordered his boat immediately, and stepped into it. Night was setting in, one of the cold spring nights of the north; and it was discovered, soon after they left the ship, that in their haste they had forgotten to provide him with a boat-cloak. He, however, forbade them to return for one; and when one of his companions offered his own great-coat, and urged him to make use of it, he replied, "I thank you very much; but, to tell you the truth, my anxiety keeps me sufficiently warm at present."

"Do you think," said he presently, "that our fleet has quitted Bornholm? If it has, we must follow it to Carlscrona."

About midnight he reached it, and once more got on board the *Elephant*.

On the following morning the Swedes were discovered; as soon, however, as they perceived the English approaching, they retired, and took shelter in Carlscrona, behind the batteries on the island, at the entrance of that port. Sir Hyde sent in a flag of truce, stating that Denmark had concluded an armistice, and requiring an explicit declaration from the court of Sweden, whether it would adhere to or abandon the hostile measures which it had taken against the rights and interests of Great Britain?

The commander, Vice-Admiral Cronstadt, replied, "That he could not answer a question which did not come within the particular circle of his duty; but that the king was then at Maloe, and would soon be at Carlscrona."

Gustavus[81] shortly afterwards arrived, and an answer was then returned to this effect: "That his Swedish majesty would not, for a moment, fail to fulfil, with fidelity and sincerity, the engagements he had entered into with his allies; but he would not refuse to listen to equitable proposals made by deputies furnished with proper authority by the King of Great Britain to the united northern powers."

Satisfied with this answer, and with the known disposition of the Swedish court, Sir Hyde sailed for the Gulf of Finland; but he had not proceeded far before a despatch boat from the Russian ambassador at Copenhagen arrived, bringing intelligence of the death of the Emperor Paul, and that his successor Alexander had accepted the offer made by England to his father of terminating the dispute by a convention: the British admiral was, therefore, required to desist from all further hostilities.

It was Nelson's maxim, that, to negotiate with effect, force should be at hand, and in a situation to act. The fleet, having been reinforced from England, amounted to eighteen sail of the line, and the wind was fair for Revel. There he would have sailed immediately to place himself between that division of the Russian fleet and the squadron at Cronstadt, in case this offer should prove insincere.

Sir Hyde, on the other hand, believed that the death of Paul had effected all which was necessary. The manner of that death, indeed, rendered it apparent that a change of policy would take place in the cabi-

81 King Gustav IV of Sweden (1778–1837), reigned 1792 to 1809. Considered hopelessly inept by his subjects, particularly following a disastrous war with Russia that resulted in the loss of Finland, Gustav abdicated in 1809 following a coup. He was succeeded by his uncle, who became Charles XIII, and who had previously served as regent during Gustav's minority.

net of Petersburgh[82]; but Nelson never trusted anything to the uncertain events of time, which could possibly be secured by promptitude or resolution. It was not, therefore, without severe mortification, that he saw the commander-in-chief return to the coast of Zealand, and anchor in Kioge Bay, there to wait patiently for what might happen.

There the fleet remained till dispatches arrived from home, on the 5th of May, recalling Sir Hyde, and appointing Nelson commander-in-chief.

Nelson wrote to Earl St. Vincent that he was unable to hold this honourable station. Admiral Graves also was so ill as to be confined to his bed; and he entreated that some person might come out and take the command.

"I will endeavour," said he, "to do my best while I remain; but, my dear lord, I shall either soon go to heaven, I hope, or must rest quiet for a time. If Sir Hyde were gone, I would now be under sail."

On the day when this was written, he received news of his appointment.

Not a moment was now lost. His first signal, as commander-in-chief, was to hoist in all launches and prepare to weigh; and on the 7th he sailed from Kioge.

Part of his fleet was left at Bornholm, to watch the Swedes, from whom he required and obtained an assurance that the British trade in the Cattegat and in the Baltic should not be molested; and saying how unpleasant it would be to him if anything should happen which might for a moment disturb the returning harmony between Sweden and Great Britain, he apprised them that he was not directed to abstain from hostilities should he meet with the Swedish fleet at sea.

Meantime he himself; with ten sail of the line, two frigates, a brig, and a schooner, made for the Gulf of Finland. Paul, in one of the freaks of his tyranny, had seized upon all the British effects in Russia, and even considered British subjects as his prisoners.

"I will have all the English shipping and property restored," said Nelson, "but I will do nothing violently, neither commit the affairs of my country, nor suffer Russia to mix the affairs of Denmark or Sweden with the detention of our ships."

---

82 Paul I was assassinated on the night of 23 March 1801. He was succeeded by his son, Alexander I (1777–1825).

The wind was fair, and carried him in four days to Revel Roads. But the Bay had been clear of firm ice on the 29th of April, while the English were lying idly at Kioge. The Russians had cut through the ice in the mole six feet thick, and their whole squadron had sailed for Cronstadt on the 3rd. Before that time it had lain at the mercy of the English.

"Nothing," Nelson said, "if it had been right to make the attack, could have saved one ship of them in two hours after our entering the bay."

It so happened that there was no cause to regret the opportunity which had been lost, and Nelson immediately put the intentions of Russia to the proof. He sent on shore, to say that he came with friendly views, and was ready to return a salute. On their part the salute was delayed, till a message was sent to them to inquire for what reason; and the officer whose neglect had occasioned the delay, was put under arrest. Nelson wrote to the emperor, proposing to wait on him personally and congratulate him on his accession, and urged the immediate release of British subjects, and restoration of British property.

The answer arrived on the 16th: Nelson, meantime, had exchanged visits with the governor, and the most friendly intercourse had subsisted between the ships and the shore.

Alexander's ministers, in their reply, expressed their surprise at the arrival of a British fleet in a Russian port, and their wish that it should return: they professed, on the part of Russia, the most friendly disposition towards Great Britain; but declined the personal visit of Lord Nelson, unless he came in a single ship.

There was a suspicion implied in this which stung Nelson; and he said the Russian ministers would never have written thus if their fleet had been at Revel.

He wrote an immediate reply, expressing what he felt; he told the court of Petersburgh, "That the word of a British admiral, when given in explanation of any part of his conduct, was as sacred as that of any sovereign's in Europe." And he repeated, "that, under other circumstances, it would have been his anxious wish to have paid his personal respects to the emperor, and signed with his own hand the act of amity between the two countries."

Having despatched this, he stood out to sea immediately, leaving a brig to bring off the provisions which had been contracted for, and to settle the accounts. "I hope all is right," said he, writing to our ambassador at Berlin; "but seamen are but bad negotiators; for we put to issue in five minutes what diplomatic forms would be five months doing."

On his way down the Baltic, however, he met the Russian admiral, Tchitchagof, whom the emperor, in reply to Sir Hyde's overtures, had sent to communicate personally with the British commander-in-chief. The reply was such as had been wished and expected; and these negotiators going, seamen-like, straight to their object, satisfied each other of the friendly intentions of their respective governments.

Nelson then anchored off Rostock; and there he received an answer to his last despatch from Revel, in which the Russian court expressed their regret that there should have been any misconception between them; informed him that the British vessels which Paul had detained were ordered to be liberated, and invited him to Petersburgh, in whatever mode might be most agreeable to himself.

Other honours awaited him: the Duke of Mecklenburgh Strelitz, the Queen's brother, came to visit him on board his ship; and towns of the inland parts of Mecklenburgh sent deputations, with their public books of record, that they might have the name of Nelson in them written by his own hand.

From Rostock the fleet returned to Kioge Bay. Nelson saw that the temper of the Danes towards England was such as naturally arose from the chastisement which they had so recently received. "In this nation," said he, "we shall not be forgiven for having the upper hand of them: I only thank God we have, or they would try to humble us to the dust."

He saw also that the Danish cabinet was completely subservient to France: a French officer was at this time the companion and counsellor of the Crown Prince; and things were done in such open violation of the armistice, that Nelson thought a second infliction of vengeance would soon be necessary.

He wrote to the Admiralty, requesting a clear and explicit reply to his inquiry, Whether the commander-in-chief was at liberty to hold the language becoming a British admiral? "Which, very probably," said he, "if I am here, will break the armistice, and set Copenhagen in a blaze. I see everything which is dirty and mean going on, and the Prince Royal at the head of it. Ships have been masted, guns taken on board, floating batteries prepared, and except hauling out and completing their rigging, everything is done in defiance of the treaty. My heart burns at seeing the word of a prince, nearly allied to our good king, so falsified; but his conduct is such, that he will lose his kingdom if he goes on; for Jacobins rule in Denmark. I have made no representations yet, as it would be useless to do so until I have the power of correction. All I beg, in the name of the future commander-in-chief, is, that the orders may be clear; for enough is done to break twenty treaties, if it should be wished, or to make the Prince Royal humble himself before British generosity."

Nelson was not deceived in his judgment of the Danish cabinet, but the battle of Copenhagen had crippled its power. The death of the Czar Paul had broken the confederacy; and that cabinet, therefore, was compelled to defer till a more convenient season the indulgence of its enmity towards Great Britain.

Soon afterwards Admiral Sir Charles Maurice Pole arrived to take the command. The business, military and political, had by that time been so far completed that the presence of the British fleet soon became no longer necessary. Sir Charles, however, made the short time of his command memorable, by passing the Great Belt for the first time with line-of-battle ships, working through the channel against adverse winds.

When Nelson left the fleet, this speedy termination of the expedition, though confidently expected, was not certain; and he, in his unwillingness to weaken the British force, thought at one time of traversing Jutland in his boat, by the canal to Tonningen on the Eyder and finding his way home from thence. This intention was not executed; but he returned in a brig, declining to accept a frigate, which few admirals would have done, especially if, like him, they suffered from sea-sickness in a small vessel.

On his arrival at Yarmouth, the first thing he did was to visit the hospital and see the men who had been wounded in the late battle—that victory which had added new glory to the name of Nelson, and which was of more importance even than the battle of the Nile to the honour, the strength, and security of England.

The feelings of Nelson's friends, upon the news of his great victory at Copenhagen, were highly described by Sir William Hamilton in a letter to him. "We can only expect," he says, "what we know well, and often said before, that Nelson *was, is,* and to the *last will ever be, the first.* Emma did not know whether she was on her head or heels—in such a hurry to tell your great news, that she could utter nothing but tears of joy and tenderness. I went to Davison, and found him still in bed, having had a severe fit of the gout, and with your letter, which he had just received;

and he cried like a child; but, what was very extraordinary, assured me that, from the instant he had read your letter, all pain had left him, and that he felt himself able to get up and walk about.

"Your brother, Mrs. Nelson, and Horace dined with us. Your brother was more extraordinary than ever. He would get up suddenly and cut a caper, rubbing his hands every time that the thought of your fresh laurels came into his head. But I am sure that no one really rejoiced more at heart than I did. I have lived too long to have ecstasies! But with calm reflection, I felt for my friend having got to the very summit of glory! the *ne plus ultra!* that he has had another opportunity of rendering his country the most important service, and manifesting again his judgment, his intrepidity, and his humanity."

He had not been many weeks on shore before he was called upon to undertake a service, for which no Nelson was required. Buonaparte, who was now first consul, and in reality sole ruler of France, was making preparations, upon a great scale, for invading England; but his schemes in the Baltic had been baffled; fleets could not be created as they were wanted; and his armies, therefore, were to come over in gun-boats, and such small craft as could be rapidly built or collected for the occasion.

From the former governments of France such threats have only been matter of insult and policy: in Buonaparte they were sincere; for this adventurer, intoxicated with success, already began to imagine that all things were to be submitted to his fortune. We had not at that time proved the superiority of our soldiers over the French; and the unreflecting multitude were not to be persuaded that an invasion could only be effected by numerous and powerful fleets. A general alarm was excited; and, in condescension to this unworthy feeling, Nelson was appointed to a command, extending from Orfordness to Beachy Head, on both shores—a sort of service, he said, for which he felt no other ability than what might be found in his zeal.

To this service, however, such as it was, he applied with his wonted alacrity; though in no cheerful frame of mind. To Lady Hamilton, his only female correspondent, he says at this time; "I am not in very good spirits; and, except that our country demands all our services and abilities to bring about an honourable peace, nothing should prevent my being the bearer of my own letter. But, my dear friend, I know you are so true and loyal an Englishwoman, that you would hate those who would not stand forth in defence of our king, laws, religion, and all that is dear to us. It is your sex that makes us go forth, and seem to tell us, 'None but the brave deserve the fair'; and if we fall, we still live in the hearts of those females. It is your sex that rewards us; it is your sex who cherish our memories; and you, my dear honoured friend, are, believe me, the first, the best of your sex. I have been the world around, and in every corner of it, and never yet saw your equal, or even one who could be put in comparison with you. You know how to reward virtue, honour, and courage, and never to ask if it is placed in a prince, duke, lord, or peasant."

Having hoisted his flag in the *Medusa* frigate, he went to reconnoitre Boulogne, the point from which it was supposed the great attempt would be made, and which the French, in fear of an attack themselves, were fortifying with all care. He approached near enough to sink two of their floating batteries, and to destroy a few gun-boats which were without the pier. What damage was done within could not be ascertained.

"Boulogne," he said, "was certainly not a very pleasant place that morning; but," he added, "it is not my wish to injure the poor inhabitants; and the town is spared as much as the nature of the service will admit."

Enough was done to show the enemy that they could not, with impunity, come outside their own ports. Nelson was satisfied by what he saw, that they meant to make an attempt from this place, but that it was impracticable; for the least wind at W.N.W. and they were lost.

The ports of Flushing and Flanders were better points: there we could not tell by our eyes what means of transport were provided. From thence, therefore, if it came forth at all, the expedition would come.

"And what a forlorn undertaking!" said he: "consider cross tides, &c. As for rowing, that is impossible. It Is perfectly right to be prepared for a mad government; but with the active force which has been given me, I may pronounce it almost impracticable."

That force had been got together with an alacrity which has seldom been equalled. On the 28th of July, we were, in Nelson's own words, literally at the foundation of our fabric of defence, and twelve days afterwards we were so prepared on the enemy's coast that he did not believe they could get three miles from their ports.

The *Medusa*, returning to our own shores, anchored in the rolling ground off Harwich; and when Nelson wished to get to the Nore in her, the wind rendered it impossible to proceed there by the usual channel. In haste to be at the Nore, remembering that he had been a tolerable pilot for the mouth of the Thames in his younger days, and thinking it necessary that he should know all that could be known of the navigation, he requested the maritime surveyor of the coast, Mr. Spence, to get him into the Swin by any channel; for neither the pilots which he had on board, nor the Harwich ones, would take charge of the ship.

No vessel drawing more than fourteen feet had ever before ventured over the Naze. Mr. Spence, however, who had surveyed the channel, carried her safely through. The channel has since been called Nelson's, though he himself wished it to be named after the *Medusa*: his name needed no new memorial.

Nelson's eye was upon Flushing. "To take possession of that place," he said, "would be a week's expedition for four or five thousand troops."

This, however, required a consultation with the Admiralty; and that something might be done, meantime he resolved upon attacking the flotilla in the mouth of the Boulogne harbour. This resolution was made in deference to the opinion of others, and to the public feeling, which was so preposterously excited.

He himself scrupled not to assert that the French army would never embark at Boulogne for the invasion of England; and he owned that this boat warfare was not exactly congenial to his feelings. Into Helvoet or Flushing he should be happy to lead, if Government turned their thoughts that way.

"While I serve," said he, "I will do it actively, and to the very best of my abilities. I require nursing like a child," he added; "my mind carries me beyond my strength, and will do me up; but such is my nature."

The attack was made by the boats of the squadron in five divisions, under Captains Somerville, Parker, Cotgrave, Jones, and Conn. The previous essay had taught the French the weak parts of their position; and they omitted no means of strengthening it, and of guarding against the expected attempt.

The boats put off about half an hour before midnight; but, owing to the darkness, and tide and half-tide, which must always make night attacks so uncertain on the coasts of the Channel, the divisions separated. One could not arrive at all; another not till near daybreak.

The others made their attack gallantly; but the enemy were fully prepared: every vessel was defended by long poles, headed with iron spikes, projecting from their sides: strong nettings were braced up to their lower yards; they were moored by the bottom to the shore, they were strongly manned with soldiers, and protected by land batteries, and the shore was lined with troops. Many were taken possession of; and, though they could not have been brought out, would have been burned, had not the French resorted to a mode of offence, which they have often used, but which no other people have ever been wicked enough to employ. The moment the firing ceased on board one of their own vessels they fired upon it from the shore, perfectly regardless of their own men.

The commander of one of the French divisions acted like a generous enemy. He hailed the boats as they approached, and cried out in English: "Let me advise you, my brave Englishmen, to keep your distance: you can do nothing here; and it is only uselessly shedding the blood of brave men to make the attempt."

The French official account boasted of the victory. "The combat," it said, "took place in sight of both countries; it was the first of the kind, and the historian would have cause to make this remark."

They guessed our loss at four or five hundred; it amounted to one hundred and seventy-two. In his private letters to the Admiralty, Nelson affirmed, that had our force arrived as he intended, it was not all the chains in France which could have prevented our men from bringing off the whole of the vessels. There had been no error committed, and never did Englishmen display more courage.

Upon this point Nelson was fully satisfied; but he said he should never bring himself again to allow any attack wherein he was not personally concerned; and that his mind suffered more than if he had had a leg shot off in the affair. He grieved particularly for Captain Parker, an excellent officer, to whom he was greatly attached, and who had an aged father looking to him for assistance. His thigh was shattered in the action; and the wound proved mortal, after some weeks of suffering and manly resignation.

During this interval, Nelson's anxiety was very great. "Dear Parker is my child," said he; "for I found him in distress." And when he received the tidings of his death, he replied: "You will judge of my feelings: God's will be done. I beg that his hair may be cut off and given me; it shall be buried in my grave. Poor Mr. Parker! What a son has he lost! If I were to say I was content, I should lie; but I shall endeavour to submit with all the fortitude in my power. His loss has made a wound in my heart, which time will hardly heal."

"You ask me, my dear friend," he says to Lady Hamilton, "if I am going on more expeditions? and even if I was to forfeit your friendship, which is dearer to me than all the world, I can tell you nothing. For, I go out: I see the enemy, and can get at them, it is my duty: and you would naturally hate me, if I kept back one moment. I long to pay them for their tricks t'other day, the debt of a drubbing, which surely I'll pay: but *when, where,* or *how,* it is impossible, your own good sense must tell you, for me or mortal man to say."

Yet he now wished to be relieved from this service. The country, he said, had attached a confidence to his name, which he had submitted to, and therefore had cheerfully repaired to the station; but this boat business, though it might be part of a great plan of invasion, could never be the only one, and he did not think it was a command for a vice-admiral.

It was not that he wanted a more lucrative situation; for, seriously indisposed as he was, and low-spirited from private considerations, he did not know, if the Mediterranean were vacant, that he should be equal to undertake it. He was offended with the Admiralty for refusing him leave to go to town when he had solicited: in reply to a friendly letter from Troubridge he says, "I am at this moment as firmly of opinion as ever, that Lord St. Vincent and yourself should have allowed of my coming to town for my own affairs, for every one knows I left it without a thought for myself."

His letters at this time breathe an angry feeling toward Troubridge, who was now become, he said, one of his lords and masters.

"I have a letter from him," he says, "recommending me to wear flannel shirts. Does he care for me? *No:* but never mind. They shall work hard to get me again. The cold has settled in my bowels. I wish the Admiralty had my complaint: but they have no bowels, at least for me. I daresay Master Troubridge is grown fat; I know I am grown lean with my complaint, which, but for their indifference about my health, could never have happened; or, at least, I should have got well long ago in a warm room with a good fire and sincere friend."

In the same tone of bitterness he complained that he was not able to promote those whom he thought deserving. "Troubridge," he says, "has so completely prevented my ever mentioning anybody's service, that I am become a cipher, and he has gained a victory over Nelson's spirit. I am kept here, for what?—he may be able to tell, I cannot. But long it cannot, shall not be."

An end was put to this uncomfortable state of mind when, fortunately (on that account) for him, as well as happily for the nation, the peace of Amiens was just at this time [25 March 1802] signed. Nelson rejoiced that the experiment was made, but was well aware that it was an experiment. He saw what he called the misery of peace, unless the utmost vigilance and prudence were exerted; and he expressed, in bitter terms, his proper indignation at the manner in which the mob of London welcomed the French general who brought the ratification saying, "that they made him ashamed of his country."

He had purchased a house and estate at Merton, in Surrey, meaning to pass his days there in the society of Sir William and Lady Hamilton. He had indulged in pleasant dreams when looking on to this as his place of residence and rest.

"To be sure," he says, "we shall employ the tradespeople of our village in preference to any others in what we want for common use, and give them every encouragement to be kind and attentive to us. Have we a nice church at Merton? We will set an example of goodness to the under-parishioners. I admire the pigs and poultry. Sheep are certainly most beneficial to eat off the grass. Do you get paid for them, and take care that they are kept on the premises all night, for that is the time they do good to the land. They should be folded. Is your head-man a good person, and true to our interest? I intend to have a farming-book. I expect that all animals will increase where you are, for I never expect that you will suffer any to be killed. No person can take amiss our not visiting. The answer from me will always be very civil thanks, but that I wish to live retired. We shall have our sea-friends; and I know Sir William thinks they are the best."

This place he had never seen till he was now welcomed there by the friends to whom he had so passionately devoted himself, and who were not less sincerely attached to him. The place, and everything which Lady Hamilton had done to it, delighted him; and he declared that the longest liver should possess it all. Here he amused himself with angling in the Wandle, having been a good fly-fisher in former days, and learning now to practise with his left hand what he could no longer pursue as a solitary diversion.

His pensions for his victories, and for the loss of his eye and arm, amounted with his half-pay to about £3,400 a year. From this he gave £1,800 to Lady Nelson, £200 to a brother's widow, and £150 for the education of his children; and he paid £500 interest for borrowed money; so that Nelson was comparatively a poor man; and though much of the pecuniary embarrassment which he endured was occasioned by the separation from his wife—even if that cause had not existed, his income would not have been sufficient for the rank which he held, and the claims which would necessarily be made upon his bounty.

The depression of spirits under which he had long laboured arose partly from this state of his circumstances, and partly from the other disquietudes in which his connection with Lady Hamilton had involved him—a connection which it was not possible his father could behold without sorrow and displeasure.

Mr. Nelson, however, was soon persuaded that the attachment, which Lady Nelson regarded with natural jealousy and resentment, did not in reality pass the bounds of ardent and romantic admiration: a passion which the manners and accomplishments of Lady Hamilton, fascinating as they were, would not have been able to excite, if they had not been accompanied by more uncommon intellectual endowments, and by a character which, both in its strength and in its weakness, resembled his own. It did not, therefore, require much explanation to reconcile him to his son—an event the more essential to Nelson's happiness, because, a few months afterwards, the good old man died at the age of seventy-nine.

Soon after the conclusion of peace, tidings arrived of our final and decisive successes in Egypt; in consequence of which, the common council voted their thanks to the army and navy for bringing the campaign to so glorious a conclusion.

When Nelson, after the action of Cape St. Vincent, had been entertained at a city feast, he had observed to the lord mayor, "that, if the city continued its generosity, the navy would ruin them in gifts."

To which the lord mayor replied, putting his hand upon the admiral's shoulder: "Do you find victories and we will find rewards."

Nelson, as he said, had kept his word, had doubly fulfilled his part of the contract, but no thanks had been voted for the battle of Copenhagen; and feeling that he and his companions in that day's glory had a fair and honourable claim to this reward, he took the present opportunity of addressing a letter to the lord mayor, complaining of the omission and the injustice.

"The smallest services," said he, "rendered by the army or navy to the country, have always been noticed by the great city of London with one exception—the glorious 2nd of April—a day when the greatest dangers of navigation were overcome; and the Danish force, which they thought impregnable, totally taken or destroyed, by the consummate skill of our commanders, and by the undaunted bravery of as gallant a band as ever defended the rights of this country. For myself, if I were only personally concerned, I should bear the stigma, attempted to be now first placed upon my brow, with humility.

"But, my lord, I am the natural guardian of the fame of all the officers of the navy, army, and marines who fought, and so profusely bled, under my command on that day. Again I disclaim for myself more merit than naturally falls to a successful commander; but when I am called upon to speak of the merits of the captains of his Majesty's ships, and of the officers and men, whether seamen, marines, or soldiers, whom I that day had the happiness to command, I then say, that never was the glory of this country upheld with more determined bravery than on that occasion: and if I may be allowed to give an opinion as a Briton, then I say, that more important service was never rendered to our king and country. It is my duty, my lord, to prove to the brave fellows, my companions in danger, that I have not failed at every proper place to represent, as well as I am able, their bravery and meritorious conduct."

Another honour, of greater import, was withheld from the conquerors. The king had given medals to those captains who were engaged in the battles of the 1st of June, of Cape St. Vincent, of Camperdown, and of the Nile. Then came the victory at Copenhagen, which Nelson truly called the most difficult achievement, the hardest-fought battle, the most glorious result that ever graced the annals of our country. He, of course, expected the medal; and in writing to Earl St. Vincent, said, "He longed to have it, and would not give it up to be made an English duke."

The medal, however, was not given:—"For what reason,"said Nelson, "Lord St. Vincent best knows."

Words plainly implying a suspicion that it was withheld by some feeling of jealousy; and that suspicion estranged him, during the remaining period of his life, from one who had at one time been essentially, as well as sincerely, his friend; and of whose professional abilities he ever entertained the highest opinion.

The happiness which Nelson enjoyed in the society of his chosen friends was of no long continuance. Sir William Hamilton, who was far advanced in years, died early in 1803; a mild, amiable, and accomplished man, who has thus in a letter described his own philosophy:

"My study of antiquities," he says, "has kept me in constant thought of the perpetual fluctuation of everything. The whole art is really to live all the *days* of our life; and not with anxious care disturb the sweetest hour that life affords—which is the present. Admire the Creator, and all His works, to us incomprehensible; and do all the good you can upon earth; and take the chance of eternity without dismay."

He expired in his wife's arms, holding Nelson by the hand; and almost in his last words, left her to his protection; requesting him that he would see justice done her by the government, as he knew what she had done for her country. He left him her portrait in enamel, calling him his dearest friend; the most virtuous, loyal, and truly brave character he had ever known. The codicil, containing this bequest, concluded with these words, "God bless him, and shame fall on those who do not say amen."

Sir William's pension of £1,200 a year ceased with his death. Nelson applied to Mr. Addington in Lady Hamilton's behalf, stating the important service which she had rendered to the fleet at Syracuse; and Mr. Addington, it is said, acknowledged that she had a just claim upon the gratitude of the country.

This barren acknowledgment was all that was obtained; but a sum, equal to the pension which her husband had enjoyed, was settled on her by Nelson, and paid in monthly payments during his life.

A few weeks after this event, the war was renewed [18 May 1803]; and the day after his Majesty's message to Parliament, Nelson departed to take the command of the Mediterranean fleet. The war he thought, could not be long; just enough to make him independent in pecuniary matters.

He took his station immediately off Toulon; and there, with incessant vigilance, waited for the coming out of the enemy. The expectation of acquiring a competent fortune did not last long.

"Somehow," he says, "my mind is not sharp enough for prize-money. Lord Keith would have made £20,000, and I have not made £6,000."

More than once he says that the prizes taken in the Mediterranean had not paid his expenses; and once he expresses himself as if it were a consolation to think that some ball might soon close all his accounts with this world of care and vexation. At this time the widow of his brother, being then blind and advanced in years, was distressed for money, and about to sell her plate; he wrote to Lady Hamilton, requesting of her to find out what her debts were, and saying that, if the amount was within his power, he would certainly pay it, and rather pinch himself than that she should want.

Before he had finished the letter, an account arrived that a sum was payable to him for some neutral taken four years before, which enabled him to do this without being the poorer; and he seems to have felt at the moment that what was thus disposed of by a cheerful giver, shall be paid to him again.

One from whom he had looked for very different conduct, had compared his own wealth, in no becoming manner, with Nelson's limited means.

"I know," said he to Lady Hamilton, "the full extent of the obligation I owe him, and he may be useful to me again; but I can never forget his unkindness to you. But, I guess many reasons influenced his conduct in bragging of his riches and my honourable poverty; but, as I have often said, and with honest pride, what I have is my own: it never cost the widow a tear, or the nation a farthing. I got what I have with my pure blood, from the enemies of my country. Our house, my own Emma, is built upon a solid foundation; and will last to us, when his houses and lands may belong to others than his children."

His hope was that peace might soon be made, or that he should be relieved from his command, and retire to Merton, where at that distance he was planning and directing improvements.

On his birthday he writes, "This day, my dearest Emma, I consider as more fortunate than common days, as by my coming into this world it has brought me so intimately acquainted with you. I well know that you will keep it, and have my dear Horatia[83] to drink my health. Forty-six years of toil and trouble! How few more the common lot of mankind leads us to expect! and therefore it is almost time to think of spending the few last years in peace and quietness."

83 Nelson's daughter by Emma Hamilton, born 31 January 1801. Southey was rather charitable in his suggestion that, prior to Sir William's death, Nelson's relationship with his wife had been merely one of very strong friendship. The reality appears to be that either Sir William was hopelessly unobservant or, more likely, knew perfectly well that his wife was sleeping with his friend and simply didn't care. It is also possible, given Sir William was 68 at the time Nelson returned to Naples in 1798, he may have actually welcomed the idea of adding a third, sexually active, partner to his household for the benefit of his much younger wife.

It is painful to think that this language was not addressed to his wife, but to one with whom he promised himself "many many happy years, when that impediment," as he calls her, "shall be removed, if God pleased; and they might be surrounded by their children's children."

When he had been fourteen months off Toulon, he received a vote of thanks from the city of London for his skill and perseverance in blockading that port, so as to prevent the French from putting to sea. Nelson had not forgotten the wrong which the city had done to the Baltic fleet by their omission, and did not lose the opportunity which this vote afforded of recurring to that point.

"I do assure your lordship," said he, in his answer to the lord mayor, "that there is not that man breathing who sets a higher value upon the thanks of his fellow-citizens of London than myself; but I should feel as much ashamed to receive them for a particular service marked in the resolution, if I felt that I did not come within that line of service, as I should feel hurt at having a great victory passed over without notice. I beg to inform your lordship, that the port of Toulon has never been blockaded by me; quite the reverse. Every opportunity has been offered the enemy to put to sea; for it is there that we hope to realise the hopes and expectations of our country."

Nelson then remarked that the junior flag-officers of his fleet had been omitted in this vote of thanks; and his surprise at the omission was expressed with more asperity, perhaps, than an offence so entirely and manifestly unintentional deserved; but it arose from that generous regard for the feelings as well as the interests of all who were under his command, which made him as much beloved in the fleets of Britain as he was dreaded in those of the enemy.

Never was any commander more beloved. He governed men by their reason and their affections; they knew that he was incapable of caprice or tyranny and they obeyed him with alacrity and joy, because he possessed their confidence as well as their love.

"Our Nel," they used to say, "is as brave as a lion and as gentle as a lamb." Severe discipline he detested, though he had been bred in a severe school. He never inflicted corporal punishment if it were possible to avoid it; and when compelled to enforce it, he, who was familiar with wounds and death, suffered like a woman.

In his whole life, Nelson was never known to act unkindly towards an officer. If he was asked to prosecute one for ill behaviour, he used to answer, "That there was no occasion for him to ruin a poor devil who was sufficiently his own enemy to ruin himself."

But in Nelson there was more than the easiness and humanity of a happy nature: he did not merely abstain from injury; his was an active and watchful benevolence, ever desirous not only to render justice, but to do good. During the peace he had spoken in parliament upon the abuses respecting prize-money, and had submitted plans to government for more easily manning the navy, and preventing desertion from it, by bettering the condition of the seamen.

He proposed that their certificates should be registered, and that every man who had served, with a good character, five years in war, should receive a bounty of two guineas annually after that time, and of four guineas after eight years. "This," he said, "might, at first sight, appear an enormous sum for the state to pay; but the average life of seamen is, from hard service, finished at forty-five. He cannot, therefore, enjoy the annuity many years, and the interest of the money saved by their not deserting would go far to pay the whole expense."

To his midshipmen he ever showed the most winning kindness, encouraging the diffident, tempering the hasty, counselling and befriending both. "Recollect," he used to say, "that you must be a seaman to be an officer; and also that you cannot be a good officer without being a gentleman."

A lieutenant wrote to him to say that he was dissatisfied with his captain. Nelson's answer was in that spirit of perfect wisdom and perfect goodness which regulated his whole conduct towards those who were under his command.

"I have just received your letter, and am truly sorry that any difference should arise between your captain, who has the reputation of being one of the bright officers of the service, and yourself, a very young man, and a very young officer, who must naturally have much to learn; therefore the chance is that you are perfectly wrong in the disagreement. However, as your present situation must be very disagreeable, I will certainly take an early opportunity of removing you, provided your conduct to your present captain be such that another may not refuse to receive you."

The gentleness and benignity of his disposition never made him forget what was due to discipline. Being on one occasion applied to, to save a young officer from a court-martial, which he had provoked by his misconduct, his reply was, "That he would do everything in his power to oblige so gallant and good an officer as Sir John Warren," in whose name the intercession had been made.

"But what," he added, "would he do if he were here? Exactly what I have done, and am still willing to do. The young man must write such a letter of contrition as would be an acknowledgment of his great fault; and with a sincere promise, if his captain will intercede to prevent the impending court-martial, never to so misbehave again. On his captain's enclosing me such a letter, with a request to cancel the order for the trial, I might be induced to do it; but the letters and reprimand will be given in the public order-book of the fleet, and read to all the officers. The young man has pushed himself forward to notice, and he must take the consequence. It was upon the quarter-deck, in the face of the ship's company, that he treated his captain with contempt; and I am in duty bound to support the authority and consequence of every officer under my command. A poor ignorant seaman is for ever punished for contempt to *his* superiors."

A dispute occurred in the fleet while it was off Toulon, which called forth Nelson's zeal for the rights and interests of the navy. Some young artillery officers, serving on board the bomb vessels, refused to let their men perform any other duty but what related to the mortars. They wished to have it established that their corps was not subject to the captain's authority.

The same pretensions were made in the Channel fleet about the same time, and the artillery rested their claims to separate and independent authority on board, upon a clause in the act, which they interpreted in their favour. Nelson took up the subject with all the earnestness which its importance deserved.

"There is no real happiness in this world," said he, writing to Earl St. Vincent, as first lord. "With all content and smiles around me, up start these artillery boys (I understand they are not beyond that age), and set us at defiance; speaking in the most disrespectful manner of the navy and its commanders. I know you, my dear lord, so well, that with your quickness the matter would have been settled, and perhaps some of them been broke. I am perhaps more patient, but I do assure you not less resolved, if my plan of conciliation is not attended to. You and I are on the eve of quitting the theatre of our exploits; but we hold it due to our successors never, whilst we have a tongue to speak or a hand to write, to allow the navy to be in the smallest degree injured in its discipline by our conduct."

To Troubridge he wrote in the same spirit: "It is the old history, trying to do away the act of parliament; but I trust they will never succeed; for when they do, farewell to our naval superiority. We should be prettily commanded! Let them once gain the step of being independent of the navy on board a ship, and they will soon have the other, and command us. But, thank God! my dear Troubridge, the king himself cannot do away the act of parliament. Although my career is nearly run, yet it would embitter my future days, and expiring moments, to hear of our navy being sacrificed to the army." As the surest way of preventing such disputes, he suggested that the navy should have its own corps of artillery; and a corps of marine artillery was accordingly established.

Instead of lessening the power of the commander, Nelson would have wished to see it increased: it was absolutely necessary, he thought, that merit should be rewarded at the moment, and that the officers of the fleet should look up to the commander-in-chief for their reward. He himself was never more happy than when he could promote those who were deserving of promotion.

Many were the services which he thus rendered unsolicited; and frequently the officer, in whose behalf he had interested himself with the Admiralty, did not know to whose friendly interference he was indebted for his good fortune. He used to say, "I wish it to appear as a God-send."

The love which he bore the navy made him promote the interests, and honour the memory, of all who had added to its glories. "The near relations of brother officers," he said, "he considered as legacies to the service."

Upon mention being made to him of a son of Rodney, by the Duke of Clarence, his reply was: "I agree with your Royal Highness most entirely, that the son of a Rodney ought to be the *protégé* of every person in the kingdom, and particularly of the sea-officers. Had I known that there had been this claimant, some of my own lieutenants must have given way to such a name, and he should have been placed in the *Victory*: she is full, and I have twenty on my list; but, whatever numbers I have, the name of Rodney must cut many of them out."

Such was the proper sense which Nelson felt of what was due to splendid services and illustrious names. His feelings toward the brave men who had served with him are shown by a note in his diary, which was probably not intended for any other eye than his own: "Nov. 7. I had the comfort of making an old *Agamemnon*, George Jones, a gunner into the *Chameleon* brig."

When Nelson took the command, it was expected that the Mediterranean would be an active scene. Nelson well understood the character of the perfidious Corsican, who was now sole tyrant of France; and knowing that he was as ready to attack his friends as his enemies, knew, therefore, that nothing could be more uncertain than the direction of the fleet from Toulon, whenever it should put to sea.

"It had as many destinations," he said, "as there were countries."

The momentous revolutions of the last ten years had given him ample matter for reflection, as well as opportunities for observation: the film was cleared from his eyes; and now, when the French no longer went abroad with the cry of liberty and equality, he saw that the oppression and misrule of the powers which had been opposed to them, had been the main causes of their success, and that those causes would still prepare the way before them.

Even in Sicily, where, if it had been possible longer to blind himself, Nelson would willingly have seen no evil, he perceived that the people wished for a change, and acknowledged that they had reason to wish for it.

In Sardinia the same burden of misgovernment was felt; and the people, like the Sicilians, were impoverished by a government so utterly incompetent to perform its first and most essential duties that it did not protect its own coasts from the Barbary pirates. He would fain have had us purchase this island (the finest in the Mediterranean) from its sovereign, who did not receive £5,000 a year from it after its wretched establishment was paid.

There was reason to think that France was preparing to possess herself of this important point, which afforded our fleet facilities for watching Toulon, not to be obtained elsewhere. An expedition was preparing at Corsica for the purpose; and all the Sardes, who had taken part with revolutionary France, were ordered to assemble there. It was certain that if the attack were made it would succeed.

Nelson thought that the only means to prevent Sardinia from becoming French was to make it English, and that half a million would give the king a rich price, and England a cheap purchase. A better, and therefore a wiser policy, would have been to exert our influence in removing the abuses of the government, for foreign dominion is always, in some degree, an evil and allegiance neither can nor ought to be made a thing of bargain and sale.

Sardinia, like Sicily and Corsica, is large enough to form a separate state. Let us hope that these islands may one day be made free and independent. Freedom and independence will bring with them industry and prosperity; and wherever these are found, arts and letters will flourish, and the improvement of the human race proceed.

The proposed attack was postponed. Views of wider ambition were opening upon Buonaparte, who now almost undisguisedly aspired to make himself master of the continent of Europe; and Austria was preparing for another struggle, to be conducted as weakly and terminated as miserably as the former.

Spain, too, was once more to be involved in war by the policy of France: that perfidious government having in view the double object of employing the Spanish resources against England, and exhausting them in order to render Spain herself finally its prey. Nelson, who knew that England and the Peninsula ought to be in alliance, for the common interest of both, frequently expressed his hopes that Spain might resume her natural rank among the nations.

"We ought," he said, "by mutual consent, to be the very best friends, and both to be ever hostile to France."

But he saw that Buonaparte was meditating the destruction of Spain; and that, while the wretched court of Madrid professed to remain neutral, the appearances of neutrality were scarcely preserved. An order of the year 1771, excluding British ships of war from the Spanish ports, was revived, and put in force: while French privateers, from these very ports, annoyed the British trade, carried their prizes in, and sold them even at Barcelona.

Nelson complained of this to the captain-general of Catalonia, informing him that he claimed, for every British ship or squadron, the right of lying, as long as it pleased, in the ports of Spain, while that right was allowed to other powers.

To the British Ambassador he said: "I am ready to make large allowances for the miserable situation Spain has placed herself in; but there is a certain line, beyond which I cannot submit to be treated with disrespect. We have given up French vessels taken within gunshot of the Spanish shore, and yet French vessels are permitted to attack our ships from the Spanish shore. Your excellency may assure the Spanish government that, in whatever place the Spaniards allow the French to attack us, in that place I shall order the French to be attacked."

During this state of things, to which the weakness of Spain, and not her will, consented, the enemy's fleet did not venture to put to sea. Nelson watched it with unremitting and almost unexampled perseverance. The station off Toulon he called his home.

"We are in the right fighting trim," said he: "let them come as soon as they please. I never saw a fleet altogether so well officered and manned; would to God the ships were half as good! The finest ones in the service would soon be destroyed by such terrible weather. I know well enough that if I were to go into Malta I should save the ships during this bad season; but if I am to watch the French I must be at sea; and if at sea, must have bad weather; and if the ships are not fit to stand bad weather, they are useless."

Then only he was satisfied and at ease when he had the enemy in view.

Mr. Elliot, our minister at Naples, seems at this time to have proposed to send a confidential Frenchman to him with information. "I should be very happy," he replied, "to receive authentic intelligence of the destination of the French squadron, their route, and time of sailing. Anything short of this is useless; and I assure your excellency, that I would not upon any consideration have a Frenchman in the fleet, except as a prisoner. I put no confidence in them. You think yours good; the queen thinks the same; I believe they are all alike. Whatever information you can get me I shall be very thankful for; but not a Frenchman comes here. Forgive me, but my mother hated the French."

M. Latouche Treville, who had commanded at Boulogne, commanded now at Toulon.

"He was sent for on purpose," said Nelson, "as he *beat me* at Boulogne, to beat me again; but he seems very loath to try."

One day, while the main body of our fleet was out of sight of land, Rear-Admiral Campbell, reconnoitring with the *Canopus*, Donegal, and *Amazon*, stood in close to the port; and M. Latouche, taking advantage of a breeze which sprung up, pushed out with four ships of the line and three heavy frigates, and chased him about four leagues.

The Frenchman, delighted at having found himself in so novel a situation, published a boastful account, affirming that he had given chase to the whole British fleet, and that Nelson had fled before him! Nelson thought it due to the Admiralty to send home a copy of the *ictory*'s log upon this occasion.

"As for himself," he said, "if his character was not established by that time for not being apt to run away, it was not worth his while to put the world right."—

"If this fleet gets fairly up with M. Latouche," said he to one of his correspondents, "his letter, with all his ingenuity, must be different from his last. We had fancied that we chased him into Toulon; for, blind as I am, I could see his water line, when he clued [*sic*] his topsails up, shutting in Sepet. But from the time of his meeting Captain Hawker in the *Isis*, I never heard of his acting otherwise than as a poltroon and a liar. Contempt is the best mode of treating such a miscreant."

In spite, however, of contempt, the impudence of this Frenchman half angered him. He said to his brother: "You will have seen Latouche's letter; how he chased me and how I ran. I keep it; and if I take him, by God he shall eat it."

Nelson, who used to say, that in sea affairs nothing is impossible, and nothing improbable, feared the more that this Frenchman might get out and elude his vigilance; because he was so especially desirous of catching him, and administering to him his own lying letter in a sandwich.

M. Latouche, however, escaped him in another way. He died, according to the French papers, in consequence of walking so often up to the signal-post upon Sepet, to watch the British fleet.

"I always pronounced that would be his death," said Nelson. "If he had come out and fought me, it would at least have added ten years to my life."

The patience with which he had watched Toulon, he spoke of, truly, as a perseverance at sea which had never been surpassed. From May, 1803, to August, 1805, he himself went out of his ship but three times; each of those times was upon the king's service, and neither time of absence exceeded an hour.

In 1804 the *Swift* cutter going out with despatches was taken, and all the despatches and letters fell into the hands of the enemy.

"A very pretty piece of work," says Nelson; "I am not surprised at the capture, but am very much so that any despatches should be sent in a vessel with twenty-three men, not equal to cope with any row-boat privateer. The loss of the *Hindostan*[84] was great enough; but for importance it is lost in comparison to the probable knowledge the enemy will obtain of our connexions with foreign countries. Foreigners for ever say, and it is true, we dare not trust England: one way or other we are sure to be committed."

In a subsequent letter he says, speaking of the same capture: "I find, my dearest Emma, that your picture is very much admired by the French Consul at Barcelona, and that he has not sent it to be admired, which I am sure it would be, by Buonaparte. They pretend that there were three pictures taken. I wish I had them; but they are all gone as irretrievably as the despatches, unless we may read them in a book, as we printed their correspondence from Egypt. But from us what can they find out? That I love you most dearly, and hate the French most damnably. Dr. Scott went to Barcelona to try to get the private letters, but I fancy they are all gone to Paris. The Swedish and American Consuls told him that the French Consul had your picture and read your letters; and the Doctor thinks one of them, probably, read the letters. By the master's account of the cutter, I would not have trusted an old pair of shoes in her. He tells me she did not sail, but was a good sea-boat. I hope Mr. Marsden will not trust any more of my private letters in such a conveyance: if they choose to trust the affairs of the public in such a thing, I cannot help it."

While he was on this station, the weather had been so unusually severe that he said the Mediterranean seemed altered. It was his rule never to contend with the gales; but either run to the southward to escape their violence, or furl all the sails, and make the ships as easy as possible. The men, though he said flesh and blood could hardly stand it, continued in excellent health, which he ascribed, in great measure, to a plentiful supply of lemons and onions.

For himself, he thought he could only last till the battle was over. One battle more it was his hope that he might fight. "However," said he, "whatever happens, I have run a glorious race."

"A few months' rest," he says, "I must have very soon. If I am in my grave, what are the mines of Peru to me? But to say the truth, I have no

84 HMS *Hindustan*, originally the Indian built East Indiaman *Born*, was purchased into the Royal Navy in 1795. Converted to a storeship in 1802, she was en route to Nelson with dispatches and supplies when she caught fire on 2 April 1804. The crew managed to ground the ship in Rosas Bay, with most of the passengers and crew getting safely ashore, but the ship was a total loss.

idea of killing myself. I may, with care, live yet to do good service to the state. My cough is very bad, and my side, where I was struck on the 14th of February, is very much swelled: at times a lump as large as my fist, brought on occasionally by violent coughing. But I hope and believe my lungs are yet safe."

He was afraid of blindness and this was the only evil which he could not contemplate without unhappiness. More alarming symptoms he regarded with less apprehension, describing his own "shattered carcass" as in the worst plight of any in the fleet; and he says, "I have felt the blood gushing up the left side of my head; and, the moment it covers the brain, I am fast asleep."

The fleet was in worse trim than the men; but when he compared it with the enemy's, it was with a right English feeling. "The French fleet yesterday," said he, in one of his letters, "was to appearance in high feather, and as fine as paint could make them; but when they may sail, or where they may go, I am very sorry to say is a secret I am not acquainted with. Our weather-beaten ships, I have no fear, will make their sides like a plum-pudding."

"Yesterday," he says, on another occasion, "a rear-admiral and seven sail of ships put their nose outside the harbour. If they go on playing this game, some day we shall lay salt on their tails[85]."

Hostilities at length commenced between Great Britain and Spain [December 1804]. That country, whose miserable government made her subservient to France, was once more destined to lavish her resources and her blood in furtherance of the designs of a perfidious ally.

The immediate occasion of the war was the seizure of four treasure-ships by the English[86]. The act was perfectly justifiable, for those treasures

85 For the benefit of the youthful, who may never have heard of this particular myth, it was once proverbial that you could capture a bird by pouring salt on its tail. This was true only to the extent that, if you could get close enough to apply the salt, you were also close enough to grab the bird.

86 This story became well known in British naval circles, and even found its way into fiction in one of the Hornblower books. Under normal circumstances, the captains and crews of the four British frigates would have received a large share of prize money, according to a standard formula, from the sale of the captured ships and, more importantly in this case, the treasure they were carrying. It was estimated the even the ordinary seamen would have received a sum equal to several years' pay. However, as it was determined that war had not yet begun, the captured ships and treasure were declared to be *droits* of the Crown, with the entire sum going into the national treasury and no prize money being awarded. There was, to be sure, a fair bit of discontent

were intended to furnish means for France; but the circumstances which attended it were as unhappy as they were unforeseen.

Four frigates had been despatched to intercept them. They met with an equal force. Resistance, therefore, became a point of honour on the part of the Spaniards, and one of their ships soon blew up with all on board.

Had a stronger squadron been sent, this deplorable catastrophe might have been spared: a catastrophe which excited not more indignation in Spain than it did grief in those who were its unwilling instruments, in the English government, and in the English people. On the 5th of October this unhappy affair occurred, and Nelson was not apprised of it till the twelfth of the ensuing month.

He had, indeed, sufficient mortification at the breaking out of this Spanish war; an event which, it might reasonably have been supposed, would amply enrich the officers of the Mediterranean fleet, and repay them for the severe and unremitting duty on which they had been so long employed. But of this harvest they were deprived; for Sir John Orde was sent with a small squadron, and a separate command, to Cadiz.

Nelson's feelings were never wounded so deeply as now. "I had thought," said he, writing in the first flow and freshness of indignation; "Fancied—but nay; it must have been a dream, an idle dream; yet I confess it, I *did* fancy that I had done my country service; and thus they use me! And under what circumstances, and with what pointed aggravation? Yet, if I know my own thoughts, it is not for myself, or on my own account chiefly, that I feel the sting and the disappointment. No! it is for my brave officers: for my noble minded friends and comrades. Such a gallant set of fellows! Such a band of brothers! My heart swells at the thought of them."

War between Spain and England was now declared; and on the eighteenth of January, the Toulon fleet, having the Spaniards to co-operate with them, put to sea.

Nelson was at anchor off the coast of Sardinia, where the Madelena islands form one of the finest harbours in the world, when, at three in the afternoon of the nineteenth, the *Active* and *Seahorse* frigates brought this long-hoped-for intelligence. They had been close to the enemy at

---

aboard the frigates, though the rest of the fleet, which would have received no benefit from the capture, was reportedly rather amused by the whole thing.

ten on the preceding night, but lost sight of them in about four hours.

The fleet immediately unmoored and weighed, and at six in the evening ran through the strait between Biche and Sardinia: a passage so narrow that the ships could only pass one at a time, each following the stern-lights of its leader.

From the position of the enemy, when they were last seen, it was inferred that they must be bound round the southern end of Sardinia.

Signal was made the next morning to prepare for battle. Bad weather came on, baffling the one fleet in its object, and the other in its pursuit.

Nelson beat about the Sicilian seas for ten days, without obtaining any other information of the enemy than that one of their ships had put into Ajaccio, dismasted; and having seen that Sardinia, Naples, and Sicily were safe, believing Egypt to be their destination, for Egypt he ran.

The disappointment and distress which he had experienced in his former pursuits of the French through the same seas were now renewed; but Nelson, while he endured these anxious and unhappy feelings, was still consoled by the same confidence as on the former occasion—that, though his judgment might be erroneous, under all circumstances he was right in having formed it.

"I have consulted no man," said he to the Admiralty; "therefore the whole blame of ignorance in forming my judgment must rest with me. I would allow no man to take from me an atom of my glory had I fallen in with the French fleet; nor do I desire any man to partake any of the responsibility. All is mine, right or wrong." Then stating the grounds upon which he had proceeded, he added, "At this moment of sorrow, I still feel that I have acted right." In the same spirit he said to Sir Alexander Ball: "When I call to remembrance all the circumstances, I approve, if nobody else does, of my own conduct."

Baffled thus, he bore up for Malta, and met intelligence from Naples that the French, having been dispersed in a gale, had put back to Toulon. From the same quarter he learned that a great number of saddles and muskets had been embarked; and this confirmed him in his opinion that Egypt was their destination. That they should have put him back in consequence of storms which he had weathered, gave him a consoling sense of British superiority.

"These gentlemen," said he, "are not accustomed to a Gulf of Lyons gale: we have buffeted them for one-and-twenty months, and not carried away a spar."

He, however, who had so often braved these gales, was now, though not mastered by them, vexatiously thwarted and impeded; and on February 27th he was compelled to anchor in Pula Bay in the Gulf of Cagliari. From the 21st of January the fleet had remained ready for battle, without a bulk-head up night or day.

He anchored here that he might not be driven to leeward. As soon as the weather moderated he put to sea again; and after again beating about against contrary winds, another gale drove him to anchor in the Gulf of Palma on the 8th of March.

This he made his rendezvous: he knew that the French troops still remained embarked; and wishing to lead them into a belief that he was stationed upon the Spanish coast, he made his appearance off Barcelona with that intent.

About the end of the month he began to fear that the plan of the expedition was abandoned; and sailing once more towards his old station off Toulon on the 4th of April, he met the *Phoebe*, with news that Villeneuve had put to sea on the last of March, with eleven ships of the line, seven frigates, and two brigs. When last seen they were steering towards the coast of Africa.

Nelson first covered the channel between Sardinia and Barbary, so as to satisfy himself that Villeneuve was not taking the same route for Egypt which Gantheaume had taken before him, when he attempted to carry reinforcements thither. Certain of this, he bore up on the 7th for Palermo, lest the French should pass to the north of Corsica, and he despatched cruisers in all directions.

On the 11th he felt assured that they were not gone down the Mediterranean; and sending off frigates to Gibraltar, to Lisbon, and to Admiral Cornwallis, who commanded the squadron off Brest, he endeavoured to get to the westward, beating against westerly winds.

After five days a neutral gave intelligence that the French had been seen off Cape de Gatte on the 7th. It was soon after ascertained that they had passed the Straits of Gibraltar on the day following; and Nelson, knowing that they might already be half way to Ireland or to Jamaica, exclaimed that he was miserable. One gleam of comfort only came across him in the reflection, that his vigilance had rendered it impossible for them to undertake any expedition in the Mediterranean.

Eight days after this certain intelligence had been obtained, he described his state of mind thus forcibly in writing to the governor of Malta:

"My good fortune, my dear Ball, seems flown away. I cannot get a fair wind, or even a side-wind. Dead foul!—Dead foul! But my mind is fully made up what to do when I leave the supposing there is no certain account of the enemy's destination. I believe this ill-luck will go near to kill me; but as these are times for exertion, I must not be cast down, whatever I may feel."

In spite of every exertion which could be made by all the zeal and all the skill of British seamen, he did not get in sight of Gibraltar till the 30th of April; and the wind was then so adverse that it was impossible to pass the Gut. He anchored in Mazari Bay, on the Barbary shore; obtained supplies from Tetuan; and when, on the 5th, a breeze from the eastward sprang up at last, sailed once more, hoping to hear of the enemy from Sir John Orde, who commanded off Cadiz, or from Lisbon.

"If nothing is heard of them," said he to the Admiralty, "I shall probably think the rumours which have been spread are true, that their object is the West Indies; and, in that case, I think it my duty to follow them—or to the Antipodes, should I believe that to be their destination."

At the time when this resolution was taken, the physician of the fleet had ordered him to return to England before the hot months.

Nelson had formed his judgment of their destination, and made up his mind accordingly, when Donald Campbell, at that time an admiral in the Portuguese service, the same person who had given important tidings to Earl St. Vincent of the movements of that fleet from which he won his title, a second time gave timely and momentous intelligence to the flag of his country. He went on board the *Victory*, and communicated to Nelson his certain knowledge that the combined Spanish and French fleets were bound for the West Indies.

Hitherto all things had favoured the enemy. While the British commander was beating up again strong southerly and westerly gales, they had wind to their wish from the N.E., and had done in nine days what he was a whole month in accomplishing. Villeneuve, finding the Spaniards at Carthagena were not in a fit state of equipment to join him, dared not wait, but hastened on to Cadiz. Sir John Orde necessarily retired at his approach.

Admiral Gravina, with six Spanish ships of the line and two French, come out to him, and they sailed without a moment's loss of time. They had about three thousand French troops on board, and fifteen hundred Spanish: six hundred were under orders, expecting them at Martinique, and one thousand at Guadaloupe. General Lauriston commanded the troops.

The combined fleet now consisted of eighteen sail of the line, six forty-four gun frigates, one of twenty-six guns, three corvettes, and a brig. They were joined afterwards by two new French line-of-battle ships, and one forty-four. Nelson pursued them with ten sail of the line and three frigates.

"Take you a Frenchman apiece," said he to his captains, "and leave me the Spaniards: when I haul down my colours, I expect you to do the same, and not till then."

The enemy had five-and-thirty days' start; but he calculated that he should gain eight or ten days upon them by his exertions. May 15th he made Madeira, and on June 4th reached Barbadoes, whither he had sent despatches before him; and where he found Admiral Cochrane[87], with two ships, part of our squadron in those seas being at Jamaica.

He found here also accounts that the combined fleets had been seen from St. Lucia on the 28th, standing to the southward, and that Tobago and Trinidad were their objects. This Nelson doubted; but he was alone in his opinion, and yielded it with these foreboding words: "If your intelligence proves false, you lose me the French fleet."

Sir W. Myers offered to embark here with 2,000 troops; they were taken on board, and the next morning he sailed for Tobago.

Here accident confirmed the false intelligence which had, whether from intention or error, misled him. A merchant at Tobago, in the general alarm, not knowing whether this fleet was friend or foe, sent out a schooner to reconnoitre, and acquaint him by signal. The signal which he had chosen happened to be the very one which had been appointed by Col. Shipley of the engineers to signify that the enemy were at Trinidad; and as this was at the close of the day, there was no opportunity of discovering the mistake.

An American brig was met with about the same time, the master of

87 (Then Rear) Admiral Sir Alexander Cochrane (1758–1832), a younger son of Thomas Cochrane, the 8th Earl of Dundonald, and uncle of the much better known Admiral Lord Thomas Cochrane, the 10th Earl.

which, with that propensity to deceive the English and assist the French in any manner which has been but too common among his countrymen, affirmed that he had been boarded off Granada a few days before by the French, who were standing towards the Bocas of Trinidad.

This fresh intelligence removed all doubts. The ships were cleared for action before daylight, and Nelson entered the Bay of Paria on the 7th, hoping and expecting to make the mouths of the Orinoco as famous in the annals of the British navy as those of the Nile.

Not an enemy was there; and it was discovered that accident and artifice had combined to lead him so far to leeward, that there could have been little hope of fetching to windward of Granada for any other fleet. Nelson, however, with skill and exertions never exceeded, and almost unexampled, bore for that island.

Advices met him on the way, that the combined fleets, having captured the Diamond Rock, were then at Martinique on the fourth, and were expected to sail that night for the attack of Granada.

On the 9th Nelson arrived off that island; and there learned that they had passed to leeward of Antigua the preceding day, and had taken a homeward-bound convoy. Had it not been for false information, upon which Nelson had acted reluctantly, and in opposition to his own judgment, he would have been off Port Royal just as they were leaving it, and the battle would have been fought on the spot where Rodney defeated De Grasse.

This he remembered in his vexation; but he had saved the colonies, and above 200 ships laden for Europe, which would else have fallen into the enemy's hands; and he had the satisfaction of knowing that the mere terror of his name had effected this, and had put to flight the allied enemies, whose force nearly doubled that before which they fled.

That they were flying back to Europe he believed, and for Europe he steered in pursuit on the 13th, having disembarked the troops at Antigua, and taking with him the *Spartiate*, seventy-four; the only addition to the squadron with which he was pursuing so superior a force.

Five days afterwards the *Amazon* brought intelligence that she had spoke a schooner who had seen them on the evening of the 15th, steering to the north; and by computation, eighty-seven leagues off. Nelson's diary at this time denotes his great anxiety and his perpetual and all-observing vigilance.

"June 21. Midnight, nearly calm, saw three planks, which I think came from the French fleet. Very miserable, which is very foolish."

On the 17th of July he came in sight of Cape St. Vincent, and steered for Gibraltar.

"June 18th," his diary says, "Cape Spartel in sight, but no French fleet, nor any information about them. How sorrowful this makes me! but I cannot help myself." The next day he anchored at Gibraltar; and on the 20th, says he, "I went on shore for the first time since June 16, 1803; and from having my foot out of the *Victory* two years, wanting ten days."

Here he communicated with his old friend Collingwood; who, having been detached with a squadron, when the disappearance of the combined fleets, and of Nelson in their pursuit, was known in England, had taken his station off Cadiz. He thought that Ireland was the enemy's ultimate object; that they would now liberate the Ferrol squadron, which was blocked up by Sir Robert Calder, call for the Rochefort ships, and then appear off Ushant with 33 or 34 sail; there to be joined: by the Brest fleet. With this great force he supposed they would make for Ireland—the real mark and bent of all their operations; and their flight to the West Indies, he thought, had been merely undertaken to take off Nelson's force, which was the great impediment to their undertaking.

Collingwood was gifted with great political penetration. As yet, however, all was conjecture concerning the enemy; and Nelson, having victualled and watered at Tetuan, stood for Ceuta on the 24th, still without information of their course.

Next day intelligence arrived that the *Curieux* brig had seen them on the 19th, standing to the northward.

He proceeded off Cape St. Vincent, rather cruising for intelligence than knowing whither to betake himself; and here a case occurred that more than any other event in real history resembles those whimsical proofs of sagacity which Voltaire, in his *Zadig*, has borrowed from the Orientals.

One of our frigates spoke an American, who, a little to the westward of the Azores, had fallen in with an armed vessel, appearing to be a dismasted privateer, deserted by her crew, which had been run on board by another ship, and had been set fire to; but the fire had gone out. A log-book and a few seamen's jackets were found in the cabin; and these were brought to Nelson.

The log-book closed with these words: "Two large vessels in the

W.N.W.:" and this led him to conclude that the vessel had been an English privateer, cruising off the Western Islands. But there was in this book a scrap of dirty paper, filled with figures.

Nelson, immediately upon seeing it, observed that the figures were written by a Frenchman; and after studying this for a while, said, "I can explain the whole. The jackets are of French manufacture, and prove that the privateer was in possession of the enemy. She had been chased and taken by the two ships that were seen in the W.N.W. The prizemaster, going on board in a hurry, forgot to take with him his reckoning: there is none in the log-book; and the dirty paper contains her work for the number of days since the privateer last left Corvo; with an unaccounted-for run, which I take to have been the chase, in his endeavour to find out her situation by back reckonings. By some mismanagement, I conclude she was run on board of by one of the enemy's ships, and dismasted. Not liking delay (for I am satisfied that those two ships were the advanced ones of the French squadron), and fancying we were close at their heels, they set fire to the vessel, and abandoned her in a hurry. If this explanation be correct, I infer from it that they are gone more to the northward; and more to the northward I will look for them."

This course accordingly he held, but still without success.

Still persevering, and still disappointed, he returned near enough to Cadiz to ascertain that they were not there; traversed the Bay of Biscay; and then, as a last hope, stood over for the north-west coast of Ireland against adverse winds, till, on the evening of the 12th of August, he learned that they had not been heard of there.

Frustrated thus in all his hopes, after a pursuit, to which, for its extent, rapidity, and perseverance, no parallel can be produced, he judged it best to reinforce the Channel fleet with his squadron, lest the enemy, as Collingwood apprehended, should bear down upon Brest with their whole collected force.

On the 15th he joined Admiral Cornwallis off Ushant. No news had yet been obtained of the enemy; and on the same evening he received orders to proceed, with the *Victory* and *Superb*, to Portsmouth.

Chapter 9
1805

Sir Robert Calder falls in with the combined Fleets—They form a Junction with the Ferrol Squadron, and get into Cadiz—Nelson is reappointed to the Command—Battle of Trafalgar—Victory, and Death of Nelson.

At Portsmouth, Nelson at length found news of the combined fleet. Sir Robert Calder, who had been sent out to intercept their return, had fallen in with them on the 22nd of July, sixty leagues off Cape Finisterre.

Their force consisted of twenty sail of the line, three fifty-gun ships, five frigates, and two brigs: his, of fifteen line-of-battle ships, two frigates, a cutter, and a lugger. After an action of four hours he had captured an eighty-four and a seventy-four, and then thought it necessary to bring-to the squadron, for the purpose of securing their prizes.

The hostile fleets remained in sight of each other till the 26th, when the enemy bore away. The capture of two ships from so superior a force would have been considered as no inconsiderable victory, a few years earlier; but Nelson had introduced a new era in our naval history; and the nation felt respecting this action as he had felt on a somewhat similar occasion. They regretted that Nelson, with his eleven ships, had not been in Sir Robert Calder's place; and their disappointment was generally and loudly expressed.

Frustrated as his own hopes had been, Nelson had yet the high satisfaction of knowing that his judgment had never been more conspicuously approved, and that he had rendered essential service to his country, by driving the enemy from those Islands where they expected there could be no force capable of opposing them.

The West India merchants in London, as men whose interests were more immediately benefited, appointed a deputation to express their thanks for his great and judicious exertions.

It was now his intention to rest awhile from his labours, and recruit himself, after all his fatigues and cares, in the society of those whom he loved. All his stores were brought up from the *Victory*; and he found in his house at Merton the enjoyment which he had anticipated.

Many days had not elapsed before Captain Blackwood, on his way to London with despatches, called on him at five in the morning. Nelson, who was already dressed, exclaimed, the moment he saw him: "I am sure you bring me news of the French and Spanish fleets! I think I shall yet have to beat them!"

They had refitted at Vigo, after the indecisive action with Sir Robert Calder; then proceeded to Ferrol, brought out the squadron from thence, and with it entered Cadiz in safety.

"Depend on it, Blackwood," he repeatedly said, "I shall yet give M. Villeneuve a drubbing."

But when Blackwood had left him, he wanted resolution to declare his wishes to Lady Hamilton and his sisters, and endeavoured to drive away the thought. He had done enough, he said: "Let the man trudge it who has lost his budget!"

His countenance belied his lips; and as he was pacing one of the walks in the garden, which he used to call the quarter-deck, Lady Hamilton came up to him, and told him she saw he was uneasy. He smiled, and said:

"No, he was as happy as possible; he was surrounded by his family, his health was better since he had been on shore, and he would not give sixpence to call the king his uncle."

She replied, that she did not believe him, that she knew that he was longing to get at the combined fleets, that he considered them as his own property, that he would be miserable if any man but himself did the business; and that he ought to have them, as the price and reward of his two years' long watching, and his hard chase.

"Nelson," said she, "however we may lament your absence, offer your services; they will be accepted, and you will gain a quiet heart by it: you will have a glorious victory, and then you may return here, and be happy."

He looked at her with tears in his eyes: "Brave Emma! Good Emma! If there were more Emmas there would be more Nelsons."

His services were as willingly accepted as they were offered; and Lord Barham, giving him the list of the navy, desired him to choose his own officers.

"Choose yourself, my lord," was his reply: "the same spirit actuates the whole profession: you cannot choose wrong."

Lord Barham then desired him to say what ships, and how many, he would wish, in addition to the fleet which he was going to command, and said they should follow him as soon as each was ready.

No appointment was ever more in unison with the feelings and judgment of the whole nation. They, like Lady Hamilton, thought that the destruction of the combined fleets ought properly to be Nelson's work; that he who had been

"Half around the sea-girt ball,
The hunter of the recreant Gaul,"

ought to reap the spoils of the chase which he had watched so long, and so perseveringly pursued.

Unremitting exertions were made to equip the ships which he had chosen, and especially to refit the *Victory*, which was once more to bear his flag.

Before he left London he called at his upholsterer's, where the coffin which Captain Hallowell had given him was deposited; and desired that its history might be engraven upon the lid, saying that it was highly probable he might want it on his return.

He seemed, indeed, to have been impressed with an expectation that he should fall in the battle. In a letter to his brother, written immediately after his return, he had said: "We must not talk of Sir Robert Calder's battle—I might not have done so much with my small force. If I had fallen in with them, you might probably have been a lord[88] before I wished; for I know they meant to make a dead set at the *Victory*."

Nelson had once regarded the prospect of death with gloomy sat-

88 Having no legitimate offspring, the titles of Viscount Nelson and his 1798 title of Baron Nelson of the Nile and Burnham Thorpe, would not be passed on. His 1801 title of Baron Nelson of the Nile and Hilborough, however, would descend to his brother, Reverend William Nelson. His brother would also later be created Earl Nelson and Viscount Merton in honor of his brother's victories. William Nelson also became Duke of Bronte on his brother's death.

isfaction: it was when he anticipated the upbraidings of his wife, and the displeasure of his venerable father. The state of his feelings now was expressed in his private journal in these words:

"Friday night (Sept. 13), at half-past ten, I drove from dear, dear Merton; where I left all which I hold dear in this world, to go and serve my king and country. May the great GOD, whom I adore, enable me to fulfil the expectations of my country! and if it is His good pleasure that I should return, my thanks will never cease being offered up to the throne of His mercy. If it is His good providence to cut short my days upon earth, I bow with the greatest submission; relying that he will protect those so dear to me whom I may leave behind! His will be done. Amen! Amen! Amen!"

Early on the following morning he reached Portsmouth; and having despatched his business on shore, endeavoured to elude the populace by taking a by-way to the beach; but a crowd collected in his train, pressing forward to obtain a sight of his face: many were in tears, and many knelt down before him and blessed him as he passed. England has had many heroes; but never one who so entirely possessed the love of his fellow-countrymen as Nelson.

All men knew that his heart was as humane as it was fearless; that there was not in his nature the slightest alloy of selfishness or cupidity; but that with perfect and entire devotion he served his country with all his heart, and with all his soul, and with all his strength; and, therefore, they loved him as truly and as fervently as he loved England. They pressed upon the parapet to gaze after him when his barge pushed off, and he was returning their cheers by waving his hat.

The sentinels, who endeavoured to prevent them from trespassing upon this ground, were wedged among the crowd; and an officer who, not very prudently upon such an occasion, ordered them to drive the people down with their bayonets, was compelled speedily to retreat; for the people would not be debarred from gazing till the last moment upon the hero—the darling hero of England!

He arrived off Cadiz on the 29th of September—his birthday. Fearing that if the enemy knew his force they might be deterred from venturing to sea, he kept out of sight of land, desired Collingwood to fire no salute and hoist no colours, and wrote to Gibraltar to request that the force of the fleet might not be inserted there in the *Gazette.*

His reception in the Mediterranean fleet was as gratifying as the farewell of his countrymen at Portsmouth: the officers who came on board to welcome him forgot his rank as commander in their joy at seeing him again.

On the day of his arrival, Villeneuve received orders to put to sea the first opportunity. Villeneuve, however, hesitated when he heard that Nelson had resumed the command. He called a council of war; and their determination was, that it would not be expedient to leave Cadiz, unless they had reason to believe themselves stronger by one-third than the British force.

In the public measures of this country secrecy is seldom practicable, and seldomer attempted: here, however, by the precautions of Nelson and the wise measures of the Admiralty, the enemy were for once kept in ignorance; for as the ships appointed to reinforce the Mediterranean fleet were despatched singly, each as soon as it was ready, their collected number was not stated in the newspapers, and their arrival was not known to the enemy.

But the enemy knew that Admiral Louis[89], with six sail, had been detached for stores and water to Gibraltar. Accident also contributed to make the French admiral doubt whether Nelson himself had actually taken the command. An American, lately arrived from England, maintained that it was impossible, for he had seen him only a few days before in London, and at that time there was no rumour of his going again to sea.

The station which Nelson had chosen was some fifty or sixty miles to the west of Cadiz, near Cape St. Marys. At this distance, he hoped to decoy the enemy out while he guarded against the danger of being caught with a westerly wind near Cadiz and driven within the Straits.

The blockade of the port was rigorously enforced, in hopes that the combined fleet might be forced to sea by want. The Danish vessels, therefore, which were carrying provisions from the French ports in the bay, under the name of Danish property, to all the little ports from Ayamonte to Algeciras, from [*sic*] whence they were conveyed in coasting boats to Cadiz, were seized.

Without this proper exertion of power, the blockade would have

89 Rear Admiral Sir Thomas Louis, Bart., (1758–1807), at the time of Trafalgar was flying his flag in Canopus. Sent to Gibraltar for supplies, Louis missed the battle, though, as Southey notes, the news of his departure may well have contributed some additional impetus to Villeneuve's decision to leave port.

been rendered nugatory by the advantage thus taken of the neutral flag. The supplies from France were thus effectually cut off.

There was now every indication that the enemy would speedily venture out: officers and men were in the highest spirits at the prospects of giving them a decisive blow; such, indeed, as would put an end to all further contest upon the seas. Theatrical amusements were performed every evening in most of the ships; and God save the King was the hymn with which the sports concluded.

"I verily believe," said Nelson (writing on the 6th of October), "that the country will soon be put to some expense on my account; either a monument, or a new pension and honours; for I have not the smallest doubt but that a very few days, almost hours, will put us in battle. The success no man can ensure; but for the fighting them, if they can be got at, I pledge myself. The sooner the better: I don't like to have these things upon my mind."

At this time he was not without some cause of anxiety: he was in want of frigates, and the eyes of the fleet, as he always called them; to the want of which the enemy before were indebted for their escape, and Buonaparte for his arrival in Egypt. He had only twenty-three ships; others were on the way, but they might come too late; and though Nelson never doubted of victory, mere victory was not what he looked to; he wanted to annihilate the enemy's fleet.

The Carthagena squadron might effect a junction with this fleet on the one side; and on the other it was to be expected that a similar attempt would be made by the French from Brest; in either case a formidable contingency to be apprehended by the blockading force.

The Rochefort squadron did push out, and had nearly caught the *Agamemnon* and *L'Aimable* in their way to reinforce the British admiral. Yet Nelson at this time weakened his own fleet.

He had the unpleasant task to perform of sending home Sir Robert Calder, whose conduct was to be made the subject of a court-martial, in consequence of the general dissatisfaction which had been felt and expressed at his imperfect victory.

Sir Robert Calder and Sir John Orde, Nelson believed to be the only two enemies whom he had ever had in his profession; and from that sensitive delicacy which distinguished him, this made him the more scrupulously anxious to show every possible mark of respect and kindness to Sir Robert. He wished to detain him till after the expected action, when the services which he might perform, and the triumphant joy which would be excited, would leave nothing to be apprehended from an inquiry into the previous engagement.

Sir Robert, however, whose situation was very painful, did not choose to delay a trial from the result of which he confidently expected a complete justification; and Nelson, instead of sending him home in a frigate, insisted on his returning in his own ninety-gun ship—ill as such a ship could at that time be spared. Nothing could be more honourable than the feeling by which Nelson was influenced; but, at such a crisis, it ought not to have been indulged.

On the 9th Nelson sent Collingwood what he called, in his diary, the Nelson-touch.

"I send you," said he, "my plan of attack, as far as a man dare venture to guess at the very uncertain position the enemy may be found in; but it is to place you perfectly at ease respecting my intentions, and to give full scope to your judgment for carrying them into effect. We can, my dear Coll, have no little jealousies. We have only one great object in view, that of annihilating our enemies, and getting a glorious peace for our country. No man has more confidence in another than I have in you; and no man will render your services more justice than your very old friend Nelson and Bronte."

The order of sailing was to be the order of battle: the fleet in two lines, with an advanced squadron of eight of the fastest-sailing two-deckers. The second in command, having the entire direction of his line, was to break through the enemy, about the twelfth ship from their rear: he would lead through the centre, and the advanced squadron was to cut off three or four ahead of the centre. This plan was to be adapted to the strength of the enemy, so that they should always be one-fourth superior to those whom they cut off.

Nelson said, "That his admirals and captains, knowing his precise object to be that of a close and decisive action, would supply any deficiency of signals, and act accordingly. In case signals cannot be seen or clearly understood, no captain can do wrong if he places his ship alongside that of an enemy."

One of the last orders of this admirable man was, that the name and family of every officer, seaman, and marine, who might be killed or wounded in action, should be, as soon as possible, returned to him, in order to be transmitted to the chairman of the Patriotic Fund, that the case might be taken into consideration for the benefit of the sufferer or his family.

About half-past nine in the morning of the 19th, the *Mars*, being the nearest to the fleet of the ships which formed the line of communication with the frigates inshore, repeated the signal that the enemy were coming out of port. The wind was at this time very light, with partial breezes, mostly from the S.S.W.. Nelson ordered the signal to be made for a chase in the south-east quarter.

About two, the repeating ships announced that the enemy were at sea.

All night the British fleet continued under all sail, steering to the south-east. At daybreak they were in the entrance of the Straits, but the enemy were not in sight. About seven one of the frigates made signal that the enemy were bearing north. Upon this the *Victory* hove to; and shortly afterwards Nelson made sail again to the northward.

In the afternoon the wind blew fresh from the south-west, and the English began to fear that the foe might be forced to return to port.

A little before sunset, however, Blackwood, in the *Euryalus*, telegraphed that they appeared determined to go to the westward.

"And that," said the admiral in his diary, "they shall not do, if it is in the power of Nelson and Bronte to prevent them."

Nelson had signified to Blackwood that he depended upon him to keep sight of the enemy. They were observed so well that all their motions were made known to him; and as they wore twice, he inferred that they were aiming to keep the port of Cadiz open, and would retreat there as soon as they saw the British fleet; for this reason he was very careful not to approach near enough to be seen by them during the night.

At daybreak the combined fleets were distinctly seen from the *Victory*'s deck, formed in a close line of battle ahead, on the starboard tack, about twelve miles to leeward, and standing to the south.

Our fleet consisted of twenty-seven sail of the line and four frigates; theirs of thirty-three and seven large frigates. Their superiority was greater in size and weight of metal than in numbers. They had four thousand troops on board; and the best riflemen who could be procured, many of them Tyrolese, were dispersed through the ships. Little did the Tyrolese, and little did the Spaniards, at that day, imagine what horrors the wicked tyrant whom they served was preparing for their country.

Soon after daylight Nelson came upon deck. The 21st of October was a festival in his family, because on that day his uncle, Captain Suckling, in the *Dreadnought*, with two other line-of-battle ships, had beaten off a French squadron of four sail of the line and three frigates. Nelson, with that sort of superstition from which few persons are entirely exempt, had more than once expressed his persuasion that this was to be the day of his battle also; and he was well pleased at seeing his prediction about to be verified.

The wind was now from the west, light breezes, with a long heavy swell. Signal was made to bear down upon the enemy in two lines; and the fleet set all sail. Collingwood, in the *Royal Sovereign*, led the lee line of thirteen ships; the *Victory* led the weather line of fourteen. Having seen that all was as it should be, Nelson retired to his cabin, and wrote the following prayer:—

"May the great *god* whom I worship, grant to my country, and for the benefit of Europe in general, a great and glorious victory, and may no misconduct in any one tarnish it; and may humanity after victory be the predominant feature in the British fleet! For myself individually, I commit my life to Him that made me; and may His blessing alight on my endeavours for serving my country faithfully! To Him I resign myself, and the just cause which is entrusted to me to defend. Amen! Amen! Amen!"

Having thus discharged his devotional duties, he annexed, in the same diary, the following remarkable writing:—

October 21, 1805.— Then in sight of the combined fleets of France and Spain, distant about ten miles.

"Whereas the eminent services of Emma Hamilton, widow of the Right Hon. Sir W. Hamilton, have been of the very greatest service to my king and country, to my knowledge, without ever receiving any reward from either our king or country.

"1. That she obtained the King of Spain's letter, in 1796, to his brother, the King of Naples, acquainting him of his intention to declare war against England from which letter the ministry sent out orders to the then Sir John Jervis to strike a stroke, if opportunity offered, against either the arsenals of Spain or her fleets. That neither of these was done is not the fault of Lady Hamilton; the opportunity might have been offered.

"2. The British fleet under my command could never have returned the second time to Egypt, had not Lady Hamilton's influence with the Queen of Naples caused letters to be wrote to the governor of Syracuse that he was to encourage the fleet's being supplied with everything, should they put into any port in Sicily. We put into Syracuse, and received every supply; went to Egypt and destroyed the French fleet.

"Could I have rewarded these services, I would not now call upon my country; but as that has not been in my power, I leave Emma Lady Hamilton therefore a legacy to my king and country, that they will give her an ample provision to maintain her rank in life. I also leave to the beneficence of my country my adopted daughter, Horatia Nelson Thomson; and I desire she will use in future the name of Nelson only.

"These are the only favours I ask of my king and country, at this moment, when I am going to fight their battle. May God bless my king and country, and all those I hold dear! My relations it is needless to mention; they will of course be amply provided for.

"*Nelson and Bronte.*
"*Witness,* {*Henry Blackwood.*
"{*T.M. Hardy*"

The child of whom this writing speaks was believed to be his daughter, and so, indeed, he called her the last time he pronounced her name. She was then about five years old, living at Merton, under Lady Hamilton's care. The last minutes which Nelson passed at Merton were employed in praying over this child, as she lay sleeping.

A portrait of Lady Hamilton hung in his cabin; and no Catholic ever beheld the picture of his patron saint with devouter reverence. The undisguised and romantic passion with which he regarded it amounted almost to superstition; and when the portrait was now taken down in clearing for action, he desired the men who removed it to "take care of his guardian angel." In this manner he frequently spoke of it, as if he believed there were a virtue in the image. He wore a miniature of her, also, next his heart.

Blackwood went on board the *Victory* about six. He found him in good spirits, but very calm; not in that exhilaration which he had felt upon entering into battle at Aboukir and Copenhagen: he knew that his own life would be particularly aimed at, and seems to have looked for death with almost as sure an expectation as for victory. His whole attention was fixed upon the enemy.

They tacked to the northward, and formed their line on the larboard tack; thus bringing the shoals of Trafalgar and St. Pedro under the lee of the British, and keeping the port of Cadiz open for themselves. This was judiciously done; and Nelson, aware of all the advantages which it gave them, made signal to prepare to anchor.

Villeneuve was a skilful seaman: worthy of serving a better master, and a better cause. His plan of defence was as well conceived, and as original, as the plan of attack. He formed the fleet in a double line; every alternate ship being about a cable's length to windward of her second ahead and astern.

Nelson, certain of a triumphant issue to the day, asked Blackwood what he should consider as a victory.

That officer answered, that, considering the handsome way in which battle was offered by the enemy, their apparent determination for a fair trial of strength, and the situation of the land, he thought it would be a glorious result if fourteen were captured.

He replied: "I shall not be satisfied with less than twenty."

Soon afterwards he asked him if he did not think there was a signal wanting.

Captain Blackwood made answer, that he thought the whole fleet seemed very clearly to understand what they were about. These words were scarcely spoken before that signal was made, which will be remembered as long as the language, or even the memory, of England shall endure; Nelson's last signal:—

"England expects every man to do his duty!"[90]

It was received throughout the fleet with a shout of answering acclamation, made sublime by the spirit which it breathed, and the feeling which it expressed.

"Now," said Lord Nelson, "I can do no more. We must trust to the great Disposer of all events, and the justice of our cause. I thank God for this great opportunity of doing my duty."

He wore that day, as usual, his admiral's frock-coat, bearing on the

90 The syntax of this signal, as received, differs slightly from what Nelson actually proposed. The original signal was to be "England confides that every man will do his duty." *Victory*'s signal officer, Lieutenant John Pasco (1784–1853), suggested changing "confides" (here used in the sense of "has confidence"), which was not contained in the signal book and would have to be spelled out, to "expects," which *was* in the book, and could be sent more quickly. Pasco was himself wounded in the subsequent action. He would eventually rise to the rank of rear admiral.

left breast four stars, of the different orders with which he was invested. Ornaments which rendered him so conspicuous a mark for the enemy were beheld with ominous apprehensions by his officers. It was known that there were riflemen on board the French ships, and it could not be doubted but that his life would be particularly aimed at.

They communicated their fears to each other; and the surgeon, Mr. Beatty, spoke to the chaplain Dr. Scott, and to Mr. Scott the public secretary, desiring that some person would entreat him to change his dress, or cover the stars; but they knew that such a request would highly displease him.

"In honour I gained them," he had said when such a thing had been hinted to him formerly, "and in honour I will die with them."

Mr. Beatty, however, would not have been deterred by any fear of exciting his displeasure from speaking to him himself upon a subject in which the weal of England, as well as the life of Nelson, was concerned; but he was ordered from the deck before he could find an opportunity.

This was a point upon which Nelson's officers knew that it was hopeless to remonstrate or reason with him; but both Blackwood, and his own captain, Hardy, represented to him how advantageous to the fleet it would be for him to keep out of action as long as possible; and he consented at last to let the *Leviathan* and the *Temeraire*, which were sailing abreast of the *Victory*, be ordered to pass ahead.

Yet even here the last infirmity of this noble mind was indulged, for these ships could not pass ahead if the *Victory* continued to carry all her sail; and so far was Nelson from shortening sail, that it was evident he took pleasure in pressing on, and rendering it impossible for them to obey his own orders.

A long swell was setting into the bay of Cadiz: our ships, crowding all sail, moved majestically before it, with light winds from the south-west. The sun shone on the sails of the enemy; and their well-formed line, with their numerous three-deckers, made an appearance which any other assailants would have thought formidable; but the British sailors only admired the beauty and the splendour of the spectacle; and in full confidence of winning what they saw, remarked to each other what a fine sight yonder ships would make at Spithead!

The French admiral, from the *Bucentaure*, beheld the new manner in which his enemy was advancing—Nelson and Collingwood each leading his line; and pointing them out; to his officers, he is said to have exclaimed that such conduct could not fail to be successful.

Yet Villeneuve had made his own dispositions with the utmost skill and the fleets under his command waited for the attack with perfect coolness.

Ten minutes before twelve they opened their fire. Eight or nine of the ships immediately ahead of the *Victory*, and across her bows, fired single guns at her, to ascertain whether she was yet within their range.

As soon as Nelson perceived that their shot passed over him, he desired Blackwood and Captain Prowse, of the *Sirius*, to repair to their respective frigates; and, on their way, to tell all the captains of the line-of-battle ships that he depended on their exertions; and that if, by the prescribed mode of attack, they found it impracticable to get into action immediately, they might adopt whatever they thought best, provided it led them quickly and closely alongside an enemy.

As they were standing on the front of the poop, Blackwood took him by the hand, saying, he hoped soon to return and find him in possession of twenty prizes.

He replied, "God bless you, Blackwood; I shall never see you again."

Nelson's column was steered about two points more to the north than Collingwood's, in order to cut off the enemy's escape into Cadiz: the lee line, therefore, was first engaged.

"See," cried Nelson, pointing to the *Royal Sovereign*, as she steered right for the centre of the enemy's line, cut through it astern of the *Santa Anna* three-decker, and engaged her at the muzzle of her guns on the starboard side—"see how that noble fellow, Collingwood, carries his ship into action!"

Collingwood, delighted at being first in the heat of the fire, and knowing the feelings of his commander and old friend, turned to his captain, and exclaimed: "Rotherham, what would Nelson give to be here?"

Both these brave officers, perhaps, at this moment, thought of Nelson with gratitude, for a circumstance which had occurred on the preceding day. Admiral Collingwood, with some of the captains, having gone on board the *Victory* to receive instructions, Nelson inquired of him where his captain was and was told, in reply, that they were not upon good terms with each other.

"Terms!" said Nelson, "good terms with each other!"

Immediately he sent a boat for Captain Rotherham; led him, as soon as he arrived, to Collingwood; and saying, "Look; yonder are the enemy!" bade them shake hands like Englishmen.

The enemy continued to fire a gun at a time at the *Victory*, till they saw that a shot had passed through her main-top-gallant sail; then they opened their broadsides, aiming chiefly at her rigging, in the hope of disabling her before she could close with them.

Nelson, as usual, had hoisted several flags, lest one should be shot away. The enemy showed no colours till late in the action, when they began to feel the necessity of having them to strike. For this reason, the *Santísima Trinidad*, Nelson's old acquaintance, as he used to call her, was distinguishable only by her four decks; and to the bow of this opponent he ordered the *Victory* to be steered.

Meantime an incessant raking fire was kept up upon the *Victory*. The admiral's secretary was one of the first who fell; he was killed by a cannon-shot while conversing with Hardy.

Captain Adair of the marines, with the help of a sailor, endeavoured to remove the body from Nelson's sight, who had a great regard for Mr. Scott; but he anxiously asked: "Is that poor Scott that's gone?" and being informed that was indeed so, exclaimed: "Poor fellow!"

Presently, a double-headed shot struck a party of marines who were drawn up on the poop, and killed eight of them; upon which Nelson immediately desired Captain Adair to disperse his men round the ship, that they might not suffer so much from being together.

A few minutes afterwards a shot struck the fore-brace bitts on the quarter-deck, and passed between Nelson and Hardy, a splinter from the bitt tearing off Hardy's buckle, and bruising his foot. Both stopped, and looked anxiously at each other, each supposed the other to be wounded. Nelson then smiled, and said, "This is too warm work, Hardy, to last long."

The *Victory* had not yet returned a single gun: fifty of her men had been by this time killed or wounded, and her main-top-mast, with all her studding-sails and her booms, shot away. Nelson declared, that, in all his battles, he had seen nothing which surpassed the cool courage of his crew on this occasion.

At four minutes after twelve she opened her fire from both sides of her deck. It was not possible to break the enemy's line without running on board one of their ships: Hardy informed him of this, and asked him which he would prefer. Nelson replied: "Take your choice, Hardy, it does not signify much."

The master was ordered to put the helm to port, and the *Victory* ran on board the *Redoutable*, just as her tiller ropes were shot away. The French ship received her with a broadside; then instantly let down her lower-deck ports, for fear of being boarded through them, and never afterwards fired a great gun during the action. Her tops, like those of all the enemy's ships, were filled with riflemen.

Nelson never placed musketry in his tops; he had a strong dislike to the practice; not merely because it endangers setting fire to the sails, but also because it is a murderous sort of warfare, by which individuals may suffer, and a commander now and then be picked off; but which never can decide the fate of a general engagement.

Captain Harvey, in the *Temeraire*, fell on board the *Redoutable* on the other side. Another enemy was in like manner on board the *Temeraire*, so that these four ships formed as compact a tier as if they had been moored together, their heads lying all the same way.

The lieutenants of the *Victory*, seeing this, depressed their guns of the middle and lower decks, and fired with a diminished charge, lest the shot should pass through, and injure the *Temeraire*. And because there was danger that the *Redoutable* might take fire from the lower-deck guns, the muzzles of which touched her side when they were run out, the fireman of each gun stood ready with a bucket of water; which, as soon as the gun was discharged, he dashed into the hole made by the shot. An incessant fire was kept up from the *Victory* from both sides; her larboard guns playing upon the *Bucentaure* and the huge *Santísima Trinidad*.

It had been part of Nelson's prayer that the British fleet might be distinguished by humanity in the victory which he expected. Setting an example himself, he twice gave orders to cease firing upon the *Redoutable*, supposing that she had struck, because her great guns were silent; for as she carried no flag, there were no means of instantly ascertaining the fact.

From this ship, which he had thus twice spared, he received his death. A ball fired from her mizzen-top, which, in the then situation of the two vessels, was not more than fifteen yards from that part of the deck where he was standing, struck the epaulet on his left shoulder, about a quarter after one, just in the heat of action. He fell upon his face, on the spot which was covered with his poor secretary's blood.

Hardy, who was a few steps from him, turning round, saw three men raising him up.

"They have done for me at last, Hardy," said he.

"I hope not," cried Hardy.

"Yes!" he replied, "my back-bone is shot through."

Yet even now, not for a moment losing his presence of mind, he observed, as they were carrying him down the ladder, that the tiller ropes, which had been shot away, were not yet replaced, and ordered that new ones should be rove immediately. Then, that he might not be seen by the crew, he took out his handkerchief, and covered his face and his stars.

Had he but concealed these badges of honour from the enemy, England, perhaps, would not have had cause to receive with sorrow the news of the battle of Trafalgar.[91]

The cockpit was crowded with wounded and dying men, over whose bodies he was with some difficulty conveyed, and laid upon a pallet in the midshipmen's berth. It was soon perceived, upon examination, that the wound was mortal. This, however, was concealed from all except Captain Hardy, the chaplain, and the medical attendants.

He himself being certain, from the sensation in his back, and the gush of blood he felt momentarily within his breast, that no human care could avail him, insisted that the surgeon should leave him, and attend to those to whom he might be useful; "For," said he, "you can do nothing for me."

All that could be done was to fan him with paper, and frequently to give him lemonade to alleviate his intense thirst. He was in great pain, and expressed much anxiety for the event of the action, which now began to declare itself.

As often as a ship struck, the crew of the *Victory* hurrahed; and at every hurrah a visible expression of joy gleamed in the eyes, and marked the countenance of the dying hero.

But he became impatient to see Captain Hardy; and as that officer, though often sent for, could not leave the deck, Nelson feared that some fatal cause prevented him, and repeatedly cried, "Will no one bring Hardy to me? He must be killed! He is surely dead!"

---

91 The exaggerated sense of honor that compelled Nelson to appear on deck in dress uniform and medals was entirely too common through much of the 19th Century. During the American Civil War, some officers died or suffered severe injury, when, despite being able to see the relatively slow approach of a cannon ball, their own misguided sense of honor, or perhaps fear of being thought a coward, kept them from dodging.

An hour and ten minutes elapsed from the time when Nelson received his wound before Hardy could come to him. They shook hands in silence, Hardy in vain struggling to repress the feelings of that most painful and yet sublimest moment.

"Well, Hardy," said Nelson, "how goes the day with us?"

"Very well," replied Hardy; "ten ships have struck, but five of the van have tacked, and show an intention to bear down upon the *Victory*, I have called two or three of our fresh ships round, and have no doubt of giving them a drubbing."

"I hope," said Nelson, "none of our ships have struck?"

Hardy answered, "There was no fear of that."

Then, and not till then, Nelson spoke of himself. "I am a dead man, Hardy," said he: "I am going fast: it will be all over with me soon. Come nearer to me. Let my dear Lady Hamilton have my hair, and all other things belonging to me."

Hardy observed that he hoped Mr. Beatty could yet hold out some prospect of life.

"Oh, no!" he replied, "it is impossible. My back is shot through. Beatty will tell you so."

Captain Hardy then, once more, shook hands with him; and, with a heart almost bursting, hastened upon deck.

By this time all feeling below the breast was gone; and Nelson, having made the surgeon ascertain this, said to him: "You know I am gone, I know it. I feel something rising in my breast,"—putting his hand on his left side,—"which tells me so."

And upon Beatty's inquiring whether his pain was very great, he replied, "So great, that he wished he was dead. Yet," said he, in a lower voice, "one would like to live a little longer too!"

And after a few minutes, in the same undertone, he added, "What would become of poor Lady Hamilton, if she knew my situation!"

Next to his country she occupied his thoughts. Captain Hardy, some fifty minutes after he had left the cockpit, returned; and, again taking the hand of his dying friend and commander, congratulated him on having gained a complete victory. How many of the enemy were taken he did not know, as it was impossible to perceive them distinctly; but fourteen or fifteen at least.

"That's well," cried Nelson, "but I bargained for twenty." And then, in a stronger voice, he said: "Anchor, Hardy; anchor."

Hardy, upon this, hinted that Admiral Collingwood would take upon himself the direction of affairs.

"Not while I live, Hardy," said the dying Nelson, ineffectually endeavouring to raise himself from the bed: "Do you anchor."

His previous order for preparing to anchor had shown how clearly he foresaw the necessity of this. Presently, calling Hardy back, he said to him in a low voice, "Don't throw me overboard:" and he desired that he might be buried by his parents, unless it should please the king to order otherwise.

Then reverting to private feelings: "Take care of my dear Lady Hamilton, Hardy take care of poor Lady Hamilton. Kiss me, Hardy,"[92] said he.

Hardy knelt down and kissed his cheek; and Nelson: said, "Now I am satisfied. Thank God I have done my duty." Hardy stood over him in silence for a moment or two, then knelt again and kissed his forehead. "Who is that?" said Nelson; and being informed, he replied, "God bless you, Hardy."

And Hardy then left him—for ever.

Nelson now desired to be turned upon his right side, and said, "I wish I had not left the deck; for I shall soon be gone."

Death was, indeed, rapidly approaching. He said to the chaplain, "Doctor, I have *not* been a *great* sinner;" and after a short pause, "Remember that I leave Lady Hamilton and my daughter Horatia as a legacy to my country."

His articulation now became difficult; but he was distinctly heard to say, "Thank God I have done my duty."

These words he repeatedly pronounced; and they were the last words which he uttered. He expired at thirty minutes after four—three hours and a quarter after he had received his wound.

Within a quarter of an hour after Nelson was wounded, above

92 Later writers have suggested that what Nelson actually said was, "Kismet, Hardy," as if he were suggesting that his impending death was a matter of fate. This suggestion is probably an application of Victorian morality to a scene that, to those remarkably prudish (in public, at least) individuals, no doubt suggested the possibility of a homosexual relationship. The original version, however, is almost certainly correct. Not only did heterosexual men of that period commonly address each other in terms we would today expect to see used only between the sexes, or by clearly homosexual individuals, but, no doubt the clincher, Hardy did, in fact, immediately kiss him on the cheek.

fifty of the *Victory*'s men fell by the enemy's musketry. They, however, on their part, were not idle; and it was not long before there were only two Frenchmen left alive in the mizzen-top of the *Redoutable.* One of them was the man who had given the fatal wound: he did not live to boast of what he had done.

An old quarter-master had seen him fire; and easily recognised him, because he wore a glazed cocked hat and a white frock. This quarter-master and two midshipmen, Mr. Collingwood and Mr. Pollard, were the only persons left in the *Victory*'s poop; the two midshipmen kept firing at the top, and he supplied them with cartridges.

One of the Frenchmen, attempting to make his escape down the rigging, was shot by Mr. Pollard, and fell on the poop. But the old quarter-master, as he cried out, "That's he, that's he," and pointed at the other who was coming forward to fire again, received a shot in his mouth, and fell dead. Both the midshipmen then fired at the same time, and the fellow dropped in the top. When they took possession of the prize, they went into the mizzen-top, and found him dead, with one ball through his head, and another through his breast.

The *Redoutable* struck within twenty minutes after the fatal shot had been fired from her. During that time she had been twice on fire in her fore-chains and in her forecastle.

The French, as they had done in other battles, made use in this, of fire-balls and other combustibles; implements of destruction which other nations, from a sense of honour and humanity, have laid aside[93]; which add to the, sufferings of the wounded, without determining the issue of the combat: which none but the cruel would employ, and which never can be successful against the brave.

Once they succeeded in setting fire, from the *Redoutable,* to some ropes and canvas on the *Victory*'s booms.

---

93 In fact, the reluctance of most nations in that period to use red-hot shot, or other combustible material against the warships of other countries, had far less to do with questions of honor than it did with practical concerns. The use of heated shot required keeping the shot furnace burning during battle, with the ever present danger that it might be hit by a well-aimed—or merely lucky—ball, scattering burning coals all over the deck. In the same way, flaming projectiles or thrown firepots were as likely to set fire to one's own ship as the enemy's—perhaps more so. When ships were made almost entirely of wood, and propelled by canvas sails, mounted to wooden masts held up by tarred rigging, fire was simply considered too great a danger to take the risk. The French did, and more than once discovered just why their enemies did not.

The cry ran through the ship, and reached the cockpit; but even this dreadful cry produced no confusion: the men displayed that perfect self-possession in danger by which English seamen are characterised; they extinguished the flames on board their own ship, and then hastened to extinguish them in the enemy, by throwing buckets of water from the gangway.

When the *Redoutable* had struck, it was not practicable to board her from the *Victory*; for, though the two ships touched, the upper works of both fell in so much, that there was a great space between their gangways; and she could not be boarded from the lower or middle decks because her ports were down. Some of our men went to Lieutenant Quilliam, and offered to swim under her bows, and get up there; but it was thought unfit to hazard brave lives in this manner.

What our men would have done from gallantry, some of the crew of the *Santísima Trinidad* did to save themselves. Unable to stand the tremendous fire of the *Victory*, whose larboard guns played against this great four-decker, and not knowing how else to escape them, nor where else to betake themselves for protection, many of them leaped overboard and swam to the *Victory*; and were actually helped up her sides by the English during the action.

The Spaniards began the battle with less vivacity than their unworthy allies, but they continued it with greater firmness. The *Argonauta* and *Bahama* were defended till they had each lost about four hundred men; the *San Juan Nepomuceno* lost three hundred and fifty.

Often as the superiority of British courage has been proved against France upon the seas, it was never more conspicuous than in this decisive conflict[94]. Five of our ships were engaged muzzle to muzzle with five of

---

94 While Southey cites the courage of the British seamen as decisive, experience may be an even greater factor. During the Napoleonic wars, British seamen were almost certainly the most thoroughly experienced in any of the world's navies, and far more so than French sailors, who spent much of time in port. The British fleets were almost constantly at sea, returning to port only out of necessity, to briefly touch shore to take on supplies, or to carry out repairs too complex to be done at sea. Blockade duty meant long months of sailing up and down enemy coasts, in all sorts of weather. Nelson himself had served almost continuously at sea from the time he was, by our standards, a small child, his periods ashore as often as not the result of sickness or injury and not leisure. At Trafalgar, it would not have been unreasonable to suggest that some of the more senior French seamen had less actual at-sea time than some of the landsmen (unrated men) in the British ships.

the French. In all five the Frenchmen lowered their lower-deck ports, and deserted their guns; while our men continued deliberately to load and fire till they had made the victory secure.

Once, amidst his sufferings, Nelson had expressed a wish that he were dead; but immediately the spirit subdued the pains of death, and he wished to live a little longer, doubtless that he might hear the completion of the victory which he had seen so gloriously begun. That consolation, that joy, that triumph, was afforded him. He lived to know that the victory was decisive; and the last guns which were fired at the flying enemy were heard a minute or two before he expired.

The ships which were thus flying were four of the enemy's van, all French, under Rear-Admiral Dumanoir. They had borne no part in the action; and now, when they were seeking safety in flight, they fired not only into the *Victory* and *Royal Sovereign* as they passed, but poured their broadsides into the Spanish captured ships; and they were seen to back their topsails for the purpose of firing with more precision.

The indignation of the Spaniards at this detestable cruelty from their allies, for whom they had fought so bravely, and so profusely bled, may well be conceived. It was such that when, two days after the action, seven of the ships which had escaped into Cadiz came out in hopes of re-taking some of the disabled prizes, the prisoners in the *Argonauta*, in a body, offered their services to the British prize-master, to man the guns against any of the French ships, saying, that if a Spanish ship came alongside, they would quietly go below; but they requested that they might be allowed to fight the French in resentment for the murderous usage which they had suffered at their hands.

Such was their earnestness, and such the implicit confidence which could be placed in Spanish honour, that the offer was accepted and they were actually stationed at the lower-deck guns.

Dumanoir and his squadron were not more fortunate than the fleet from whose destruction they fled. They fell in with Sir Richard Strachan, who was cruising for the Rochefort squadron, and were all taken.

In the better days of France, if such a crime could then have been committed, it would have received an exemplary punishment from the French government. Under Buonaparte it was sure of impunity, and perhaps might be thought deserving of reward.

But if the Spanish court had been independent, it would have become us to have delivered Dumanoir and his captains up to Spain, that they might have been brought to trial, and hanged in sight of the remains of the Spanish fleet.

The total British loss in the battle of Trafalgar amounted to 1,587. Twenty of the enemy struck; but it was not possible to anchor the fleet, as Nelson had enjoined. A gale came on from the S.W., some of the prizes went down, some went on shore; one effected its escape into Cadiz; others were destroyed; four only were saved, and those by the greatest exertions.

The wounded Spaniards were sent ashore, an assurance being given that they should not serve till regularly exchanged; and the Spaniards, with a generous feeling, which would not perhaps have been found in any other people, offered the use of their hospitals for our wounded, pledging the honour of Spain that they should be carefully attended there.

When the storm, after the action, drove some of the prizes upon the coast, they declared that the English who were thus thrown into their hands should not be considered as prisoners of war; and the Spanish soldiers gave up their own beds to their shipwrecked enemies.

The Spanish vice-admiral, Alva, died of his wounds. Villeneuve was sent to England, and permitted to return to France.

The French Government say that he destroyed himself on the way to Paris, dreading the consequences of a court-martial; but there is every reason to believe that the tyrant, who never acknowledged the loss of the battle of Trafalgar, added Villeneuve to the numerous victims of his murderous policy.[95]

It is almost superfluous to add, that all the honours which a grateful country could bestow were heaped upon the memory of Nelson. His brother was made an earl, with a grant of £6,000 a year. £10,000 were voted to each of his sisters; and £100,000 for the purchase of an estate

A public funeral was decreed, and a public monument. Statues and

95 Vice Admiral Pierre Charles Jean Baptiste (de) Villeneuve (1763–1806), after being paroled and returned to France, was found dead the Hôtel de Patrie in Rennes, en route to Paris. His death was ruled a suicide, it being found that he had taken his own life by stabbing himself six time in the chest, the final thrust penetrating the heart. While Southey and other British writers of the time were entirely willing to put this death down to the work of an assassin dispatched by Napoleon, Villeneuve's death is not inconsistent with suicides of this type, which often result in several, usually shallow, penetrations before a final deep thrust completes the act.

monuments also were voted by most of our principal cities. The leaden coffin in which he was brought home was cut in pieces, which were distributed as relics of Saint Nelson—so the gunner of the *Victory* called them; and when, at his internment, his flag was about to be lowered into the grave, the sailors who assisted at the ceremony with one accord rent it in pieces, that each might preserve a fragment while he lived.

The death of Nelson was felt in England as something more than a public calamity; men started at the intelligence, and turned pale, as if they had heard of the loss of a dear friend. An object of our admiration and affection, of our pride and of our hopes, was suddenly taken from us; and it seemed as if we had never, till then, known how deeply we loved and reverenced him. What the country had lost in its great naval hero—the greatest of our own, and of all former times—was scarcely taken into the account of grief.

So perfectly, indeed, had he performed his part, that the maritime war, after the battle of Trafalgar, was considered at an end: the fleets of the enemy were not merely defeated but destroyed; new navies must be built, and a new race of seamen reared for them, before the possibility of their invading our shores could again be contemplated. It was not, therefore, from any selfish reflection upon the magnitude of our loss that we mourned for him: the general sorrow was of a higher character.

The people of England grieved that funeral ceremonies, and public monuments, and posthumous rewards, were all which they could now bestow upon him, whom the king, the legislature, and the nation would have alike delighted to honour; whom every tongue would have blessed; whose presence in every village through which he might have passed would have wakened the church bells, have given schoolboys a holiday, have drawn children from their sports to gaze upon him, and "old men from the chimney corner" to look upon Nelson ere they died.

The victory of Trafalgar was celebrated, indeed, with the usual forms of rejoicing, but they were without joy; for such already was the glory of the British navy, through Nelson's surpassing genius, that it scarcely seemed to receive any addition from the most signal victory that ever was achieved upon the seas: and the destruction of this mighty fleet, by which all the maritime schemes of France were totally frustrated, hardly appeared to add to our security or strength; for, while Nelson was living, to watch the combined squadrons of the enemy, we felt ourselves as secure as now, when they were no longer in existence.

There was reason to suppose, from the appearances upon opening the body, that in the course of nature he might have attained, like his father, to a good old age. Yet he cannot be said to have fallen prematurely whose work was done; nor ought he to be lamented who died so full of honours, at the height of human fame. The most triumphant death is that of the martyr; the most awful that of the martyred patriot; the most splendid that of the hero in the hour of victory: and if the chariot and horses of fire had been vouchsafed for Nelson's translation, he could scarcely have departed in a brighter blaze of glory. He has left us, not indeed his mantle of inspiration, but a name and an example which are at this hour inspiring thousands of the youth of England: a name which is our pride, and an example which will continue to be our shield and our strength. Thus it is that the spirits of the great and the wise continue to live and to act after them; verifying, in this sense, the language of the old mythologist:

> Σοὶ μὲν δαίμονες εἰσί, Διὸς μεᾴλου διὰ βουλᾴς,
> Ἐσθλοί, ἐπιχθόνιοι, φύλακες θνητῶν ἀνθρώπων
> [They are gods, I tell you, through the counsels of mighty Zeus, good beings, dwellers on earth, the guardians of mortal men.]

CPSIA information can be obtained
at www.ICGtesting.com
Printed in the USA
BVHW031834100821
614112BV00011B/71